CW01213281

# HU JINTAO

## CHINA'S SILENT RULER

# HU JINTAO

## CHINA'S SILENT RULER

Kerry Brown

Chatham House, UK

World Scientific

NEW JERSEY · LONDON · SINGAPORE · BEIJING · SHANGHAI · HONG KONG · TAIPEI · CHENNAI

*Published by*

World Scientific Publishing Co. Pte. Ltd.
5 Toh Tuck Link, Singapore 596224
*USA office:* 27 Warren Street, Suite 401-402, Hackensack, NJ 07601
*UK office:* 57 Shelton Street, Covent Garden, London WC2H 9HE

**Library of Congress Cataloging-in-Publication Data**
Brown, Kerry, 1967–
　Hu Jintao : China's silent ruler / by Kerry Brown.
　　p. cm.
　Includes bibliographical references.
　ISBN-13: 978-981-4350-02-0
　ISBN-10: 981-4350-02-8
　1. Hu, Jintao, 1942–　2. Heads of state--China--Biography.　3. China--Politics and government--2002–　I. Title.
　DS779.29.H785B76 2012
　951.061092--dc23
　[B]
　　　　　　　　　　　　　　　　　　　　　　2012004360

**British Library Cataloguing-in-Publication Data**
A catalogue record for this book is available from the British Library.

Copyright © 2012 by World Scientific Publishing Co. Pte. Ltd.

*All rights reserved. This book, or parts thereof, may not be reproduced in any form or by any means, electronic or mechanical, including photocopying, recording or any information storage and retrieval system now known or to be invented, without written permission from the Publisher.*

For photocopying of material in this volume, please pay a copying fee through the Copyright Clearance Center, Inc., 222 Rosewood Drive, Danvers, MA 01923, USA. In this case permission to photocopy is not required from the publisher.

In-house Editors: Agnes NG
　　　　　　　　　DONG Lixi

Typeset by Stallion Press
Email: enquiries@stallionpress.com

Printed in Singapore by B & Jo Enterprise Pte Ltd

*In Memory of Ivy Rose Cole, 1918–2011.*

*My winter world, that scarcely breathes that bliss
Now, yields you, with some sighs, our explanation.*
— Gerald Manley Hopkins, `To R.B'

*Men's faults are written in bronze and their virtues on water.*
— Shakespeare

*And I knew at once, I had an immediate idea, that the person sitting beside Mr Philips was my landlord, the man in the manor, the man I had got used to not seeing… So this glimpse of my landlord — this glimpse of someone unexpectedly ordinary — made him, after all, more mysterious… So that more than ever for me the personality of the man continued to be expressed by his setting, by these beeches on the public road, but the permanently closed front gate of the manor and the overgrown garden at the back… Neither picture, neither the man I thought I had seen, nor the man I had invented, answered to what I was told about my landlord by people in London, who know him and sometimes came to visit him. That other man, coming to me in fragments as it were, remained far away.*
— V.S Naipaul, The Enigma of Arrival

# ACKNOWLEDGMENTS

I am very grateful to Han Li for research assistance while writing this book and to World Scientific for commissioning it. I am also very grateful to Rod Wye, Stephanie Kleine-Ahlbrandt, Marya Arian, David Goodman and Loh Su Hsing for comments on the original draft.

# CONTENTS

| | | |
|---|---|---|
| *Acknowledgments* | | vii |
| *List of Abbreviations* | | xi |
| *Foreword* | | xiii |
| *Map of China* | | xv |
| *Introduction* | | xvii |
| Chapter 1 | Life | 1 |
| Chapter 2 | The Hu Era: Politics and Internal Affairs | 27 |
| Chapter 3 | A Strong Rich Country: The Chinese Economy Under Hu | 77 |
| Chapter 4 | China's International Face Under Hu | 101 |
| Chapter 5 | What Does Hu Think? Ideology in the Hu Era | 141 |
| Chapter 6 | Always the Party Man: Hu and the CCP | 171 |
| Conclusion | Hu Jintao: A Provisional Assessment | 197 |
| *Bibliography* | | 215 |
| *Index* | | 221 |

# LIST OF ABBREVIATIONS

CCP — Chinese Communist Party
CCRG — Central Cultural Revolutionary Group
CIC — China Investment Corporation
CMC — Central Military Commission
CNOOC — China National Overseas Oil Corporation
CR — Cultural Revolution
ECFA — Economic Framework Co-operation Agreement
EU — European Union
IMF — International Monetary Fund
KMT — Kuomintang (Nationalist Party)
NATO — North Atlantic Treaty Organisation
OECD — Organisation of Economic Co-operation and Development
PLA — People's Liberation Army
PRC — People's Republic of China
SARS — Severe Acute Respiratory Syndrome
TAR — Tibet Autonomous Region
USD — US dollars
WHO — World Health Organisation
WTO — World Trade Organisation

# FOREWORD

During the last decade China has further developed its transformation from pariah state of the 1960s to leading international presence in the 21$^{st}$ century. Thirty years of sustained high economic growth that has seen China become the factory of the world has now been joined by the cultural and technological achievements of its leading universities, high-speed rail, and the Shanghai Expo of 2009. The Chinese Communist Party has taken the credit for much of this change and not simply the maintenance of stability and the necessary policy settings.

One man — Hu Jintao — has been China's leader for most of the last decade, as both Secretary General of the Party and President of the People's Republic. Yet the outside world knows very little about President Hu. Even by the standard of a political system in which public presence is usually regarded as a sign of weakness, Hu Jintao's apparently purposeful self-effacement is quite remarkable. Kerry Brown in his political biography refers to President Hu as 'a silent ruler'. The picture of the man that emerges is one not just of silence, but of an extreme desire not to be in any kind of public spotlight while still mindful of the responsibilities of rule.

Whimsy and charisma are completely absent from President Hu's political persona. Instead there is a commitment to the continued rule of the Chinese Communist Party, to a resurgent Chinese nationalism, and to social justice. The latter is likely to be the most long-term legacy of President Hu's term of office. During the Mao-dominated years of China's development the country was one of the most equal in the world, albeit an equality of poverty. By the middle of the first decade of the 21$^{st}$ century China had become one of the most unequal countries in the world.

Health and welfare provisions were simply becoming unavailable to all but the better off. Starting in 2005 President Hu and the Premier of the People's Republic of China, Wen Jiabao, combined to ensure the diversion of the government expenditure to health and welfare programmes. New urban and rural health programmes were introduced, together with increased expenditure on education, wage support and subsidised housing projects.

Kerry Brown's study of Hu Jintao and his time as leader of the Chinese Communist Party and President of the People's Republic of China is a timely and insightful analysis of the man and his world. Very little has been written for English-speaking audiences about Hu Jintao. It is particularly timely because in 2012 Hu Jintao will step down from office to make way for the next generation of leadership. In its analysis of the last decade the book presents a thorough and balanced appreciation of the trials and tribulations, as well as the successes achieved. Reform after state socialism, a discourse of modernisation, and indeed, simply just development in itself are complex processes that are not easily negotiated; these processes always bring the unexpected and rarely go smoothly. So it has been with China. As Kerry Brown argues, possibly the most significant achievement of the regime is that it has brought continuity and political stability to China, despite all the potential challenges. Hu Jintao may have been self-effacing but his approach to depersonalise politics has been an essential part of the recipe for a China continually expanding its influence and importance in world affairs. *Hu Jintao: China's Silent Ruler* is a book no one with an interest in China and its impact on the world can afford not to read.

Professor David S G Goodman
Professor of Chinese Politics
University of Sydney

# MAP OF CHINA

# INTRODUCTION

Over the six-month period from late 2012 to early 2013, Hu Jintao, President of China, Chair of the Central Military Commission, and Party Secretary of the Chinese Communist Party (CCP), will relinquish at least two of his three key positions. According to the Constitution of the Chinese Communist Party, his time as Party head will come to an end, given that he has already served two terms of five years. He will be well over the supposed retirement age of 68. His time as supreme leader of the Party with a monopoly of power in the world's most populous country will be over, and he will, at the 18th Party Congress to be held in 2012 in Beijing, have to hand over to a new generation of leaders.

Hu has presided over the People's Republic of China (PRC) at a critical period. He came to power in 2002 just a few months after his country had entered the World Trade Organisation (WTO). The Tiananmen Square uprising was just over a decade before, and the stain it had left on the memories of the elite leaders in the central government still remained. The period under Jiang Zemin and Zhu Rongji was one that was dominated by bold moves to scale down state owned enterprises, but also by increasing levels of inequality and corruption. A seminal moment in the 1990s was when Jiang himself had needed to move against fellow Politburo member and Party Secretary of Beijing Chen Xitong in 1996, placing him under house arrest and then prosecuting him for massive embezzlement. Interestingly, most commentators at the time smelt a rat and assumed that rather than Chen's main crime being corruption, he was prosecuted for being a supporter of the left, more conservative wing of the Party.

China's entry to the WTO had been an epic in its own right, spanning over 14 years, starting off in the 1980s, during a highly liberal, experimental phase in China's development.[1] It was a negotiation that had ebbed and flowed with the fortunes of China and its economy, being briefly locked into a deep freeze after the 1989 Tiananmen Square massacre, kick-started once more in 1992 when Deng famously re-energised the reform and opening up process with his legendary Southern Tour, and intimately linked with the more reformist, outward looking elements in the Chinese leadership around Jiang Zemin and Zhu Rongji. Their battles to finally reform the state owned enterprise system, which had been the backbone of China's industry until the 1990s, resulted in over 60 million workers being laid off. To many more cautious policy makers, entry to the WTO would only create even greater competitive pressures on China's already vulnerable domestic economy.

The theatrical build up of events to China's final full agreement to the terms of its entry in late 2001 are now the stuff of anecdote and legend. The chief negotiator for the US was on her way to the airport, about to give up on any final agreement, when she was summoned back to get the okay to the Agreement from then Chinese Premier Zhu. For the Europeans, there were epic negotiating sessions over financial services and telecoms before a final agreement was settled on. The WTO Communiqué was finally signed in November 2001.

There can be few more symbolic moments by which to plot the start of the era of Hu Jintao than entry to the WTO. Although he was not formally to be made Party Secretary of the CCP and President of the Country till late in 2002 and early in 2003 respectively, it was already pretty much certain that he was to be Jiang Zemin's successor as the 'core' of the Fourth Generation leaders. He had been taking on an increasingly prominent role in international

---

[1] See Yasheng Huang, *Capitalism with Chinese Characteristics*, Cambridge University Press, Cambridge, 2009, for a very good account of this period.

affairs since 1998 and in speaking about domestic policy. And yet, when he was finally elevated to the number one slot, the most common question asked about him was 'Who is Hu?' which fronted the covers of international magazines like *The Economist*. Hu has remained largely unknown, his position on policy issues mostly a mystery.

We have now had almost a decade to watch Hu as he has led China. His period in power is coming to a close, although, as later parts of this study will show, whether we can be confident he will finally disappear from political life after the next transition of leadership in 2012 is a moot point. In Chinese politics, the act of retirement is surprisingly difficult. But as this study will argue, Hu has been, first and foremost throughout his life, a man for Party process and rules. So if anyone can disappear in a quiet and anonymous retirement, he can. He was, at least on the surface, after all, pretty anonymous while in power.

Hu is a difficult politician to write about for many reasons. The culture in which he has exercised power does not welcome transparency, despite attempts during his tenure to deliver greater openness through what has come to be called 'inner Party democracy'. The Politburos over which he has presided have been famously unleaky. Even the Wikileaks telegrams in 2010 revealed little of that so-called confidential government interaction with the leadership around him and himself. Maoism, Dengism and even a form of ideology around Jiang Zemin are all valid labels. But Hu's contributions to the intellectual life of modern China, while hastily enshrined in the country's constitution in 2007, have no specific traction. His speeches are famously generic, avoiding any hint of a personal voice, with one of them famously drafted by a committee and passing through over 50 different iterations before being delivered at the 17th Party Congress in 2007.

Hu aroused deep interest before he came to power, largely because so little was known of him. He is allegedly gifted with a phenomenally good memory, understated, calm and almost wholly devoid of small talk. Whether he was a reformer, a liberal, or a leftist was unknown. Hopes of him hiding some huge hinterland in his path towards the top were more fond fancies than based on wise analysis. The assumption that he simply could not reveal much about himself in China's claustrophobic political atmosphere was held fast to by some, even several years into his period in power. Now the vast majority of that time has gone, and we have to start looking at this record as being indicative of him as a leader and as telling us something about him as a person. This is in place of any willingness on his part to speak directly about these issues.

For Hu, despite being judged one of the modern world's most powerful figures, is also one of its least willing to communicate. While US Presidents like Barack Obama and George W Bush, or European leaders like former British Prime Minister Tony Blair or French President Nicholas Sarkozy, were willing to sit with domestic and international journalists for long periods while in office, Hu gave no one-to-one interviews with any foreign journalists (apart from one with the Russian Interfax agency), and only held the most stilted, stage-managed interactions with Chinese reporters. His silence has been so faithfully maintained that it is hard to see this as an affectation but more likely as being in keeping with his own personality. Unlike his predecessor Jiang Zemin, there were no outbursts of karaoke singing during trips abroad, nor, for that matter, any explosions of anger at intrusive Hong Kong journalists, something Jiang famously did in 2000 when visiting the Special Administrative Region. Hu maintained the same visage whether he was celebrating success (like the opening of the 2008 Beijing Olympics) or facing down disaster (in his response to the tragic natural calamities of his era — the Wenchuan earthquake in Sichuan in May 2008, or the Gansu earthquakes in 2010). One of the two cartoons produced by mainland artists while he was in power showed him weeping while writing a letter to an unfortunate citizen. Even such a light and friendly caricature was to see its makers suspended from their jobs. Hu's image belonged, at least in the PRC, to the Party and to himself. No one else could mess with it.

This combination of China's political culture and the man's own diffidence and silence, mean that uncovering the person behind the image constructed of him publicly, especially at this stage, for any assessment of him, is very hard. This is, therefore, very much a political analysis of him and an assessment of his time in power. It is based on the assumption that he has been the most influential and important political figure in contemporary China from 2002 to 2012, and that therefore there must be some link between him, his personal beliefs and the way that China has actually developed over this period.

After almost a decade of Hu's role, China presents itself as an immense paradox. It is a country that, with entry to WTO (and this will be dealt with in the chapter on economics under Hu), has simply exceeded most expectations in terms of its own growth and productivity. It was under Hu that China became the world's largest holder of foreign reserves (overtaking Japan in 2006), the world's largest exporter (overtaking Germany in 2009) and the second largest economy (overtaking Japan, again, in 2010). Under Hu, China became the world's largest user of automobiles and the largest emitter of carbon greenhouse gases. Hu's China is a place of dazzling statistics and bewildering, rapid growth. It is also a country where as much is spent on internal security as on defence.[2] It is a country where, for the first time in its history, as many people live in its cities as in the countryside. It is also a country where official statistics for protests have risen from around eight thousand a year when Hu came to power, to over 90 thousand a year by 2010, proof perhaps of a new-found sense in the rights of citizens to express their discontent about specific issues.

---

[2] This came out in the National People's Congress in 2010. The figure for the first is assessed as USD75 billion and USD80 billion for the second.

When Hu was elected to be Party Secretary of the CCP in 2002, capitalists had only just been allowed to enter the Party, after many years of being regarded with deep distrust. By the midpoint of Hu's era, they were contributing to as much as half of all GDP growth according to the Organisation of Economic Co-operation and Development (OECD). The compact made with business people has been one of the most striking features of the 2002 to 2010 period. Business people have, on the whole, been left to do business; they have largely put their political ambitions, if any, in the hands of the CCP, or simply on hold. The rule of the market has been dominant, with the general parameters of Deng Xiaoping's initial vision of China's future maintained. Celebrations in 2008, and again in 2010, of various aspects of this whole process only saw Hu stand close to that vision, by making it clear that China would not, and could not, return to the isolationism of the past, nor the economic blueprint of heavy central state planning adhered to then.

But Hu's era has also been one of profound contention. Towards its end, 150 million people are still judged, even by the central government, to be living in poverty, surviving on less than USD2 a day. China is a country that has met almost all of its UN Millennium Development Goals many years earlier than expected. And yet, over 20 million people are still malnourished. It is a society that has seen an unprecedented growth in the size of its middle class, and yet is still riddled with conflicts between different sectors of society, from migrant workers, to poor city dwellers, to farmers, university graduates, local officials, and the new wealthy. Understanding the key political personality at the centre of all this is important, despite the challenges mentioned above.

This book will follow a simple plan. The first chapter will look at Hu's personal life, following his progress from Tsinghua University to his first Party appointment in Gansu and then Guangxi and Tibet. In the process, the chapter also describes the experience of many of those from his generation who had to live through the excitement, and trauma, of the final years of the Cultural

Revolution. I will look at the period during which, in the early 1980s, he caught the eye of then paramount leader, Deng Xiaoping, possibly while he was the head of the China Youth League, and how he made this one of the fundamental networks by which he was able to eventually rise to power over a decade and a half later. I will look at his return to Beijing in the early 1990s and the steps by which he was raised, first into the Politburo, then to the Vice Presidency, and finally to become Party Secretary in 2002.

From the second chapter onwards, I will discuss thematic issues around his period in power, particularly his performance in terms of internal politics (the second chapter), China's economy (the third) and China's international role (the fourth). The chapter on internal politics will look at Chinese society as it has developed over the period from 2002, and in particular the impact of rapid economic growth on social development and the creation of new groups in society, as well as the management of relations between these. It will also look at the events in elite politics and Hu's role in these and in facing key challenges like the SARS crisis in 2003, the removal of former Shanghai Party Secretary Cheng Liangyu in 2006, and the handling of the uprisings in Tibet and Xinjiang in 2008 and 2009 respectively.

In the third chapter, I will look at economic growth in the Hu decade, the area of strongest achievements, specifically focusing on Chinese investment abroad, the development of the non-state sector, and the response to the global economic crisis of 2008.

In the fourth chapter, I will look at Hu's international record — at the way in which he has related to the world outside China, both in his visits to other countries and his responses to international crises, from the wars against Iraq and Afghanistan from 2003, to the relations with the US, European Union (EU) and other key partners. Most critically of all for China's own interests, I shall discuss the attempts by him and others to articulate a narrative for China's increased dominance in the international system which can assert what the country's legitimate interests are, but also reassure others that it plans to be a cooperative, positive force in global affairs. The key contribution Hu has made to cross-strait relations is of particular importance here and may well be put down as one of his most successful achievements.

In the fifth chapter, I will deal with the crucial question of ideology as it is expressed in key statements and speeches Hu has made since 2002, and the ways in which this has contributed to the CCP's narrative of its power and authority in China, how it relates to Hu's own methods of exercising power, as well as the sort of changes and adaptations that Hu has sponsored in contemporary ideology in the PRC.

In the sixth chapter, I will look at the more practical issue of Hu's actions as a Party man — his record in promoting, and impeding, reform in China, and in developing key parts of the Party self-governance. Inner Party democracy and the struggle to reform the CCP will be the focus of this chapter, with some assessment of just how Hu has been able to manage the various threats and challenges to the CCP as it moves into the 21$^{st}$ century, as one of the final surviving systems where the Communist Party has a monopoly on power, both externally and internally.

In the final chapter, I will go where angels fear to tread and try to make some provisional assessment of the Hu era. In particular, I will look at its record of success in terms of economic development and international relations, as well as challenging areas like the rise in inequality, the failure to craft a coherent narrative of China's international role, and its own specific vision of modernity. I will in particular look at what might be called the vision that Hu and his fellow elite leaders have of China and its role, of human development and the limitations in this.

That such a significant world leader, in a period of intense media attention, should remain so shrouded in mystery is one of the more remarkable aspects of Hu's leadership. That he would probably pass through most major thoroughfares in western capitals and not be recognised, is as much an indictment of widespread ignorance outside China of who is leading it and what their political programme, is as anything else. Hu has been complicit in this, presenting a 'non-ego' style of leadership. According to one anecdote when asked in the early 2000s by former French President Giscard D'Estaing why there were no direct presidential elections in the PRC, Hu replied that was because few would know who he was in his own country. I will argue in this book that, with China's unhappy history of egotistic leadership in modern times like Mao's, Hu's reasons for keeping a very low profile had very good intentions.

But it would be wrong to see Hu as a man without power constrained in a system where he has been swamped by the interests and influence of other powerful figures around him. It is clear that in key areas, from policy on Taiwan, to Tibet, to China's international relations, to its internal economic and political development, he has been the most significant voice in the country in the first decade of the 21st century, and this has become clearer as the decade has continued. His views may well have been hard to clarify, but at least in actions they are clear. His regime has been risk-averse, highly conservative in some aspects, but surprisingly bold in others. As a person he is regarded as something of a control freak. As we start to deal with the legacy he might leave in China, we have to search a little harder for what he has said, to interpret this and be clearer about the sort of politician he was. This is an initial attempt to do that.

# Chapter One

# LIFE

Hu Jintao presents particular challenges to those who wish to write about the man, rather than his public life and political career. His speeches are devoid of any personal detail, and he had never submitted to an interview with the western media until his visit to the US in early 2011 when he deigned to meet foreign journalists from the *New York Times*, but only with prepared questions. His personal background, beyond the baldest statement of his key career milestones, has not appeared on any Party publicity, nor figured in any campaign. While the wartime childhoods of former elite leaders like Jiang Zemin and Li Peng, and their being sons of martyrs in the struggle against the Japanese was made into a part of their public persona, and figured in accepted biographies of them in Mainland China, for Hu, almost every aspect of his early years and rise to power is unclear.

First of all, his birthplace. According to the authoritative databank of Chinese elite politicians, China Vitae, he was born in Jixi, Anhui province, in December 1942.[1] This is the same place as is recorded on his official CV issued by the *People's Daily* (though there it is carefully and somewhat ambiguously worded as "a native of", leaving room for him to be physically born elsewhere).[2] According to expert on contemporary Chinese politics Willy Lam, however, his family had left this place over a century before,

---

[1] www.chinavitae.com/biography/Hu_jintao/career [22 December 2011].
[2] http://english.peopledaily.com.cn/data/people/hujintao.shtml [22 December 2011].

and he was actually born in Taizhou, in neighbouring Jiangsu province.[3] Another report has him supposedly born in Shanghai.[4]

In fact, if it is true that he was born in Jiangsu province, it would mean that since 1989, the Communist Party has been led by two natives of this rich coastal province, for this was where Jiang Zemin also came from. Anhui, a vast middle province, with an economy largely based on agriculture even today, was perhaps a good place to claim a strong link with, as it suited Hu's programme of presenting himself as a man from the true grassroots, from a modest background.

Hu's mother was to die just at the dawn of the founding of the People's Republic of China in 1949. His father was a relatively wealthy tea merchant, who according to some reports died in the Cultural Revolution (CR), and to others, died in 1978. What is not in dispute is that Hu was largely bought up by an aunt. He had two sisters, both of whom still live in Jiangsu, one of them occupying a relatively modest position in the local Party.

Very little is known about Hu's schooling and childhood. He himself has never mentioned any experiences from that time to whether foreign visitors, or when he has travelled abroad. The most important event happened in 1959 when he went to Tsinghua University, one of the elite educational establishments re-generated by the Communists in Beijing, to study in the Water Conservancy Engineering Department. In view of China's massive water issues during his time in power, it is ironic that his early career was spent learning about hydrology, an issue he was to have to deal with at some length almost half a century later. He seems to have been a good student, with a formidable memory for facts and details, and a politically reliable background — from

---

[3] Willy W Lam, *Chinese Politics in the Hu Jintao Era: New Leaders, New Challenges*, M E Sharpe, London, 2006, p 5.
[4] John C Tkacik, 'Who's Hu? Assessing China's Heir Apparent, Hu Jintao', Lecture at the Heritage Foundation, US, April 19, 2002, at http://www.heritage.org/Research/Lecture/Whos-Hu [22 December 2011].

a family of petit bourgeoisie with no damaging capitalist links. All this meant that on his graduation in 1964, he was able to stay on to be a postgraduate and political instructor.

Tsinghua had a very special place in the political firmament of post-1949 China. According to American-based scholar Cheng Li, the formidable Jiang Nanxiang, the President of the University from 1952, wished to make the institute "the cradle of red engineers", creating a system of political counsellors to do this.[5] This network was there to ensure ideological training amongst students, and to make them reliable future administrators and leaders. The fruits of Jiang's work become clear over three decades later when the Politburos from the 1990s onwards were dominated by graduates of the college from this period. It created an elite which brought together capable, ambitious people who were potential leaders and, most importantly, who were all faithful to the concept of the unified rule of the CCP.

Of these, Hu Jintao was to eventually become the golden boy. He fitted all the requirements of Jiang's vision of a member of a technocratic elite, the kind that the latter was trying to create, with some success, not just at Tsinghua, but also through his consecutive position as Minister of Education. Aware of the decimation of China's human capital through both the terrible toll of the Sino-Japanese war (1937–1945), and then the fleeing of many of the country's intellectuals and scientists either to Taiwan with the Kuomintang (KMT), or abroad when the PRC was founded after the Civil War (1946–1949), Jiang had the support of the new leaders around Mao Zedong to build up a small class of well trained, capable young scientists and intellectuals. But their training had to fit the specific needs of China as defined through the Five Year Plans implemented since 1953 — to rebuild the country's infrastructure, to create a technical culture, and to address the huge defence needs the country had. These only grew more urgent after the rift

---

[5] Cheng Li, *China's Leaders: The New Generation*, Rowman and Littlefield, Lanham Boulder, 2001, p 89.

with the USSR in the late 1950s, when many of the Soviet experts were simply sent home, and China's largest technical co-operation and assistance partner simply disappeared.

All this was to be rudely interrupted by the Cultural Revolution, which started to have impact in 1966. The Cultural Revolution, the movement 'to touch the soul', as one of its leading protagonists Jiang Qing was to call it, had its roots deep in complex elite conflicts and social contradictions stretching back into the late 1950s. Mao's clash with his defence minister Peng Dehuai at the Lushun Meeting in 1959 was only the precursor to a series of conflicts amongst senior leaders throughout the early 1960s. A few years of relatively stable, pragmatic governance by then President Liu Shaoqi and Secretary General of the Communist Party Deng Xiaoping (this was a different, and less powerful position than the General Secretary position created later) was replaced by distant murmurs of radical change from 1965. A seemingly esoteric argument about Vice Mayor of Beijing Wu Han's play 'Hai Rui Dismissed from Office' was the trigger for an escalating series of commentary and attack, into which Mao Zedong eventually made a spectacular intervention, marking what was in effect his political comeback after several years of near-silence.

By the summer of 1966, China was preparing for what was to be three years of frenzied political activity, extending from the centre out to all of the provinces and autonomous regions, and deep into rural areas. But in the early months, it was very much a political campaign like those which had prefigured it in the 1950s, including the Three Antis Movement of 1953 and Five Antis Movement of 1954–1955, and the Anti Rightist Campaign after the Hundred Flowers Movement in 1957 inviting intellectuals and others to offer criticisms and ideas to the authorities. Just like these campaigns, the media spread highly systematic messages about the need to attack certain carefully defined enemies. An atmosphere of vigilance quickly became one of hysteria. Victims were identified, and in some cases struggled against, in others dismissed from their offices, and in the worst cases suffered violence and ostracism from the Party, leading in the most extreme cases to death. Quite soon after its inception, however, the Cultural Revolution was to transform into something far more ambitious. The stakes were much higher than in previous conflicts, with two of the most powerful figures in the CCP directly raged against each other. Mao Zedong remained almost untouchable, because of his leadership in the Sino-Japanese War and the long struggle for the Communists to come to power. But Liu Shaoqi was equally revered in parts of the Party, as someone who had been an activist almost from the foundation of the CCP in the 1920s, and had played a key role in some of the defining battles during the wars.

By 1966, it was clear that the objective this time was not just the 'enemies' within society who had been targeted in previous campaigns — ex nationalist KMT supporters, those with bad class backgrounds, capitalists and other 'black' classes. While these were still around and needed to be 'dug out' (a phrase much loved by Cultural Revolution era demagogues and propagandists) the real enemy this time was within, deep in the ranks of the CCP. Mao's target, for much of the CR era, was the very Party that he had been so instrumental in bringing to power, and which he had led since the early 1940s without any major challenge. The most vicious aspect of the CR was this inner-Party feuding, where the Communist Party simply ripped into itself. This also gave the vast, complex movement an unpredictability that meant the CCP was only fully reunified and cohesive after Mao's death in 1976.

Those of Hu's generation who came to adulthood at this period were profoundly marked by their experiences during this political movement. Its impact on them cannot be underestimated. This is especially true of the very small proportion of Chinese who were at university in the mid to late 1960s. Someone of Hu's age would have taken the full brunt of this wild, ambitious, sometimes exhilarating, sometime terrifying movement, and would have had their thinking changed and affected at one of the most formative and important periods of their life by the very agitated atmosphere in which they were living. The impact was strong enough to talk, later, of set groups in society — the 'sent down youth' (*xia xiang*), who left the cities on Mao's invitation to work amongst the people in the countryside, and the 'wounded' (*shang kou*), those who were to be victimised by the CR movement, and suffer during it, and who were to write in a whole genre afterwards of what they had endured.

One of the most perplexing aspects of dealing with the ongoing assessment of the impact of the CR is the difficulty of dividing people into victims and agitators. This was a battle over a long period in which there were no clear sides, and in which those agitating for the 'digging out and exposure of class enemies' one week were to become themselves victims of backlashes and changes of direction within the movement as a whole the next. In recent years, as the great Chinese writer Ba Jin was to say in the 1980s when he recalled the CR, it has sometimes been assessed as a movement in which everyone was a perpetrator, and all held some responsibility, and where people just as easily shifted one moment from victims to the next as culprits, and often back again.

Stories of Hu's life during this time are scarce. The most that can be said is regarding the atmosphere at Tsinghua at this period. This was the world in which he was living, and playing at least some part, and it was a relatively small community. An idea of its violence can be gleaned from William Hinton's *Hundred Days War at Tsinghua*, an eyewitness account by an American farmer who had been in China in the 1940s and author of *Shenfan*, one of the great descriptions of the land reform movement then. His descriptions of the struggle sessions at Tsinghua, where he was then working as a teacher, and the inter-factional struggles between students and the groups they established was one of the earliest, and remains a classic.[6]

It was in this world that radical groups were allowed space. Groups like the *Liandong* Red Guard faction, which believed

---

[6] William Hinton, 'Hundred Days War at Tsinghua University', *Monthly Review Press*, New York, 1973.

deeply in 'blood inheritance' and 'bloodline', talked about something that resembled a Communist royalty. Later elite leaders like future Politburo member Bo Xilai were to be tarred by association with this group, linked to acts of violence against fellow members. If Hu was active in such groups, no one in them, or associated with them has ever subsequently spoken. His later skills at being a silent, anonymous onlooker were already apparent even at this stage. He also had the great good fortune to be posted out of Beijing in 1968 for his first job in the administration of Gansu, far over in the north west.

One of the most complete accounts of the CR in Tsinghua is contained in American scholar Andrew Walder's *Fractured Rebellion: The Beijing Red Guard Movement*.[7] For each of the universities and colleges in Beijing, which, after all, only embraced a tiny fraction of the capital's population then, there was a complex interplay between the college authorities as they existed on the eve of the Cultural Revolution, the newly created groups that cropped up once the movement had started, and then a whole new establishment, mostly under the umbrella of the Central Cultural Revolutionary Group (CCRG), set up to be the chief centre of authority once the movement was underway.

For every university that Walder looks at in his study, the situation was slightly different. In Beijing University, perhaps the best known and understood example from this period, the movement was dominated by Nie Yuanzi, a member of the philosophy department. It was she who had posted a big character poster on May 25th 1966 declaring attacks on the current authority figures legitimate, and labelling them as bourgeois counter-revolutionaries. This had been brought to the attention of Mao Zedong, possibly by his newly politically active wife Jiang Qing (part of the condition of her original marriage to him set by the Party leadership in the 1930s was that she would keep out of politics), and published in the *People's Daily*, the ultimate mouthpiece of

---

[7] Andrew G Walder, *Fractured Rebellion: The Beijing Red Guard Movement*, Harvard University Press, Cambridge, MA and London, 2009.

the Party. As Walder and others have made clear, however, Nie was by no means typical of the student leaders. She was, for a start, considerably older than them, being in her early forties. Despite being affiliated to the philosophy department, she also had no particular academic training. More importantly, she had a history, from the Yan'an period when the Party had taken refuge in a revolutionary base in the central province of Shanxi. It was here that she had first crossed the path of the man who was ultimately to run China's security services, Kang Sheng. She was wise to fear him. Newly prominent in the Cultural Revolution himself, he was to be one of the key movers of the moment, and his influence, paranoid and sinister, is claimed to lay behind some of the worst excesses of this time.[8]

The movement in Tsinghua University was led by a much younger student, Kuai Dafu. It was he who led one of the first Red Guard groups, established under the inspiration of Mao Zedong to rebel. The process, however, by which each university in Beijing experienced the movement was slightly different. For Tsinghua, its particular significance was the role of Jiang Nanxiang, its President. As Walder states, "he was an obvious target for any purge of academic circles."[9] At the heart of the disruption for universities and critically important for the world in which Hu Jintao had his first political experience, were the creations of factions and work teams, which were to grow into rebellion groups and the Red Guard movement. Tsinghua was at the centre of this, as a place of political innovation and radical activism. In 1966, students had a choice: they "had to decide how to allocate their time between the pursuit of academic excellence and the compilation of a strong record as a political activist."[10] Political instructors like Hu "regularly placed formal evaluations in political dossiers that were kept on every student and that would follow them throughout their careers."[11]

---

[8] See the biography on him by John Byron and Robert Pack, *The Claws of the Dragon: The Evil Genius Behind Mao and His Legacy of Terror in the People's Republic*, Touchstone Books, New York, 1993.
[9] Walder, p 38.
[10] Walder, p 7.
[11] *Ibid*.

Radicals raged against conservatives, generating vicious internal battles, many of which ended in bloodshed, and often death. As institutions ground to a halt (most of China's universities ceased to function after the summer of 1966) the only organised life were through these groups, all battling for legitimacy with each other. For Tsinghua, Jiang Nanxiang was removed in June, replaced by officials from the central ministries (the leading one of them from the State Economic Commission).[12] All school officials were suspended from their posts, with those accused of the most serious crimes forced to undertake manual labour all day. "Tsinghua's work team conducted the most militant purge of any university," Walder concludes.[13] Kuai Dafu, a twenty-year-old third year student in the chemical engineering department was not even a Party member when he became the leader of one of the most radical groups, and the face of rebellion at the university. What he had going for him most was an excellent class background, something that trumped almost all other considerations. From June 1966, once President Jiang had been removed, he organised a number of radical, provocative acts, from struggle sessions to the posting of wall posters, denouncing the authorities and other groups. This culminated in him holding a hunger strike in July, which eventually, after the withdrawal of the work teams, led to him being partially rehabilitated by the Central Cultural Revolutionary Group, even being visited by Premier Zhou Enlai later in the month.[14] By August 5th, the first Red Guard group appeared, leading to the formal establishment of the Tsinghua Red Guards on August 19th, who stressed the need for blood line in choosing members — only the sons and daughters of revolutionary households were considered.[15]

From this point on, the Red Guard movement, particularly at Tsinghua and Beijing University, became wrapped up in the elite struggles in the central political apparatus even more. Attacks

---

[12] Walder, p 38.
[13] Walder, p 39.
[14] Walder, p 73.
[15] Walder, p 98.

on the then President Liu Shaoqi in late August in big character posters on Tsinghua campus, one of which was authored by his own daughter, confirmed that he was in deep trouble. High schools started getting dragged into the movement, and links were made between Red Guard groups in one institution and those in another. At this point it became clear that these university and school groups were of great political interest, and use, to the powerful figures within the newly created Central Cultural Revolutionary Group, with their own radical programme and agenda. There was one problem, however, and that was that even after the bedlam and havoc that the rebel groups had wreaked on life in Beijing, their ambitions proved hard to control, and their anger started being directed not just against the myriad of enemies they saw in society around them, but also against the very figures in the top new radical leadership that they were meant to be serving. A number of big character posters at Tsinghua University specifically aimed their attention at the CCRG, accusing it of secretiveness and being a new anti-Mao power centre. Their challenge of the Maoist elite elicited, in late 1966, a brutal response, led by Jiang Qing who declared in December, "we educated them poorly; forty and sixty-year-olds have not taught them properly. Their aristocratic arrogance, thinking that their bloodline is so noble, treating others so rudely — what nonsense."[16] At Tsinghua and other universities and institutes across Beijing, leaders of dissident groups who were seen as criticizing the new Maoist elite were arrested. This did not prevent Kuai Dafu from organising a mass event from Tsinghua in early February 1967, in which five thousand students marched through the city demanding the arrest of Liu Shaoqi and offering criticism of such figures as another Politburo member Bo Yibo. By the spring of 1967, the city was convulsed in violence, with a huge struggle session held against the wife of Liu Shaoqi, Wang Guangmei on April 10th. This was the infamous occasion on which Wang was forced to wear ping pong balls connected together by a piece of string around her neck, a humiliating reference to the

---

[16] Walder, p 187.

pearl necklace she had worn on a state visit to Indonesia in 1964. Further struggle sessions were held by the end of the year, but by the beginning of 1968, Tsinghua was put under martial law, with the military called in, as they would be elsewhere in China in and after September that year, to hammer out differences between radical groups and attempt to return things to something approaching normality.

Inter-factional conflict had its last major turn in the middle of 1968, when a radical group led by Kuai had an armed clash with another faction on the campus. "By early May," Walder writes, "Tsinghua campus was a patchwork of fortified buildings and ill defined front lines."[17] The first death in May from this conflict led to a demonstration in Tiananmen Square, and a further large scale assault at the end of the month. With the army called in en masse in July, Mao himself finally intervened. The Cultural Revolution was to move on to other forms and manifestations, with many students sent down to the countryside, or deployed in other activities. But the most violent phase had passed.

Unless Hu Jintao himself, or a direct witness is able to speak more clearly about what he did in Tsinghua during this violent and unsettled period, it is impossible to do anything except speculate. Ren Zhichu, in an unauthorised biography published in Canada in 1997, states that at the time he came under criticism for being "too individualistic" and a member of "a carefree clique."[18] By the standards of invective of the period, these were fairly bland denunciations. Whatever Hu's role in Tsinghua during this period, the campus is physically not so big, and the people involved were relatively small in number.[19] Many of the events laid out above

---

[17] Walder, p 244.
[18] See Ren Zhichu, *Zhong gong kua shi ji jie ban ren: Hu Jintao* (*Hu Jintao: China's First Man in the 21st Century*) Ontario, Mingjing chubanshe, 1997, p 38, quoted in Richard D Ewing, 'Hu Jintao, the Making of a Chinese General Secretary', *China Quarterly*, 2003, 173, p 19.
[19] According to Walder, at the time there were less than 4,500 students, staff, administrative and service people at Tsinghua.

must have been ones he was at least aware of, and perhaps for some, directly involved. As a political instructor, he would have been associated with the old establishment, which the Red Guards were created to smash. In that sense, it is unlikely he would have been involved in the more radical activity. Whether he was present at the famous humiliation of Wang Guangmei, or any of the other mass events, too, is unclear. But all of this would have been the backdrop to his life. And his departure in 1968 to Gansu was characteristic of the man's future — leaving a scene of trouble at the right time. His long years in the hinterland were about to begin.

## Gansu

To this day, Gansu province remains one the poorest, least developed amongst all of the PRC's 31 regions. A thin, long area, sandwiched between Qinghai in the west, Inner Mongolia in the east, and Sichuan in the south, it even has one international border with the Mongolian People's Republic.

Gansu's great fame to this day rests on it being the main land corridor by which people could enter China from Central Asia. What was subsequently called the Silk Route runs through the province, continuing on down to the ancient city of Xi'an, which had been historically one of the world's great political and cultural centres. In 21$^{st}$ century China, Gansu exploits this link for the few tourists that visit. The area's arid, sparsely populated hinterland is speckled with evidence of some of the ethnic groups that lived here thousands of years before. Ancient earthworks from the Qijia and Mijiayao periods can still be seen, a few miles from the current capital of the province, Lanzhou.

As a graduate in hydrology, Hu's first post was in the House Construction Team in the Liujiaxia Project Bureau. This dam had been one of several which were part of a major programme of water management projects announced in the mid 1950s, and work started on it formally in the fateful year of 1958, which also marked the start of the Great Leap Forward, the push instigated by Mao to make China a fully industrialised country within the next decade. Construction had been interrupted in the early 1960s, during the great famines, but when Hu arrived, it was only a year from completion. Hu's first home outside of Beijing as an adult, therefore, was an isolated, incomplete project 70 kilometres outside of Lanzhou, in Linxia Hui Autonomous Prefecture, one of the many dominated by one of China's 55 ethnic minorities with a notional self-administration.

In 1969, as the 9th Party Congress in Beijing was summoned, marking an end of the Cultural Revolution's most violent period, Hu moved into the bureaucracy proper, as an official for the hydroelectric ministry, joining one of its local bureaus, first as a secretary, then as Deputy Secretary, the first formal Party positions he was to have since Tsinghua.

For all its isolation, Gansu was to give Hu three major advantages. Firstly, he was to have experience as a Mishu (private secretary), from 1974 to 1975, when he served the Chair of the Gansu Construction Committee. As Cheng Li has noted, these positions next to powerful figures in the local and national leadership have been the foundation for many elite political careers since the 1970s.[20] Current Premier Wen Jiabao is perhaps the most famous example of this, serving as the head of the General Office of the CCP under first Party Secretary Hu Yaobang, and then Zhao Ziyang in the 1980s. Secondly, it was in Gansu, in 1980, that Hu was to meet his first, and most influential political patron, the then Party Secretary of the area, Song Ping. Song was to serve as Party boss of Gansu from 1977 to 1981, before returning to the central government in 1981. As head of the all-important personnel department of the CCP (called the Organisation Department) he was the key mentor for the careers of not just Hu, but also Wen. Finally, Hu's years in Gansu gave him the perfect credentials when rising to national leadership later the ability to say, with conviction, that

---

[20] Cheng Li, p 147.

he understood the situation in non-metropolitan, provincial China, and that he was an elite leader with an authentic understanding of the grassroots.

It is ironic that Hu Jintao worked in the same, small province for almost the same time as Wen Jiabao, whom he was ultimately to rule with over three decades later. But the two avoided talk of a 'Gansu Gang' with any similarity to the Shanghai Gang that was suspected of having such powers in the 1990s and 2000s under Jiang Zemin's leadership of the CCP. Hu's two final positions in Gansu were as the Deputy Director of the Provincial Construction Committee from 1975 to 1980, and finally, from 1980 to 1982, Vice Chairman of the same committee. It was from these vantage points that he would have observed the changes brought in from 1978 and the Plenum held late that year in a military hotel in Beijing, which was to kick off the reform and opening up process and mark the return to almost complete political control of Deng Xiaoping after the death of Mao Zedong two years earlier.

Gansu was also to be the place where two major events happened in Hu's personal life. It was here that he married his girlfriend from Tsinghua, Liu Yongqing (two years older than him), and where his two children, a boy, Hu Haifeng, and Hu Haiqing, a girl were born.

## Return to the Centre and Out Again — Hu in the Eighties

Hu's return to the central government in the early 1980s was largely as a result of attracting the eye of his first major mentor, the then Party Secretary of Gansu, Song Ping, mentioned above. Song Ping's wife, Chen Shunyao, had been deputy Party Secretary of Tsinghua University for part of the time that Hu had been studying there,[21] and had recommended the young official to Song, soon after his arrival in Gansu. In this, Hu, and Wen, was to enjoy a

---

[21] Ewing, p 20.

great stroke of good luck. Song returned to Beijing in 1982–1983 to be head of the powerful State Planning Commission. But it was as head of the Central Organisation Department of the CCP from 1987 to 1992, that Song offered Hu the most help, and it was indeed during this period that he was elevated into the Politburo. The role of patronage in Chinese politics has been intensely studied. The informal networks that can make — and break — careers lie at the heart of the *guanxi* system, where connections between individuals matter more than institutional factors. For all Deng's talk from 1978 onwards of creating a 'rule of law' rather than 'rule of man', which was epitomised by the utter lack of regulations in the Maoist era, China's elite political culture was to prove not so easy to change, even in the new reform era.

Hu was to gain the support of one other patron during his period in Beijing in the mid 1980s — one who was to prove far more contentious in later years. Hu Yaobang had been appointed Party Secretary of the national CCP in 1982, the same year in which Hu had returned to Beijing from Gansu. A military veteran from the gruelling horrors of the Long March, and the Sino-Japanese War, where he had survived attempts at execution, he had worked his way up as an official in Shaanxi, and in the Communist Youth League, before being appointed by Deng because of his reformist record to be head of the Party. Hu was marked out as a liberal, promoting rehabilitation of those who had been persecuted during the Cultural Revolution, and supporting Deng in his battles to move from the rigid centralised command economy structure favoured during the Maoist era to a market oriented one.

Hu Yaobang was also mandated by Mao in the search for younger cadres to take greater levels of responsibility. At the end of the late Maoist period, the CCP's ranks were depleted, many of its most talented former officials simply sidelined, or existing in political limbo, and a large number prematurely dead through ill treatments during the Cultural Revolution years. Deng himself was already 76 at the start of the decade, with a group of elite leaders around him like Chen Yun, Peng Zhen, and Bo Yibo who were also deep into their seventh or eighth decades. They were very aware that a new generation of leaders needed to be found and prepared. Hu Jintao was one of these.

The portfolio he was given was an attractive one too. Co-opted into the Central Committee, the central decision-making body of the CCP at national level, with, at the time, over 300 members, he was made the Secretary of the China Youth League, and of the All China Federation of Youth. This was to supply him with a critical network for the rest of his career, meaning that he was able to have input into the careers of younger officials at the very start of their working lives.

The China Youth League predates the Communist Party itself by a year, founded in 1920, months before the first Congress of the CCP itself in Shanghai, under the influence of the Soviet Union International Comintern. By the 1980s, its formal role was to act as a training ground for Party membership. Most university students, and those in high school, up to the ages of 26, were members. So were members of the PLA and others working in an official capacity. It had, in fact, more people in it than the CCP itself.

By 1985, at the height of China's liberalisation, a period fondly recalled as one of the most open and free in post-1949 history, Hu was assessed as ready to become Party Secretary of a province, the youngest to achieve this in the history of the PRC. Once more, he was sent down to one of the poorest regions, Guizhou, in the south west, sandwiched between Yunnan, Guangxi, Hunan, and Sichuan. Guizhou is a province which has a diverse mix of ethnic groups but undeveloped industry, despite its natural resources. "From the first day I arrived here," Hu is quoted as saying soon after he arrived in the province, "I have identified myself with developing and invigorating Guizhou's 176,000 sq kilometres of land and making the province's 29 million people of all nationalities rich and happy."[22] It was while in Guizhou that the first wave of student demonstrations in Beijing

---

[22] Ewing, p 21.

in 1987 forced Hu Yaobang to leave office, to be replaced by Zhao Ziyang. By 1988, Hu Jintao was considered ready to be given his greatest challenge to date, Party leadership of Tibet Autonomous Region (TAR).

## Hu Jintao and Tibet

Hu's four years in Tibet were to be tumultuous, and to throw unexpected, and unwanted, problems at him. It is also clear that physically, he did not enjoy life in the region, reportedly only staying there for 18 months of his full four year posting, spending the rest of his time in Beijing recovering from high altitude sickness.[23] For Guizhou, the challenges were social development and poverty. But Tibet offered a wholly different level of difficulty. A region of the PRC with a very separate cultural, linguistic and ethnic feel from any other in the vast country, it had only become formally part of the PRC in 1951 with the 17 Point Agreement between the central government and the leaders in Tibet. Complex arguments about its historic status, and the long-term interference of powers like Great Britain and the US had meant that the central government had a high level of uneasiness about just how securely the huge area assimilated into the Chinese political entity.

None of this was helped by the aggressive Maoist policies during the Cultural Revolution which saw widespread attacks on monasteries, the decimation of religious communities, and violent struggles between separate rebellious groups that would have put the unrest at the universities in Beijing during the 1980s to shame. Hu Yaobang's visit to the region in 1980 was a seminal moment of recognition that central policy had gone badly wrong. More central money was sanctioned to ease some of the huge developmental and social issues in the area, and liberal policies allowing the reopening of monasteries and the use of Tibetan language in

---

[23] Lam, p 9.

schools were implemented. Dialogue was even restarted with the Dalai Lama, and his 'government in exile'.

All of this, however, had little traction when the student unrest started in 1989. Corruption, the influence of international events like the reforms in the Soviet Union, and social discontent fired by rising inflation all played their part in a series of demonstrations that grew sharper in intensity as the year went on. For Tibet, the moment of crisis came sooner than for the central leaders in Beijing. On the night of March 5th, demonstrations around a police station in Lhasa became increasingly agitated. According to one account, Hu played a skilful game, refusing to give the local police chief open sanction to move on the protestors for most of the day, and then simply disappearing at night, so that, when things became critical, the police on their own authority had no choice but to take action, firing into the crowd, killing many demonstrators and dispersing the rest. By the morning of March 6th, things had been pacified, despite the loss of lives.[24]

While at least in this account, Hu never gave the final authorisation, he enjoyed the plaudits. He had shown himself to be tough when it mattered, and won the admiration of the central leadership. The greatest influence was through the aging patriarch, paramount leader Deng Xiaoping, who apparently stated in the early 1990s that "this person Hu Jintao is not bad at all."[25] Further plaudits were to fall from the paramount leader's lips during his Southern Tour in early 1992.[26] These were taken as signs that somewhere down the line, after the end of Jiang Zemin's period in office, Hu would be national leader. The comments were ascribed almost mythical sanctity, and were taken as the greatest tangible clue of what Hu's fate would be.

In this way, Tibet, through the tragic violence and upheaval that unfolded there in 1989, became the crucible where Hu's leadership

---

[24] Lam, p 8–9.
[25] Ewing, p 25.
[26] Peter Yu, 'Hu's the one to succeed Jiang Zemin?' *The Straits Times*, Singapore, August 28, 1998.

was tested and found fit. In the words of one analyst, "Hu's actions showed utter faithfulness to the central line, and to the Party. This streak of ruthlessness certainly took back some who had seen him as a quieter, more scholarly figure."[27] Unsurprisingly, Hu's time in Tibet gave him a close interest in the region, so that, even in 2010, confidential cables leaked to the Wikileaks site made clear that Hu remained very much engaged and in charge of central policy towards the region.[28]

## Return to the Centre: Hu's Elevation to the Politburo

The combination of being perceived to have done a good job in Tibet under very difficult circumstances, pacifying it no matter what the cost at a time when the CCP was under great threat; the role of Song Ping, a patron, in the crucial Organisation Department of the CCP (the one with a key role in deciding personnel decisions) and; the words of support from paramount leader Deng Xiaoping meant that in late 1992, at the 14th Congress, Hu was given a raft of positions, the most important of which was that he was put in charge of the CCP Secretariat and made a member of the Standing Committee of the Politburo, the formal summit of power and decision making in contemporary China. The ascent of this relatively young official (he was merely fifty at the time) from relative obscurity to the seven-strong Standing Committee (it was subsequently increased to nine in 2002) was both surprising and unprecedented. He had, after all, only been a member of the Central Committee of the CCP since 1982. That he was now one of the most powerful figures in China, and yet almost hardly known to the outside world, was an apt symbol of how opaque, and introspective, the world of elite Chinese politics remained, even after the reforms under Deng Xiaoping.

---

[27] Personal communication.
[28] Press Trust of India, 'Wikileaks: Hu Jintao in Charge of Tibet Issue', 19 December 2010, http://ibnlive.in.com/news/wikileaks-hu-jintao-incharge-of-tibet-issue/137927-2.html [22 December 2011].

One of Deng's great battles had been to introduce more formal, institutionalised processes of decision making and governance into the Communist Party itself. Under Mao, it had been, more often than not, the servant, sometimes the victim, of his own immense power. No Congress had been held from 1956 to 1969. The one in 1969 had been a gruesome affair in which many of the previous members were either dead, or in prison. It became dominated by military leaders till the next one, in 1973, during which a new group of radical leftist figures had been elevated. Many of these too had been dismissed when what became known as the Gang of Four fell in 1976. When the first Congress after Deng had gained full control of the CPC was held in 1982, there was a deliberate attempt to set down some new ground rules so that no single ruler could dominate the system and abuse it in the way that Mao had. Congresses were to be regularised, and held every five years. Party Secretaries and Politburo members started to have set terms of appointment. In a series of deals in the 1980s, the most senior, and aged, leaders, were convinced of the need to step down, so that fresh blood could enter the Party. Bo Yibo, for instance, one of the most influential Communist leaders from the 1930s onwards, was persuaded to retire, in return for one of his sons enjoying a political career after him.

By 1992, Congresses had started becoming the key moments at which future policy directions and leadership positions were made clear. And the 1992 Congress occurred at a critical period, soon after paramount leader Deng Xiaoping's famed Southern Tour in which he had expressed frustration with the slow pace of economic reform, and asked that more be done to open China's economy up and accelerate its liberalisation. These were taken at the time as criticisms of the man put in to lead the Party after the uprising in 1989, Jiang Zemin.

Jiang himself, having been abruptly placed at the head of the Party in 1989, was highly cautious before 1992, carefully balancing the concerns of conservatives in the Party, who were against more reform because they believed it had partly led to the problems in

1989 which had so badly affected the Party, and those of liberals who had wanted more reform, faster and deeper. It was not helped by the fact that he had as his Premier Li Peng, a key figure in the June 4th crackdown, and someone who sided with the conservative hardliners. Deng's talks in early 1992, while in some of the key places which had developed under the economic reforms he had sanctioned a decade before, were taken as signs that Jiang now had the legitimacy to push further ahead with opening up China's economy, allowing greater flows of foreign investment, and reforming its industrial and agricultural sectors. By the Congress in late 1992, therefore, the start of a new era of economic reformism was already clear.

Hu was to maintain a low profile throughout the mid 1990s. He met occasional delegations, and focussed on his job as head of the Secretariat in the Politburo. But his appointment in 1993 to head the Party School, the key central think tank for the CCP, at least gave some scope for him to be involved in the framing of new thinking and ideas about how the Party ruled and its ideological orientation. The collapse of the Soviet Union in 1991 had provoked deep soul searching within the CCP, with many convinced that with further reforms, the same fate that befell the Soviet Communist Party would happen to the CCP.[29] From 1991 a long period of reflection and research at the Central Party School began to draw some conclusions about how China might be able to marketise its economy, without jeopardising the monopoly on power by the CCP. Economic growth was seen as key to the country's stability and the CCP's hold on power. But as this book will later argue, the need to maintain ideological coherency, and cohesiveness, was still important. In the period during which Hu was the head of the Party School, it was seen as a place where Party officials and thinkers could ponder matters freely. It was considered one of the more liberal institutions in China, despite its location so close to those in power. It was this more than anything that made observers at the time believe that Hu Jintao might be a liberal.

---

[29] See Neil Munro, 'Democracy Postponed: Chinese Learning from the Soviet Collapse', *China Aktuell*, 2008, 37(4), p 42.

Re-elected to the Standing Committee at the next Congress, the fifteenth, in 1997, Hu was made a Vice President only a year later. Most significantly of all, in 1999 he was elevated to the vice chairmanship of the Central Military Commission (CMC), the group comprised both civilians and military officers in charge of policy for the People's Liberation Army (PLA). With this position secured, he had combined the key areas he needed to — executive political responsibility as Vice Premier, and military responsibility. It was also in 1999 that he was given the high profile job of speaking publicly about the accidental bombing of the Chinese embassy in Belgrade during the NATO-led attack on Yugoslavia, an event which caused huge anger in China, and demonstrations against NATO embassies and consulates in Beijing and other cities. He had the critical job of calling off outraged patriotic violence while himself not appearing unpatriotic.

By 2000, it was already clear that Hu Jintao was almost certain to replace Jiang Zemin as leader at the next Congress in 2002. What role Jiang might play after his retirement (Deng, for instance, had remained highly active as a politician, despite retiring from all his formal positions except as head of the CMC in 1987), and how the transition might happen remained unclear.

The following chapter will look in more detail at the succession process, by which Hu became General Secretary, and Country President. From 2002, in fact, Hu's story becomes that of China, and it is necessary to treat them together. In effect, the story of the last decade of his life has also been that of the last decade of China's development; it is impossible to separate the two. That will be dealt with in the rest of the book.

## Who is Hu: The Man of No Qualities?

What we can do here is to address the vexed question of what kind of man Hu seems to be, through his career, and the way he has managed his rise to power. This presents particular challenges, since Hu himself uses no personal register at all in his speeches, and gives no clues away about what has motivated and driven him to be the dominant political force in China in the first ten years of the 21st century. He is one of the most opaque and mysterious figures of modern global politics. It would be unwise to expect him to surrender his secrets too easily.

There are three aspects of his career, however, which do say something about him. The first is that he enjoyed the patronage of very different, very demanding, and very powerful figures from quite early in his career. Song Ping, Hu Yaobang, and Deng Xiaoping were all tough, shrewd men, but each very different in their focus. Hu, however, managed to impress each of them in different ways, getting their support at key stages in his career. The second is that Hu managed to avoid creating any major enemies, at least within the Communist Party elite. His elevation was not opposed by anyone powerful enough to prevent it, and he managed to keep on the right side of almost everyone that mattered. In the savage world of Chinese politics, this is a formidable achievement. Finally, he managed to belong to a number of different factions, and yet was not controlled by any of them. A graduate of Tsinghua University, he was initially given a power base by the Communist Youth League, but he was also someone who had once been a *Mishu* (Private Secretary), and a technocrat. The two groups he did not clearly belong to which were identified and heavily researched later were the Shanghai Group, and the princelings (those related to former high level leaders of the CCP, usually accepted as Vice Minister level or above). Ironically, his lack of association with these groups was also helpful.

In addition to these three features, there are two others, which are of more personal importance. The first is that Hu appears, to those who have met him, and those who have dealt with him, to be a man with immense self control. Order and control are central to his personal habits, and to his political persona. He is a man who likes his overseas visits to be conducted with rigorous planning. He makes speeches in which his sole objective is to deliver no surprises. None of them contain a word about him as a person. He conducts interviews only under the fiercest strictures, where questions are vetted beforehand, and nothing might happen to unsettle him. His response to anything unexpected is icy coldness. His performance at the opening of the 2008 Beijing Olympics was par for the course — a few words, uttered with almost mechanical tonelessness, and then silence. This connects to the second aspect of his time in power — the peculiar demonstrations of egolessness. Hu has allowed no collected works to be published in his name, and has maintained the lowest of profiles. He has carried out Deng Xiaoping's instructions about not allowing a political career in China to be corrupted into arrogance and egomania. Hu operates by what seems like consensus, and rarely takes central stage. There is no Hu Jintao Thought as there was for Deng and Jiang, no talk at least by the CCP of 'Hu as the core of the fourth generation of leadership' and no hefty investment in anything approaching a personality cult.

This lack of ego is puzzling. Combining hugely effective ambition, which allowed him to become the youngest ever Party Secretary of a province, the youngest member of the Politburo, and then to succeed, despite vigorous opposition, in securing the leadership of the CCP and the country, with a lack of ego seems contradictory. In fact, it has proved to be a brilliant strategy. Hu's 'egolessness' is, in fact, almost certainly highly deliberate, and it remains at the heart of his political success.

As in any political culture, the choice of a political persona happens quite early, and defines the rest of a leader's life. In most western democracies, this is often tightly related to the choice of political orientation, left or right. But in China, where one party rules supreme, the issue is more about how one manages the tight web of relations around one, negotiating the myriad pitfalls that exist in order to balance as many of these as possible, and leave as few of them destroyed. Hu has been masterly as doing this, as his networks described above show.

His highly controlling manner indicates that in fact he is more than capable of creating this discipline. Rumours of his being a sharp dancer in his youth betray at least some original, more spontaneous spark. But the long years of life in the remote Gansu province, perhaps, gave Hu a far tougher patience.

The way in which he has expunged all indications of any underlying personality away from his public, political one has been done with ruthless self-discipline. Hu Jintao lives in a world where he does not make gaffes, or lose his temper, or have public clashes with people, simply because the opportunities for these are removed. It is no small irony that in an era, as we shall see, in which China is beset by contentiousness between different social and economic groups, and in which the impact of very rapid economic change on society has been so unsettling, creating inequality, argument and a society that frequently looks like it is in ferment, its key leader is a man almost wholly devoid of any strong characteristics, who demonstrates by his very existence, huge control.

One of the more intriguing possibilities to understand Hu's inner self is to look at words written by the philosopher Immanuel Kant, one of the great fathers of the Enlightenment. In his 'Groundwork of the Metaphysics of Morals',[30] Kant discusses the question of how to define morality. Arguing that only the good will is something intrinsically and wholly good, he moves on to look at personal actions, and how these might be construed as moral or not. "As I have deprived the will of every impulse which could arise to it from obedience to any law, there remains nothing but the universal conformity of its actions to law in general, which alone is to serve the will as a principle, i.e., I am never to act otherwise that so that I could also will that my maxim should become a universal law."

---

[30] Immanuel Kant, 'Groundwork for the Metaphysics of Morals', at http://evans-experientialism.freewebspace.com/kant_groundwork_metaphysics_morals01.htm, [23 December 2011].

It is a further irony that the Enlightenment and its values, things criticised by, amongst others, intellectuals like Wang Hui, should find such a perfect practitioner in President Hu, a man who has expunged all trace of personal desire and impulse in order to become the image of the type of person described by Kant — a man who speaks as though he wills that all his words were scientific, impersonal, objective, and universal.

Reading Hu's speeches, therefore, is to read statements of consensus, and of collective agreement. He exists on one level as merely the mouthpiece for these. They are written and circulated and drafted by committees, with no overt personal input in terms of style by Hu himself. Hu's ideological interests have been expressed through the unwieldy slogans 'scientific development' and 'harmonious society' — expressing, once more, selflessness, consensus, and the push to what are presented as universal truths. At the heart of Hu's project of himself, therefore, is the extraordinary belief in creating a perfect political persona, someone who is, in fact, not a person at all, but a symbol of the belief system of the whole Party, a belief system still dominated by the idea of Truth. It is with this particularly powerful carapace that Hu has dominated Chinese politics for the first part of the 21$^{st}$ century. He is, paradoxically, a man who has willed himself with iron determination to have no personal qualities. But his silence has created huge problems at a time when, far quicker than he or the leaders around him ever expected, his country has become a globally dominant force, and its voice can no longer be that of a control freak, but of a human being that others outside of China can relate to and understand. In that sense, Hu's greatest success — his creation of this very particular, consensus driven personality, perfectly suited to success in China's hugely difficult internal politics — is also the root of his greatest failure, the inability to help people around the world understand China, and feel at ease with what it is doing. All that will be discussed in the following chapters.

## Chapter Two

# THE HU ERA: POLITICS AND INTERNAL AFFAIRS

Hu Jintao's rise to supreme power was carefully choreographed, and while it was widely foreseen, it was fraught with potential risks. The CCP, seemingly appearing unified from the outside, has in its history been sometimes famously divided over key issues (the most famous of which was the reform process itself). Its history of delivering smooth successions has been a poor one. Mao Zedong dominated political life, with large ebbs and flows, for almost three decades once the CCP came to power. But his chosen successors either ended up dead or in prison. Liu Shaoqi, for many years his number two, and President of the country up to 1966, was felled during the violent chaos of the Cultural Revolution, and, by most accounts, died of untreated cancer on a prison floor in his native Hunan. His replacement as Mao's successor Lin Biao fared little better, enjoying a few brief years of glory, but coming under a cloud of suspicion from the Ninth Party Congress in 1969 onwards. He was either killed, or murdered, on a flight which crashed in Mongolia while attempting to flee the country in September 1971. Mao's final choice as successor, Hua Guofeng, managed to do what all the others had failed to, by outliving Mao, but he was in the end, slowly, but highly effectively outmanoeuvred by Deng Xiaoping, who reigned as paramount leader for the next decade.

For all Deng's many talents, either for institutional reasons or bad luck, he was no better at picking a successor than his predecessor had been. The only difference was that his choices managed at least to remain alive once their time as the chosen one had passed. Hu Yaobang, from Mao's native Hunan province, occupied the position of Party Secretary of the CCP as it was rebuilding its institutional capacity in the early 1980s. But a spate of demonstrations in 1986 and 1987 mobilised opposition against him in the CCP amongst the many who opposed the whole reform process, and he was removed from his position, although he maintained a place on the Politburo. His replacement, Zhao Ziyang, fared little better, and was ironically felled by protests partially brought about by the death of Hu of a heart attack in April 1989, although a more complex constellation of issues like corruption, inflation, and the international situation in Eastern Europe and the USSR played a part too.[1]

The final choice of Jiang Zemin, formerly Party Secretary in Shanghai, was one that puzzled many at the time. He was someone who Deng and others had never expressed any strong opinion about, and was largely regarded as a well-meaning but unimpressive technocrat. His one major positive mark was from his handling of the protests in Shanghai in 1989 where he had managed to calm the situation down without loss of life. A more politically meaningful reason may well have been that Jiang alone was the candidate who was disliked the least by all the other factions, from those who were supporters of the June 1989 crackdown, to those who were still liberals at heart.

Jiang was able to consolidate his position over the coming years, taking Deng's strong hint in 1992 during the Southern Tour by restarting the reform process and further opening up China's internal market. But the idea that Jiang might exercise power in the same way that Deng or even Mao had was simply not acceptable to the CCP. Instead, in incremental steps, and for different reasons, retirement limits were brought in. A political elite that had been dominated by people in their seventies in the 1980s was now brought down to the mid sixties age range. And more thought was put into institutionalising the length of time that leaders were in power, as well as the processes and mechanisms by which power was exercised. The vexing question of dividing responsibilities between the government and the Party was revisited, though

---

[1] Zhao Ziyang refers to these in some detail in his memoirs, released a few years after his death in 2010. These are referred to in Chapter six.

remained unresolved. The final formulation was that while the government executed and implemented policy, it was all within the political rubric set out by the CCP. Authority for that flowed from the Politburos, where consensus was created and then articulated.

While it was often said that Hu Jintao rose to power smoothly because of Deng Xiaoping's patronage, in fact it was largely under Jiang Zemin that he was effectively promoted to his most important positions first as Vice Premier in 1997, and then as Deputy of the CMC in 1999. This imputes to him a far broader support base in the Party than merely the favour of one hugely powerful leader — and one who was dead by the time Hu finally came to power. Deng may have been seen as supporting Hu — but he had his reasons for doing so, which we will discuss later, and in the end, these were also recognised by others.

The process of transition from an elder to a younger generation of leaders was an uncertain one. There was a sense that the rules needed to be made up as the process continued. There was no lack of competing options. With a history of botched transitions between elite leaders, the challenge in the late 1990s was to manage this without the personal intervention of senior, retired leaders, only a few of whom were alive in the period from 2000 to 2003 when the process was scheduled to happen. A whole number of objectives had to be achieved. First the CCP's elite leadership had to change at the Party Congress in 2002. The results of this could not be a surprise. Groundwork had to be done, both within the Party, and then amongst the broader population. There needed to be continuity between the third and fourth generation leaders, in terms of personnel and ideology. A sudden change, especially at a time when China was wrestling with implementing the terms of the WTO, was too risky. The various parts of the CCP needed to be prepared for this change, to buy into it. Influential blocs on the left and right of the CCP needed to be recruited and convinced that what was about to happen was a good outcome.

The left could not be underestimated. Its most vociferous ring leader was Deng Liqun, who in the late 1990s as the impact of the Zhu Rongji and Jiang Zemin reforms on the state owned enterprises sector really bit in, had issued a 'ten thousand character' essay, saying that Jiang's leadership was ignoring the increasing gap between rich and poor which had come about as a result of over-aggressively implementing anti-socialist policies.[2] This drew on a long debate against some of Deng Xiaoping's reforms going right back to the early 1980s.[3] The scaling down of the state sector was seen as producing a new social stratification in which former favoured social groups like state workers and farmers were being marginalised. Their concerns needed to be addressed. The 'banner' of socialism, Deng declared, had to be maintained. Jiang's ideological solution for what to do about an increasingly significant non-state sector was achieved with the 'Three Representatives' theory, introduced in the late 1990s, and then implemented into Party ideology in 2002, where it was also made part of the Party and state constitution.[4] Jiang had first articulated his theory while in Guangdong in 2000, stating that "throughout the historical periods of revolution, construction and reform, it [the CCP] has always represented the development trend of China's advanced productive forces, the orientation of China's advanced culture, and the fundamental interests of the overwhelming majority of the Chinese people."[5] This was a convoluted way of saying that the Party now had to do a deal with a group of people who were not necessarily Party members but

---

[2] Joseph Fewsmith, 'China since Tiananmen,' Second Edition, Cambridge University Press, Cambridge, 2008, p 183–185.

[3] For an overview of the series of Ten Thousand Character Essays around the 1997 15th Party Congress, see Kalpana Misra, 'Neo Left and Neo Right in Post Tiananmen China', *Asian Survey*, 2003, 43(5), p 717–744, especially 716–718.

[4] The Constitution of the CCP adopted at the 16th Party Congress in 2002 has, in its preamble, the statement: "The Communist Party of China takes Marxism-Leninism, Mao Zedong Thought, Deng Xiaoping Theory and the important thought of Three Represents as its guide to action." See http://news.xinhuanet.com/english/2007-10/25/content_6944738.htm [accessed February 14, 2011].

[5] 'On the Three Represents' from the website of the Communist Party International Liaison Department, http://www.english,cpc.com.cn/66739/4521344.html [22 December 2011].

were becoming some of the most important sources of growth and employment in the country.

Having built up consensus over the value of the non-state sector, and argued forcefully that it now had to be enfranchised and embraced by the CCP, Jiang was able to propose that entrepreneurs could enter the Party, something which had been banned since the 1950s and reinforced because of claimed links between them and the unrest that occurred in June 1989.[6] This was a highly pragmatic move. It was hard to see how the Party could achieve its ambitious economic growth objectives without enlisting the entrepreneurial class, and it had already turned its back on a wholly state dominated economy. Bringing business people into the bosom of the Party meant that they were at least more politically controllable.

This was Jiang's major innovation, a legacy he clearly wished to protect. Part of his means of doing this was also to secure his own people in key positions in the succeeding Politburo from 2002 onwards. The central figure here was his close political confidant, Zeng Qinghong, and others clustered around him in what had become called the 'Shanghai Group' either because of their service in senior office in the city, or being natives there. The claims that these figures represented a particular Jiangist faction which maintained his power in the coming years even as Hu replaced him would recur time and again over the next decade, with varying levels of evidence and credibility.

Alice (Lyman) Miller describes the actual mechanics of a Party Congress for the modern Party in the first issue of the China Leadership Monitor. "Party congresses are the most authoritative public events in the politics of the CCP. By Party statute, Party

---

[6]An overview of the gradual 'decontamination' of China's entrepreneurial class from 1978 onwards, and especially the crucial period of change from non-recognition to authorisation to join the CCP can be found in Jie Chen and Bruce J Dickson, *Allies of the State: China's Private Entrepreneurs and Democratic Change*, Harvard University Press, Cambridge, MA, 2010, p 22.

congresses convene every five years and fulfil three basic functions. First, they assess the work of the Party in major policy areas over the preceding five-year period since the last Party congress. Second, they define the Party's overarching 'general task' as well as the priorities and approaches — the Party's 'line' — for all significant policy areas for the coming five-year period. Last, they appoint (or reappoint) the Party's top leadership."[7] In this context, the 16th Party Congress had two key achievements to focus on – one, the transition to a new leadership, and two, the demonstration of continuity through agreement on key policy areas. These were the maintenance of the reform and opening up period, and commitment to implement China's WTO promises.

That Hu would be appointed Party Secretary in late 2002 was something few doubted in the lead up to the event. The main question was what sort of powers he would have in view of the likelihood of Jiang Zemin staying around, either as Chair of the CMC, or in other capacities where he was able to exercise influence backstage. The issue of whether Hu would finally be able to be his own man was a controversial one, and widely debated. As a clue to this, the composition of the Politburo around him, which was increased to nine in membership, was important. Were it to be stacked with people seen as close to Jiang Zemin, then questions about Hu's real viability to operate as his own boss would have been rife. All the suspicions about a Shanghai Group would, in the eyes of many, be proved right.

As it was, the 2002 Politburo turned out to be exactly what it should be — a gathering of figures who created consensus and compromise. The critical position of Premier went to Wen Jiabao, a figure Hu had worked with for many years, and someone with a similar background and patronage. Critically, he was also someone hard to place in any of the clear categories for factions — he was

---

[7] Alice Miller, 'The Road to the Sixteenth Party Congress', *China Leadership Monitor*, Issue 1, Winter, 2002, at http://media.hoover.org/sites/default/files/documents/clm1_LM.pdf [22 December 2011].

a Tsinghua graduate, but not a princeling, a technocrat but with no link to the Communist Party Youth League, and, perhaps most importantly, a former *Mishu* whose formidable bureaucratic skills had long been admired by others in the Party. He had enjoyed the patronage of Song Ping, as had Hu, from his time in Gansu, and he had also been a close protégé of Hu Yaobang, and then Zhao Ziyang, whom he had famously served as Private Secretary of the Politburo Secretariat. Wen's final great attribute was that he had worked with Zhu Rongji on the economic portfolio as Vice Premier from 1997.

So while Hu Jintao had to deal with the potentially formidable opposition of Zeng Qinghong at number five in the 2002 Politburo Standing Committee, and other Jiang protégés like Jia Qinglin and Huang Ju at number four and six respectively, he had more neutral figures like Wen Jiabao to counter this. Even so, Wu Bangguo and Luo Gan, the security chief, could all be said to be members of the so-called Shanghai Group. And in the broader Politburo there were people like Chen Liangyu, Party Secretary of Shanghai, and definitely someone close to Jiang. To confirm the suspicion that Jiang had no intention of fading away quietly, he did indeed maintain his position in the CMC as Chair. The Hu era began, therefore, with a whole series of questions about just how free the new Party Secretary would be to exercise power with so many constraints seemingly around him.

## The First Great Challenge: SARS

Hu Jintao's new government experienced its first real challenge in 2002, and from an unexpected direction. In Guangdong province on November, 16th 2002, the first known case of someone being afflicted with the Severe Acute Respiratory Syndrome (SARS) was recorded. By February 11th the following year, there were 300 officially recognised cases, with the first five fatalities. SARS was a wholly new disease, and this was the reason for the enormous panic which it managed to create once it had been diagnosed properly.

With symptoms similar to fever, the origins of the disease were unclear, but seemed to have come from other species like civet cats, raccoon dogs, or badgers. Ten thousand masked palm civets were destroyed in Guangdong because of this suspicion in 2003. With the memories of avian flu and mad cow disease still strong, huge efforts were put into preventing any chance of cross-species contagion. (Subsequent research proved that in fact the disease was linked to civet cats.[8])

The initial confusion about what the disease was, how contagious it was, and where it would spread, was compounded by the refusal of officials to be open with the information they were receiving about the disease, even to the extent of suppressing information. On March 11th, Hong Kong health officials confirmed that hospital workers had contracted SARS. A few days later, on March 15th, the WHO confirmed that SARS existed and that it had occurred in countries as far apart as Canada, Indonesia, the Philippines, Singapore, Thailand and Vietnam. Travel warnings were issued and the disease was labelled as highly contagious.

From initial denial, the Chinese government began its formal response in late March. However, the then Minister of Health Zhang Wenkang gave a press conference on April 3rd in Beijing claiming that the disease offered no threat to public health, that the country had only a handful of cases, and that it was safe to visit. This did little to reassure the public. The capital became like a ghost town, most citizens who went out wore white face masks, roads around the country had disinfection stations, and a surreal air of a place in the midst of crisis, while its politicians kept on saying everything was normal, reigned. In many ways, the suppression of information only made the eventual fallout far worse than it would have been had there been full disclosure from the beginning.

---

[8] Quanlin Qiu, 'Scientists Prove SARS Civet-Cat Linked', *China Daily*, November 23, 2006, at http://www.chinadaily.com.cn/china/2006-11/23/content_740511.htm [22 December 2011].

It was a veteran surgeon based at Beijing PLA General Hospital No. 301, seventy one-year-old Dr Jiang Yanyong, who issued a public statement which he signed, stating that according to his survey of admissions with the disease to hospitals in Beijing alone, there were considerably more cases than those claimed by Health Minister Zhang.[9] After the ensuing international publication of this statement, the central government heeded the advice of the World Health Organisation (WHO) later in the month, admitting that it was not 37 cases of the disease that had occurred, as it had originally stated, but almost ten times this number (339). Minister Zhang and the Mayor of Beijing were both fired. From April 21st, a huge campaign to raise awareness of the disease was mounted, and proactive measures were introduced to stop the spread of the disease.[10] Entertainment venues were closed, on May 5th, ten thousand people were quarantined in Nanjing, on May11th, spitting in public places was banned in Guangdong, and tough sentences were threatened for people who contravened the main quarantine orders. After a peak in early June, by June 23rd China was lifted from the WHO list of infected areas. A small outbreak a year later was contained, and by 2004, WHO could declare that SARS was a dormant disease.[11] The WHO final figure for cases in China was 2537, with 349 deaths.[12]

SARS highlighted some of the systemic problems that Hu inherited. One of them was an almost institutional inability to admit problems as they were occurring and deal with them before they became full blown crises. The lack of transparency in the system, and the desire to maintain control by refusing to allow open

---

[9] Susan Jakes, 'Beijing SARS Attack', *Time Magazine*, April 8, 2003.
[10] Susan Jakes, 'Jiang Yanyong: Time People Who Mattered, 2003', *Time*, at http://www.time.com/time/asia/2003/poypm2003/jiang_yanyong.html [15 February 2011].
[11] Chronology from the BBC 'Timeline: SARS Virus', July 7, 2004, at http://news.bbc.co.uk/1/hi/world/asia-pacific/2973415.stm [22 December 2011].
[12] 'Summary of Probable SARS Cases with Onset of Illness from 1 November 2002 to 31 July 2003',' World Health Organisation at http://www.who.int/csr/sars/country/table2004_04_21/en/index.html [15 February 2011].

dissemination of information, was one of the worst characteristics of the CCP system. Huge efforts, in particular, were put into the control over information, with the Ministry for Propaganda (later renamed the Ministry for State Information) being one of the most powerful. The causes behind this resistance to openness were as much internal as external. Separate parts of the government machinery maintained control over the information in their areas, refusing to share it with each other. Rumours of some leaders from the Jiang era being embarrassed if there was open disclosure abounded, with the idea that Jiang and those in the so-called Shanghai Group around him were in fact still largely in charge refusing to lay down, despite the changes in personnel that had happened on the surface.

The intervention of the WHO, and the whistleblowing of a figure as respected as Dr Jiang, a member of the CCP and therefore someone who could not have been accused of having an ulterior motive, meant that the government was forced to devise a more active strategy. The final accountability was taken by a Minister and a Mayor. The vast mobilisation of resources and people in containing the threat of the disease and combating it was impressive. Those flying in and out of Beijing at the time of the crisis were met by a range of health workers screening people, putting some groups in quarantine, and detaining others till further checks were made. Less impressively, long after the crisis had passed, Dr Jiang suffered reprisals, in an act that could only be interpreted as political vindictiveness.

Perhaps the main lesson from the whole crisis for the government was that it showed how little it was trusted. Suspicions of cover up proved hard to shift. Years of hearing highly optimistic language from government officials about everything from economic data to the situation in rural areas had created a profound scepticism by the vast majority of people about the state line on most issues. There was wide recognition that one of the key problems in China was the lack of an open media able to dig a little deeper and get better information, or hold government agencies to account, even though things had moved on a long way from the absolute control of the Maoist era.

Administratively, Hu's government had passed the first major test of its time in power. But the SARS issue had been a scare. It had shown a government being challenged, and at times losing control of the agenda. While it finally managed to recover, for someone with such a strong interest in control and management, Hu must have found the spring of 2003 a tough period, and one that reminded him that running a country as complex and huge as the PRC was never easy.

## Addressing Internal Inequalities

In fact, the deeper issue was not a potential pandemic that proved itself in the end to be relatively ephemeral. The Hu era's greatest challenges lay in the inequality that existed in society, after over two decades of fast growth. One of the shocks of the SARS crisis had been that many migrant labourers and those living in the cities with rural registration documents had found themselves going back to country areas where there was next to no health infrastructure. In the cities, China's health service functioned reasonably well. The wealthier the sick person was, the better it worked for him. But in huge parts of the countryside, it was in effect decimated, either by poor funding or lack of personnel.

What had rural dwellers really gained from the whole opening up and reform process? For Mao, farmers had been the great soldiers of the revolution. Contrary to how Marx had envisaged things, it was not in the semi-industrialised cities that the Communist Party had made its great recruitment — China's proletariat in the 1920s and 1930s was barely a few million. It was in the more impoverished areas of central and north China, initially in the provinces of Hunan, Henan and Jiangxi, and later in Shaanxi, Shanxi and Shandong where the real mobilisation had happened. The countryside had starved in the era of the Great Leap Forward and the famines of the early 1960s, in order to feed the cities. An internal passport system based on that which existed in Stalin's USSR had been introduced in 1958, severely differentiating between rural and urban dwellers — something that still left a mark in 2002 when dependency on your household registration (*hukou*) status dictated where you could work, what social services you might have access to, what schools you could go to, and a host of other benefits.

And yet, just as farmers had fought in Mao's armies which won the war against the Nationalists and gained the CCP power, so were they the bulk of the people who worked in China's new factories, generating prosperity during the Reform Era, and on the construction sites, building its great new cities. Migrant labourers had moved from their rural places with little security, establishing famous 'villages' in Beijing and Shanghai where they worked in a number of sectors, often for low wages and long hours. Migrant labourers suffered discrimination, and were more often than not almost invisible in the cities in which they worked. And yet their contribution to growth was critical. For a country relatively poor in easily accessible resources and energy, labour from a vast workforce was the great gift which it had. Unfortunately, China's rural migrant workforce was also one of the worst treated, and one of the greatest sources of discontent.

One of the most powerful expressions of this had been a book by two journalists who came from the same province that Hu claimed was his native one — Anhui. When Chen Guidi and Wu Chuntao wrote their *Life of China's Peasants* (*Zhongguo Nongmin Diaocha*) in 2001, they were building on a tradition of reportage about the situation in the various parts of the vast Chinese countryside that went back decades.[13] One of the most celebrated examples had been an epic study undertaken by the sociologist and Shanghai scholar Cao Jinqing in *China Along the Yellow River: Reflections*

---

[13] Some of the most celebrated had been written by non-Chinese scholars. William Hinton, *Fanshen: A Documentary of Revolution in a Chinese Village*, University of California Press, California, 1967, and Jan Myrdal, *Report from a Chinese Village*, Heinemann, London, 1966 were two of the most notable.

*on Rural Society*.[14] This was based on travels that Cao had made in 1996, in the central province of Henan. His account of his encounters with local officials, and observations of the embattled relationship they had with farmers in the areas in which they were in control was widely read inside and outside China. Chen and Wu's work was to enjoy even greater success, simply because it focused much more than Cao's book had on the popular topic of corruption in the rural areas, and the huge burdens of taxation placed on the backs of farmers — a grievance that had its roots deep in history, and had been one of the great motivators of dynastic failure when popular unrest had swirled up from the countryside and overwhelmed, sometimes even toppling dynasties.

While Chen and Wu's book enjoyed some initial success, the government ban placed on it meant it became a runaway bestseller in samizdat versions, selling a reported ten million illegal copies. Their description of violent, thuggish local officials evidently touched a nerve. An example of the cases they dealt with occurred in Zhang Village, Tangnan Township, Guzhen County, Anhui Province. An official there, Deputy Party Chief Zhang Guiquan, on being accused of embezzling funds, had responded by arranging a posse of heavies to attack those he suspected of being his main accusers.[15] When confronted with an attempt to audit the accounts of the village, Zhang and his sons had stabbed four of the other villagers to death. As Chen and Wu comment, "the power of organisation is considerable and can be formidable when combined with political power. The sheer number of Chinese peasants could make them overwhelming, but they are scattered and have no organisational resources to counter oppression. The rural cadres, on the other hand, are highly organised; they are the legal representatives of state power in the countryside."[16] Deputy

---

[14] Jinqing Cao, *China Along the Yellow River: Reflections on Rural Society*, Routledge Curzon, New York, 2005.
[15] Guidi Chen and Chuntao Wu, *Will the Boat Sink the Water: The Life of China's Peasants*, Public Affairs Ltd, New York, 2006, p 29–30.
[16] *Ibid.*, p 37.

Party Secretary Zhang was literally able to get away with murder in his own village. "The case," Chen and Wu state, "of Zhang Guiquan and his sons killing people in broad daylight, though exceptionally horrific, was not so unique. In our investigation we discovered that local bullies who lorded over the peasants was a common phenomenon of village life, Zhang Guiquan being just one of the products of China's peculiar mechanism of power at the rural grassroots level."[17] Zhang was able to escape the attention of the courts, the local and national press, and even the Party for several months. This sort of local power figure was something common throughout China. But even greater than the suffering farmers experienced at the hands of these officials was the burden on them in terms of taxation. According to the two journalists, by 1990, the various ministries in the central government had authorised taxation on 149 items.[18] From 1990 to 2000, "the total taxes the state had extracted from the peasants had increased by a factor of five."[19] Local governments listed about 269 types of taxation, from 'fund raising' (raising money to build local public structures), to management fees for repairing offices, village cadres allowances for business trips (a particularly contentious entry), 'stipends for villages non-production personnel' (allowances given to figures like the street cleaners, village group leaders, etc), education expenses, village birth control projects, militia training, and social services.[20]

The Jiang and Zhu period had been seen as one associated with radical restructuring of the state owned enterprises, leading to perhaps as many as 60 million losing their jobs, and of acceptance, finally, of the role of entrepreneurs in society after 1993. Even so, it had also been seen as an era in which inequality had crept up. According to economist Barry Naughton, "around 1983–1984, China was probably the most equal that it has ever been, even more equal than under

---

[17] Ibid., p 40.
[18] Ibid., p 172.
[19] Ibid., p 151.
[20] Ibid., p 152–154.

[Maoist] socialism."[21] Since this time, however, inequality has steadily increased, with sharp rises in the early 1990s, and then towards the end of the decade. "By 2001, China's overall Gini Coefficient [a measure of inequality where 1 is ownership of everything by just one person, and 0 is absolute equality] had increased to 0.447. China's increase in inequality is unprecedented. China is now more unequal that the average middle income country and about as unequal as the average low income country."[22] Thus, Naughton concludes, "in the course of two decades China has gone from being one of the most egalitarian societies, about as equal as Japan, to being more unequal than the United States."[23] China's long march to prosperity has also, in the last two decades, been a very fast march towards increasing inequality in society. The Jiang and Zhu period was seen as only aggravating this with pro-private enterprise policies, and a dismantling of the control mechanisms and socialist legacy structures that had existed before.

Hu Jintao showed a high awareness of this problem from the first months when he became Party Secretary. It was to eventually surface in the talk of 'socialist countryside' and 'harmonious society' that appeared around 2004–2006. But tackling the inequality and the situation in the countryside was one of the main areas of policy difference with their predecessors which the Hu–Wen leadership wanted to stress. The countryside, despite the declining importance of agricultural productivity in GDP, was still a quarter to a third of the Chinese economy. It was still where the majority of the people lived, at least in 2001. One of the remarkable transitions that occurred while Hu and Wen were to hold power was a shift towards an almost equal balance between rural and town dwellers, something confirmed by the census held in 2010 which showed that China now had as many living in the urban areas as in the countryside.

---

[21] Barry Naughton, *The Chinese Economy: Transitions and Growth*, MIT Press, Cambridge, MA, 2007, p 217.
[22] *Ibid.*, 218.
[23] *Ibid.*

The greatest challenge was what to do about the powers of local officials. These had been the figures which aroused the most distrust and hate. In surveys later in the decade, by *Xiaokang* ('Moderately Prosperous') Magazine, local officials were shown to be universally regarded with loathing by the public, blamed for the embezzlement of state funds, and seen as larcenous individuals who supported narrow, family interests. Like the case of Zhang cited by Wu and Chen in their book, local officials were often accused of getting away with daylight robbery and even murder. There was plenty of evidence that in fact this is often exactly what happened. Even so, corruption was sometimes more about perception than reality, and this meant it remained a source of constant anger and irritation. In an essay on corruption, Andrew Wedeman asked whether China was really a country where corruption was serious enough to be the state's undoing. This is the belief of many commentators, among them the respected economist Xu Xiaonian, former employee in Goldman Sachs. Estimates as high as 12 percent of GDP have been allocated to business associated with the black market and official embezzlement and malfeasance. With the significant caveat that collecting data in the area is notoriously complicated, Wedeman looks at the figures for those officials who have been investigated by the Party Discipline and Inspection Commission, in effect the CCP's internal police. He describes the process by which they were formally examined in great detail, and then crunches the numbers to show that in fact, for those about whom an investigation starts, the chances of ending up in jail are quite high — far higher, and for far longer, than the US.[24]

To be fair, local officials were often damned whatever they did, partly because they had been asked to do the state's dirty work, in collecting taxes and in implementing unpopular land and family planning policies. The sole attempt to give them

---

[24] In Jean Oi, Scott Rozelle, and Xueguang Zhou (Eds), *Growing Pains: Tensions and Opportunity in China's Transformation*, Walter A Shorenstein Asia Pacific Research Center, Stanford, 2010.

some legitimacy had been the process of village elections, started in the early 1980s and then given legal basis first in a law from 1987, and finally, nationally, in a comprehensive law from 1998. But the successes of this experiment, as it came to be called, were not straightforward.

As will be discussed later, Hu Jintao was no supporter of deepening the moves towards township elections, something very tentatively done in the early 2000s. He stood more for introducing greater accountability into the Party itself. Even so, the need to proactively jump on corrupt officials more was important, and here, just as with the celebrated case of the Mayor of Beijing and Politburo member Chen Xitong in 1996, he was able to kill a number of birds with one stone by focusing on the powerful Party Secretary of the great city of Shanghai, supposedly a key member of the eponymous group.

## The Fall of Chen Liangyu

Chen Liangyu had spent his political career in Shanghai, elevated, in 2002, to be Party Secretary, replacing the respected Xu Kuangdi who was shifted sideways to Beijing. That Chen was closely associated with Jiang Zemin was no secret. He had worked his way up the local political system in the 1980s, at the time when Jiang was the head of the CCP there. Apart from a short sabbatical on a British government scholarship to Birmingham in the UK, Chen had never worked in any other place.

The background to Chen's clash with Hu was centred on the Shanghai Social Insurance Agency (SIA). And at the heart of this was the immense challenge of trying to provide viable local funds to sustain massive pension liabilities that local governments across China had worked up over the previous decade. "It may come as a surprise to many...," writes Mark Frazier in his book on pensions in China, "that the most expensive function of the Chinese government (including central and local levels) is not urban construction, infrastructure or even national defence but, instead, the provision of public pensions."[25] It was in order to address some of the burden of this pension commitment that the Shanghai Social Insurance Agency had been established. The head of the Labour Exchange and Social Security Bureau Zhu Junyi, was the first to have serious accusations levelled against him, being blamed by the investigators from the central government for taking more than USD 474 million and loaning it to local real estate developers and other businesses. A survey completed in 2007 by the National Audit Office revealed that the Shanghai SIA had illegally diverted, as loans and other investments, the colossal total of 32.9 billion yuan (USD 4.2 billion).[26] Much of the commercial property in the city had been funded by this huge misappropriation of funds. It wasn't that this was a new or surprising story, as there had been rumblings for some time that there were serious issues in the city's finances. From the private sector, one of the biggest figures felled as the scandal unfolded was Zhou Zhengyi, at one time China's 11th richest man, who was detained as early as 2003 for illegally acquiring state land and loans. He was finally arrested in early 2007 and convicted of offering bribes, a crime for which he was tried and convicted in November that year and handed a 16-year sentence.

Shanghai was paralysed for much of the end of 2006 by the Chen scandal. Part of the problem, as Frazier points out, is that local governments had very little clarity from the central government on what to do about making their social security funds viable, and had to operate at the edges of what the regulations allowed. "The Shanghai Pension Scandal is more than a story of how factional politics brought down the Shanghai leadership. The scandal also revealed the extremes to which urban officials could go in fulfilling the ambiguous and largely unfounded mandates handed down

---

[25] Mark W Frazier, *Socialist Insecurity: Pensions and the Politics of Uneven Development in China*, Cornell University Press, New York, 2010, p 2.
[26] *Ibid.*, p 15.

by the central government in the 1990s to enact social welfare measures."[27]

Chen was certainly not a universally popular local leader, despite the fact that he came from the city. He was regarded as aloof, greedy, and was accused after his fall of having up to 17 mistresses. His backing over a number of years to host one of the Formula One Tracks in suburban Shanghai had also been accused, despite its eventual success, of creating an immense white elephant at huge cost, while the general levels of wealth in the city had stagnated for households. A large part of this was due to the soaring property prices over this period. Economist Yasheng Huang dissected the city's real economic basis in a chapter in his book, *Capitalism with Chinese Characteristics* crisply titled 'What is Wrong With Shanghai?'[28] Huang argues that "the 'Shanghai Miracle' is assumed but not demonstrated"[29], going on to say that while "it is true that Shanghai has had an excellent GDP performance, much of this performance seems to have only moderately improved the living standard of the average Shanghainese." Prosperity has come the way of enterprises, most of them state owned, and not into household incomes, where rising living costs have eaten away at whatever growth that had been generated. He also accuses the city of pursuing 'anti-poor' growth policies, and being, despite appearances, not a city full of entrepreneurial energy, but of stifled government-led activity.[30]

Chen Liangyu, along with former Party Secretary, the late Huang Ju (who preceded him before joining the full Standing Committee of the Politburo in Beijing) was intimately linked with the celebration of modernity that is now Pudong district's skyline. The vast World Trade Building, briefly the tallest in Asia, had begun

---

[27] *Ibid.*, p 16.
[28] Yasheng Huang, *Capitalism with Chinese Characteristics*, Cambridge University Press, Cambridge, 2008, p 175 onwards.
[29] *Ibid.*, p 176.
[30] *Ibid.*, p 176–177.

under Chen, as had the Maglev railway line that goes between the newly built Pudong airport 50 kilometres from the centre of the city at speeds of up to 430 kilometres an hour. This was a place that the world came to admire, both for the rapidity with which it had been built and the daring modernity of the physical landscape after a few years of radical renovations. Even so, listening to Chen's own words, one can see that in modern China appearances can be very deceptive. "If I am not mistaken," Chen had bragged while still Party boss of the city, "in our country, private businesses contribute 40 percent of GDP. In our Shanghai, SOES [state owned enterprises] create nearly 80 percent of Shanghai's GDP. Who upholds socialism more vigorously? Who else if not Shanghai?"[31] The maintenance of government control over Shanghai's economy was evident in the way its main enterprises were state owned, and its chief economic actors were linked closely to the government. Even the Pudong redevelopment area was built on what could be claimed was illegality, with the farmers who had been the owners of leases on the land before the building started in the 1990s being largely unrecompensed for their moves to other, far less lucrative and useful land.

Hovering around Hu's treatment of Chen, however, was a sense that it was more about politics than any specific economic crimes that he had committed. Deep down, Chen was a highly expendable figure, someone who, according to rumours at least, had committed the fatal error of openly disagreeing with the consensus line from the Politburo not once, but twice. Stories of open shouting matches at the Politburo stood uneasily beside the penchant that Hu had of convening cerebral study days. According to one analyst at the time, Hu's removal of Chen had been like a chess player suddenly simply removing a key piece from the board, and daring the opposing player to challenge them. It had reconfigured the political balance, at a key time just before the 17th Party Congress to be held a year later in 2007, showing that after four years at the

---

[31] *Ibid.*, p 210.

helm, Hu was indeed in charge. It was also a useful preparation for the other significant removal of Shanghai Group members that Hu and those around him were evidently planning. That Jiang Zemin had inevitably had to be informed as senior retired leader of the planned purge of Chen meant that, by the time the investigators descended on Shanghai, the case against him was watertight. By 2008, after almost two years in detention, he was charged with corruption, found guilty, and, like the businessman Zhang, sentenced to 16 years under house arrest. There were rumours that he was able to live in a luxury compound, as long as he remained silent. There, apparently, he lives to this day.

## 2007: The Party Congress

Party Congresses are the great stage events of CCP life in the late 20th and early 21st century. Under Mao, they had happened infrequently and were largely irrelevant. From 1958 to 1969, there were none. In 1973, as the Cultural Revolution wound to its end, there was the bizarre Tenth Party Congress, during which the young Wang Hongwen (sarcastically nicknamed 'The Helicopter' because of the rapidity of his ascent), a factory activist from Shanghai, was elevated into the Politburo and marked as a potential successor to the ageing and ill Mao Zedong. But all of this was swept away once the radical leaders (amongst them, Wang) in the group that came to be called the Gang of Four were arrested a few weeks after Mao's death in September 1976.

The new leadership around Deng Xiaoping was keen to create stronger institutions within the CCP, and to give it greater structural coherence and strength. In the 1981 'Resolution on Party History', there was a complaint, justified on many levels, that the Party had itself become one of the chief victims of Mao, and that it had been merely a servant of the whims of one man in the last decade from mid 1966, criticising his wayward behaviour from 1957 onwards. From 1982, therefore, Congresses were held with much greater regularity, and started to have more influence and importance. This only grew in the years from 1990 onwards when senior leaders from the so-called first and second generations of leadership began to either retire or die. In 1982, the membership of the Politburo after the 12th Party Congress that year predominantly comprised people who had fought in the Sino-Japanese and the Civil War. Almost all had military backgrounds. None had been to university. As the decade wore on, and the great senior leaders like Bo Yibo and Chen Yun grew older, an unwritten rule seemed to allow that they were able to designate one of their children to occupy positions of responsibility while they 'retired', so that they could remain influential through their children.[32] In Bo Yibo's case, of his two children Bo Xilai and Bo Xicheng, it was the former who was allowed to pursue a political career within the Party, and the latter who pursued a business career — though there are, obviously, pleasing synergies between these two areas in the PRC.

The deepening institutionalisation of the Congress and the roles of the Party Central Committee, as well as the Politburo meant that there was less talk after the death of the paramount leader Deng Xiaoping in 1997 of a shadowy backstage in Chinese politics where 'retired' leaders still remained hugely influential. While some of the former elite leaders like Bo Yibo managed to live on into the 2000s, on the whole the most powerful people in China were those who sat on either the full or the Standing Committee of the CCP — something that was partially acknowledged by increasing the numbers on the Standing Committee from the seven positions which had existed in the 1990s, to nine in 2002 at the 16th Party Congress.

The 2002 Congress had seen the first smooth transition of power from one generation of leaders to another. But for the first five years of Hu's era as General Secretary, he inevitably had to deal with the powerful imprint of those leaders from the generation before who had 'retired', but remained influential. Of these, the

---

[32] Cheng Li, *China's Leaders: The New Generation*, Rowman and Littlefield, Lanham Boulder, 2001, p 130–131.

most important by far was Jiang Zemin, his theatrical, extroverted predecessor, a man who had been woefully underestimated when brought up from Shanghai in 1989 under emergency conditions to head the Party after the Tiananmen Square clampdown. Many had expected Jiang to be an interim leader.[33] That he had not only managed to survive, and to respond to the challenge set by Deng Xiaoping in his Southern Tour in 1992 to start faster economic growth and greater liberalisation, but also managed to build up his own power base proved what a formidable operator he was.

Even after 2002, and Jiang's relinquishment of his leadership of the CCP, he was able to maintain influence by being head of the CMC till 2004, and maintained his Party leadership of the same body into 2005. Jiang's 'long goodbye', while no way as lengthy as that of Deng, who had been relinquishing formal positions of power throughout the 1980s, still cast a shadow over Hu, and meant that at least in terms of outside speculation, the latter's early period in office was dogged by the question of how much he could be his own man. In the 16th Congress Politburo, he had to work with those closely connected with Jiang, perhaps the most prominent being Zeng Qinghong, a powerful Party operator, and someone very much associated with Jiang both during his time in Shanghai and in his career as a central leader after 1989.

Zeng's greatest influence came from a similar area to that of Wen Jiabao, as head of the Central Committee and Party Secretariat, a small group in charge of the leadership logistics, diaries and briefings. From 1993, Zeng had served in this position, closely linked to the elite leaders at the time and operating as the consummate administrator and central government insider. Like Wen, he had been able to use this position to create a dense web of support amongst many different areas in the Party. And as, in effect, the

---

[33] See Willy Lam, *The Era of Jiang Zemin*, Prentice Hall, New York, 1999.

gatekeeper to the most powerful leaders, particularly Jiang, Zeng had huge prominence. While admired for his intelligence and his political skills, however, Zeng was also seen as someone who was manipulative and devious. He was famed for keeping a low profile and acting humbly in meetings, but his elevation into the Politburo in 2002 was seen by many commentators as a sign that Jiang had only agreed to depart so easily as long as someone trusted was to serve on his behalf and maintain his influence, protecting his legacy, on the supreme decision-making body. Perhaps this was not so irrational — at least a couple of experienced politicians still being in senior slots in the new Politburo could make sure that critics could not easily claim that the political direction of China was now in the hands of relative novices.

In the lead up to the Party Congress of 2007, rumours of whether Hu Jintao would be able to secure stronger representation in the Politburo, for those seen as closer to him than the Jiang group, abounded. There was also speculation about just what sort of ideological imprint the 17th Congress would make which would further Hu's policy goals. Many had noticed that Hu operated in a much lower key way than Jiang. At the 16th Central Committee Fifth Plenum in October 2005, there were no big personnel changes, giving clues to how much Hu was able to imprint his authority on the Party in what should have been the Post-Jiang era. But as one analyst commented, Hu's power was mainly focused on the General Office of the CCP (that which Zeng Qinghong had headed in the 1990s), and in the Personnel Department. These were two crucial areas, one of them in charge of information and briefing, and one of them appointments to senior political positions. But it meant that, for instance, the propaganda portfolio, and important trade and economics functions, still remained under the control of other influential voices. Hu, unlike Jiang and his Premier Zhu Rongji, seemed to have established an era of 'shared leadership', where 'Hu–Wen' were talked of more than one particular person (the Jiang era was seldom referred to as the 'Jiang–Zhu' era). Nor, at least in official documents like those produced by Xinhua or

*People's Daily*, were there uses of phrases like "Hu as the Core Leader."[34]

Such self-effacement did not mean that Hu was Jiang's yes man. It was never overt, but there were clear signs from his first year in power that the new Party Secretary was patiently building up his own political identity and willing to flex his muscles when he wanted. The whole point of his 'collective leadership' mode, indeed, was to show precisely that the Party, and its institutions and processes, was preeminent and stood above individuals. A return to rule centred on one charismatic figure was not a possibility. A major part of Hu's political programme from the moment he came to power was to show that process, inner Party institution building, and strengthening the Party as an organisation against manipulation by cliques, factions or specific vested interests was the overarching strategy.

Hu's facelessness was belied by the rumours swirling around during the fall of Chen Liangyu in Shanghai that it had been on his instigation that the Party Secretary of Shanghai had been singled out, and that instruction for his removal had been sent, in the final stages, to Jiang for his information only, rather than for any formal approval. Many at the time interpreted Hu's move as being one directly against a key member of the 'Shanghai Group', those linked to the city, and therefore to Jiang and Zhu during their time there, forming a significant clique in the inner sanctum of the Party itself. Quite what held figures as disparate as Wu Bangguo, an arch conservative, Huang Ju (before his death in 2007), Zeng Qinghong and Li Changchun, all reputedly members of the clique, together in terms of ideas was far harder to spell out. The sense that there was a powerful grouping however, and that somehow it remained a means of Jiang retaining at least some influence, was not so easily dispelled. And so part of the storm of speculation in the lead up to the 17th Party Congress in 2007 was how much Hu would be able to

---

[34] Alice Miller, 'Hu's In Charge', *China Leadership Monitor*, Issue 16, Fall, 2005, p 1 and 4.

clear away some of the main figures from this group, and slip some of his own people into influential positions.

As the major show pieces of Party life, Congresses are meticulously planned. Candidates to sit on the Party National Congress, usually about 2,000 people, are selected from provincial and national lists over several months, screened, and then finally approved by the sitting Politburo. This process alone, with its painstaking assessment of the political, regional and social affiliation of figures, consumes much of the year leading up to the Congress itself. This group in fact then elects the Central Committee, the approximately 350-strong Party elite, who in turn elect the Politburo. This series of elections, while being highly managed, can sometimes fling up surprises. A prominent leftist in the 1990s, Deng Liqun (author of the 'Ten Thousand Character' essays criticising Jiang as mentioned earlier) failed despite strenuous efforts by his supporters to get him voted into the Politburo by the Central Committee in 1997.[35] But for the main positions, the idea of either the General Secretary or Premier failing to be elected is unthinkable.

At the same time as the personnel are being arranged, the Party undergoes a huge exercise to start drafting the main leadership speeches to be made at the Congress. The most important of these is the Work Report, made by the Party General Secretary, which gives an overview of achievements since the last Congress, and then sets out the main objectives for the coming five years. Putting aside questions of the content of Hu's speech in October 2007 (that will be dealt with in Chapter Five), one has to simply focus on the immense efforts that go into producing a statement which all government ministries, Party departments, provincial leaders, and other key figures in Chinese political life can listen to and approve. A speech at this level is usually delivered to the delegates in the Great Hall of the People who listen, in central Beijing in total, stupefied boredom, quite simply because most

---

[35] He had also been voted off the 13th Central Committee in 1987.

of them would have seen its contents many times and be utterly familiar with what it would be saying.

For Hu's 2007 speech, portions of it were reportedly drafted and redrafted over 50 times. It was sent to provincial leaders, fellow Politburo members, central committee members, and heads of ministries and major state owned corporations for comments. One of the drafters Li Junru, at that time one of the deputies of the Party School in Beijing, worked on elements of the speech that dealt with ideology and international affairs. Other parts were left to Hu's key policy advisor Wang Huning.

While the whole idea behind a Work Report at the Congress by the General Secretary, especially one as focused on control and order as Hu, was that it should contain no surprises for anyone, the actual line up of leaders on the final day of the Congress, those who had been voted in to sit on the Politburo, was much more important, and there speculation swirled around till almost the last minute. According to one BBC report just before the conference, "No-one knows for certain who will be promoted and who will leave high office, but a number of key names do keep cropping up."[36] Of these, the most persistent were a protégé of Hu's, Party Secretary of Liaoning Li Keqiang, and the then Party Secretary of Shanghai Xi Jinping. Both of them had attracted interest because they were not even, at the time of the Congress, on the full Politburo, the usual launch pad for entry to the Standing Committee.

Leadership change at the 17th Party Congress was not as wholesale as during the 2002 Congress, where five of the seven strong membership were up for retirement, and only Hu and Wen remained in place after the changes had happened. A similar sweeping change happened at the same time in important jobs within the Party, making this truly a moment, where power shifted from the war generation, to those who were first politically active

---

[36] BBC News, 'Q and A: China's Party Congress', October 16, 2007, at http://news.bbc.co.uk/1/hi/world/asia-pacific/7039876.stm [22 December 2011].

during the Cultural Revolution.[37] Changes slated for 2007 were not as large — only four new slots were likely to be available, caused by the retirement of leaders, and in one case the death of Huang Ju. But they were seen as immensely significant for showing who might be in pole position to replace Hu and Wen at the end of their various Party and government terms in five to six years time.

Of those elected in 2002, Luo Gan (born in 1935) and Wu Guanzheng (1938), being both over the age of 68 at the time of the Congress, were the likeliest to take retirement. Jia Qinglin had been mired in claims about his involvement in the massive smuggling scandal in Fujian, where he had been Party Secretary from 1993 to 1996 before moving to Beijing. He was seen as very close to Jiang, and therefore someone Hu might want to gently move into retirement. Zeng Qinghong, while on the border of retirement (he was born in 1939) was in theory still very much eligible to serve another term. Early speculation had him slated as a potential Vice President.

When the final moment came, however, the extension of the Congress by a day aroused suspicion that all was not well with the process of electing new leaders. When the line-up of new members was finally announced on 21st October, there were some surprises. Jia Qinglin, despite his unpopularity amongst the public and the accusations made against him, survived, remaining at No. 4, the head of the United Front Organisation, the China People's Political Consultative Conference. Luo Gan had indeed departed, as had Wu Guangzheng. But Li Changchun had been elevated from the 8th to the 5th ranking member. Perhaps the most startling change at the Congress was that Zeng Qinghong had gone, replaced by Xi Jinping and Li Keqiang, but crucially with Xi in a position one slot higher than Li, at numbers 6 and 7 respectively. The two other new faces were He Guoqiang, as head of the discipline and inspection portfolio, and Zhou Yongkang, a veteran of China's energy sector, in 9th slot in charge of security.

---

[37] Cheng Li, *China's Leaders*, p 4–5.

Hu Jintao's comments when introducing the new line-up that Xi and Li were 'two younger men' was widely reported (it was hard to tell if they were injected with any irony or humour!). Xi was born in 1953 and Li in 1955. That Xi was in a higher position than Li was the strongest indication yet that he was in the main position to replace Hu in 2012. The other Li who had been talked of as a possible Politburo Standing Committee entrant, Li Yuanchao, was left just outside, at the number 10 slot in the full Politburo, but crucially in charge of the Organisation Department, in effect in charge of the Party's human resources. And as Richard McGregor, the Financial Times journalist, pointed out in his study of the modern CCP, the Communist Party's two great levers of control in recent times have been power over information, and equally as important, power over personnel appointments.[38]

Li Keqiang was previously seen as someone much closer to Hu than Xi. Described as a "rising star" by Cheng Li in 2001,[39] he was in charge of demanding provinces like Henan, and then Liaoning in the north east, at times when they had been struck with particular challenges (for Henan, it was the devastating HIV-contaminated blood disaster that had been exposed there in the late 1990s.)[40] Someone regarded as a bold economic reformer, and politically highly reliable, Li shared Hu's own modest background. This stood in stark contradiction to Xi Jinping, the princeling son of Xi Zhongxun, Party Secretary of Guangdong in the early 1980s when the economic reforms piloted by Deng Xiaoping's government were at their critical early stage. Apart from his stellar family background, Xi was not linked particularly to any clique though he was talked about as being more in Jiang's camp than Hu's. His 'victory' in managing to rise from being the member of the Central Committee with the lowest number of votes in 1997,

---

[38] Richard McGregor, *The Party: The Secret World of China's Communist Rulers*, HarperCollins, New York, 2010.
[39] Cheng Li, *China's Leaders*, p 10.
[40] For the background to the AIDS crisis, see Jonathan Watts, *When a Billion Chinese Jump*, Faber and Faber, London, 2010, p 198 onwards.

to being the likeliest to replace Hu in 2012 was as much due in the end to these profound family links to almost all areas of the Party, and a lack of affiliation which narrowed down his support base. He could, indeed, be all things to all men and avoid debilitating attachments to any specific factions.

The success of others reputably favoured by Hu to get into the full Politburo only served to strengthen the impression that five years into his time in power, Hu was moving out from under the shadow of Jiang. Liu Yandong, another colleague from the China Youth League, Li Yuanchao, Wang Qishan and Wang Yang were all brought in. According to one assessment, with these personnel changes, along with the ideological ones discussed in the next chapter, "Hu has emerged from the 17th CCP Congress with his hand strengthened".[41]

## A Historic Year: 2008

One of the victories of the Jiang Zemin era had been the successful bid, in 2001, to host the 2008 Olympics. This had been a risky move. In 1993, China had made an early bid, competing against Sydney, and using this as an attempt to rid itself of some of the pariah status that it had had since the 1989 Tiananmen Square massacre. The failure to secure this bid by a mere two votes had been greeted by a bitter nationalist backlash in China. To try again, only eight years later, even when China's rehabilitation had largely been achieved and many of the political obstacles had been cleared out of the way, was regarded by some as a case of Jiang taking a big risk.

The night that Beijing citizens heard that they had successfully won the bid, an explosion of firecrackers and fireworks were let off throughout the city. In the hot July evening, tens of thousands convened in Tiananmen Square. The Politburo members led the

---

[41] Alice Miller, 'China's New Leadership', *China Leadership Monitor*, Issue 23, Winter, 2008, p 7.

celebrations, with a heavy lashing of nationalistic pride — this was China's moment to show that it was a truly global power. In the ensuing seven years, the Chinese government would reportedly spend over USD 30 billion on the 2008 Games.[42] The capital city would be rebuilt in parts, particularly around the centrepiece Bird's Nest stadium (this alone cost USD 250 million), and the national swimming stadium, with 1.5 million people relocated, and the huge third terminal at the Capital Airport constructed (in a mere three years). Metro lines would be added, and new ring roads laid, with parts of the centre of the city unrecognisable even to those who had only visited a year or so before.

For Hu and the new leadership, the burden of hosting the Olympics rapidly became a heavy one. In 2006, the Vice Mayor of Beijing Liu Zhihua had been sacked and then prosecuted for taking massive backhanders off deals associated with the games. According to one report, he was finally exposed after demanding a bribe from a foreign businessman over the sale of a piece of land that was being bidded for. But the fact that an official who was probably earning only a few hundred dollars a month was in charge of procurement and infrastructure bids potentially worth billions of dollars only highlighted again the systemic root causes of corruption in contemporary China.[43]

The nervousness of the Hu leadership was compounded in March 2008, a few months before the event, when, on the 49th anniversary of a massive revolt against Communist rule in Tibet, a group of monks started protesting in the provincial capital of

---

[42] 'The Cost of the Beijing Olympics', *The Guardian*, July 28, 2008, at http://www.guardian.co.uk/sport/2008/jul/28/olympicgames2008.china1 [22 December 2011].
[43] See Richard Spencer, 'Corruption Scandal Hits Beijing', *Telegraph*, June 24, 2006, at http://www.telegraph.co.uk/news/worldnews/asia/china/1522194/Corruption-scandal-hits-Beijing-Olympics.html and Oliver August, 'Sacked Olympics Chief had "pleasure palace" full of Concubines', *The Times Online*, June 12, 2006, at http://www.timesonline.co.uk/tol/news/world/asia/article673988.ece [22 December 2011].

Lhasa. The demonstrations escalated so that, by 17th March, James Miles, *The Economist* correspondent and one of the few western journalists in the city when the unrest started, reported that he had seen "a Bank of China branch with its windows smashed, the guardroom of the Tibet Daily, the Communist Party's main mouthpiece in the region, similarly damaged, a multi-storey internet café gutted by fire, and shop after Chinese-owned shop burned or destroyed." He concluded, "The scale of the unrest was probably the biggest the city had seen since the Tibetan uprising of 1959 which prompted the Dalai Lama to flee into exile."[44] Tensions simmered in the region deep into the next month, despite a massive influx of security personnel. While the central government did not repeat the imposition of martial law which Hu Jintao had authorised when he was Party Secretary there in 1989, the sheer number of soldiers, armed police and public security personnel meant that by the end of April, while the region had been stabilised, it remained closed to foreigners and a huge number of Tibetans had been detained. Analysing the event afterwards, Pankaj Mishra wrote "the most surprising thing about the, eruption of Tibetan rage is that it didn't occur sooner... Tibetans... confront a capitalist modernity more destructive of tradition and more ruthlessly exploitative of the sacred land they walk on than any adversary they have known in their tormented history".[45]

From his days in charge of the area, Hu had maintained a close interest in it and was probably (though this was never publicly confirmed) the head of the Central Leading Small Group on Tibet, the body with the final decision on key areas affecting the autonomous region. One of the points of discussion in the aftermath of the riots was how the security services had failed to

---

[44] 'Lhasa Under Siege', *The Economist*, March 17, 2008.
[45] Pankaj Mishra, 'At War With the Utopia of Modernity', in Kate Merkel-Hess, Kenneth L Pomeranz, and Jeffrey N Wasserstrom (Eds), *China in 2008: A Year of Great Significance*, Rowman and Littlefield, Lanham Boulder, 2009, p 42.

see such major trouble coming.[46] Since being linked more closely to the rest of China with the construction of the train line from Qinghai province across to Lhasa in July 2006 (at the opening of which, President Hu had enthusiastically stated that "This is a magnificent feat by the Chinese people, and also a miracle in world railway history"[47]), it was widely believed by the central leadership that Tibet's rapid economic growth rate would integrate it more deeply with the rest of the country and appease the majority of the discontented ethnic Tibetans in the region.[48] That such a huge uprising could happen, at such a sensitive time, only aggravated the central government's nervousness. It was to have a profound effect on an already obsessively controlling leadership, with an impact lasting for the rest of the Hu era.

This internal nervousness was not helped in the lead up to August 2008 by a rising cacophony of international criticism about the Olympics. A particular sore point had been exposure of China's newly emerging trade interests in African countries like Sudan and Zimbabwe (this will be dealt with more in Chapter Four on China's international profile under Hu). "Beijing's relationship with the Sudanese regime had become a major cause célèbre that threatens to tarnish China's reputation," Ian Taylor, an expert on China-Africa relations wrote near the time. "This forced policy

---

[46] There were some, however, who believed that the CCP had actually manipulated the riots so that they happened before the Olympics, rather than during them, and in that way justified a major clampdown. Such conspiracy theories remain extremely popular in the PRC, and join a long and distinguished history of similar stories, all characterised by threadbare evidence.
[47] BBC News, 'Hu opens World's highest railway', July 1, 2006, at http://news.bbc.co.uk/1/hi/5133220.stm [22 December 2011].
[48] This was spelt out clearly in the seventh section of the State Council White Paper issued in 1993, in which the Chinese government had stated that their "goal is to narrow as soon as possible the gap in economic development between Tibet and other areas of the nation in order to lay a solid foundation for the common prosperity of Tibetan and other ethnic groups." See 'Tibet, Its Ownership and Human Rights Situation', at http://www.china.org.cn/e-white/tibet/9–7.htm [22 December 2011].

makers in Beijing, after the 2008 Olympics were dubbed by some critics the 'genocide Olympics' from 2007 onwards, to mount a 'full scale foreign policy [offensive] that played up China's contribution to conflict resolution and encouraged more proactive explanations of Sino-African diplomacy".[49] On 13th February, much to the embarrassment of the organisers of the games, the internationally acclaimed American film director Stephen Spielberg pulled out of being one of the advisors for the opening and closing ceremonies, citing that, as a result of the Chinese involvement in problematic countries in Africa, his "conscience would not allow [him] to continue with business as usual".[50] The appointment of a senior Chinese government rapporteur for Africa, the veteran diplomat Liu Guijin, only served to calm the criticism a little — as the year wore on, far from bringing China immense soft power benefits, the Olympics was focusing unwelcome light on areas where it wished to continue observing the foreign policy mantra imputed to Deng Xiaoping in the 1980s, of 'keeping a low profile and never taking leadership positions'.

Natural disasters did not make the year easier. Heavy snow during the Chinese New Year festival in late January left millions stranded at the one time in the year when migrant labourers were given their chance to return home.[51] On May 12th, 2008, an earthquake of an altogether more devastating scale occurred. At 2.28 in the afternoon, in Wenchuan, in the south western province of Sichuan, a quake measuring 7.8 on the Richter Scale shook the region, with five reported dead in the first few hours after the shock. That figure was to rise massively in the next day, with a final figure of over 68 thousand dead. The central government's initial response was praised, with Premier Wen going to the region quickly (something which he had also done during the Spring Festival snowstorms,

---

[49] Ian Taylor, *China's New Role in Africa*, Lynne Rienner, Boulder, 2009, p 51.
[50] Helene Cooper, 'Spielberg Drops Out as Adviser to Beijing Games in Dispute Over Darfur Conflict', *New York Times*, February 13, 2008.
[51] See Jane Macartney, 'Chinese Snow Storms Strand 200,000 at Station in New Year Exodus', *Times*, January 29, 2008.

which had gained him the popular nickname 'Uncle Wen', but which apparently irritated his colleagues on the Politburo, and in particular Hu, to such an extent that he had to maintain a lower profile for much of the rest of the year). International assistance was welcomed, with crisis specialists from non-government organisations and volunteers, from dozens of countries, involved in the relief and clear up effort, in sharp distinction from China's earlier massive earthquake in the summer of 1976 where a quarter of a million had died only weeks before Mao Zedong's own death, and when the radical leadership then in the ascendant in Beijing turned their backs on all offers of outside help, claiming they were self-sufficient and needed no foreign assistance.[52]

While the immediate relief effort had been praised (Hu himself visited the crisis region on May 17th), the aftermath raised many questions about the ways in which many of the schools and other public buildings, which had been built shoddily on land vulnerable to quakes, had collapsed, killing many young people, while the local government buildings had survived. Chinese state media were the first to address this, with one stating that "We cannot afford not to raise uneasy questions about the structural quality of school buildings."[53] Protests by parents who had tragically lost their children in the disaster were soon repressed, with some of the main parent activists placed under arrest and a clampdown on activities arranged by parents trying to get answers.[54]

When Hu Jintao stood before world leaders and over four billion television spectators on August 8th, 2008, at eight minutes past eight in the evening, to announce the opening of the Games, he must have been doing so through tense lips. The stress of the last

---

[52] Particularly significant here was the involvement of Japanese relief workers and government aid organisations, despite the tetchy nature of their relationship since the Koziumi Prime Ministership from 2000 to 2005.
[53] BBC, 'China anger over shoddy schools', May 15, 2008 at http://news.bbc.co.uk/1/hi/world/asia-pacific/7400524.stm [22 December 2011].
[54] See Mathew Weaver, 'Police Break Up Protests of China Earthquake Victims', *Guardian*, June 3, 2008.

few months had been high. One of the few positive developments had been the Party allowing a freeing up of media, to fulfil China's obligations under the International Olympic Committee host country agreement. The internet, which had been carefully screened till then, was allowed a little more openness. There were even reports of a protest space in Beijing, but reporters researching this were unsurprised to learn that no group that had applied for permission to use the place had been granted it. But on the whole, the Games exemplified tight control, with nothing left to chance. Despite the extraordinary logistic achievement of hosting such an enormous event, one of the few initial criticisms was that it seemed a somewhat regimented, joyless occasion. For Hu, it must have been a relief to finally get the Games out of the way.

Indeed, the Opening Ceremony with its legion of drummers and hi-tech special effects that inspired gasps of amazement from the audience, and the success in particular of Chinese athletes (they ended up for the first time ever with the most number of gold medals) were all impressive, and in keeping with the narrative of China as a newly emerging major player on the world stage, there were many in the political elite who must have felt that China got a poor return for its vast investment. They were not alone. Popularist writers like Wang Xiaodong in the incendiary 'China is Unhappy' (*Zhongguo Bu Gaoxing*) published in the early part of 2009, were quick to exploit the ways in which the year 2008 had highlighted big differences, as they saw it, between China and the rest of the world. One author in the collection, in looking back on 2008, stated that "this year saw too many things happen, and seemed to go so quickly. But because so much happened, it is hard to forget... The words that best describe 2008 are 'hard', because in 2008, China and the world saw many complex things when they faced each other, things without precedent".[55] But as the author goes on to state, the 'happy business' of the Olympics,

---

[55] Xiaodong Wang *et al.*, *Zhongguo Bu Gaoxing* ('China is Unhappy'), Phoenix Media Publishing and Jiangsu Publishing House, Nanjing, 2009, p 36 (Author's translation).

in which China received most gold medals and organised things so successfully, was also the same occasion during which the tale of the troubled procession of the torch throughout the world as it made its way to Beijing happened. Here, many Chinese could see the conflicted emotions that the country's rising prominence were creating outside (the torch ceremonies in France, the UK and the US in particular had created huge controversy, with the most contentious scenes happening in Paris when a disabled Chinese athlete was manhandled there, creating a massive anti-French backlash in the PRC).

The main lesson coming from the Olympics for Hu and the new leaders around him, therefore, was a sharp reminder of their relative isolation in the world, and it underlined their need to remember that they had to rely on themselves. And while Hu's speech at the Party Congress, and at the end of the year when he was celebrating the 30th anniversary of the reform and opening up process launched in December 1978, were full of strong words (see Chapter Five) and statements maintaining the commitment to continuing to develop China through internationalisation, from after the Olympics, the main legacy was to be a gradual but increasingly intense tightening of pressure on internal protest, even further cautiousness on the part of the leadership, and, most particularly because of Tibet, an empowerment of the security services.

## Xinjiang, and Charter 08

Only a few weeks after the close of the Games, the veteran activist Liu Xiaobo, an academic once based at the prestigious Beijing University, joined together with over 2000 others from areas as diverse as academia, law, and civil society, to issue an open manifesto for political change in the PRC. They chose to use the model of the Charter 77 document from Czechoslovakia, which was one of the seminal moments in the move towards political reform and the fall of the Communist Party there. They also chose to issue it on December 10th, International Human Rights Day. This provocative combination almost inevitably pushed deep into the territory of unease and insecurity and provoked an immediate, strong response. Liu in particular had form. He had already spent years in prison in the 1990s because of his role in the 1989 uprising, and for his other activities as a writer and lecturer. He had been in and out of jail ever since. But Charter 08, with its direct challenge to the Party, was raising the stakes.

Hu Jintao had used the word 'democracy' over 60 times in his key speech at the 17th Party Congress (see Chapter Five, on Hu and Ideology). But as the authors of a blueprint for political change in China, 'Storming the Fortress', had made clear just after the Congress, while it was critical to talk about political reform, "in contemporary China, pushing forward reform must be under the leadership of the CCP. This is the choice of history, and of the people. Fundamentally, following the leadership of the CCP derives from the nature of political reform and from the conditions in our country. Without the leadership of the CCP, then there can't be any reform of the political system, and there will be no future for development in China".[56] The authors of this highly influential book were all academics based at the Central Party School, the very place where Hu had been President before being replaced first by Zeng Qinghong, and then, in 2007, Xi Jinping. What they said represented strands of opinion within the elite. Even for relative liberals like them, having the CCP out of the equation was unthinkable.

Liu Xiaobo and his co-authors' challenge was somewhat different. "The Chinese government's approach to 'modernization' has proven disastrous", Charter 08 states in its preamble. "It has stripped people of their rights, destroyed their dignity, and corrupted normal human intercourse. So we ask: Where is China

---

[56] Tianyong Zhou, Changjiang Wang, and Anling Wang, *Gong Jian: Shiqida hou Zhongguo Zhengzhi Tizhi Gaige Yanjiu Baogao*, ('Storming the Fortress: A research report on political reform after the 17th Party Congress', Xinjiang Production Corps Publishing House, Xinjiang, 2007, p 7, (Author's translation).

headed in the 21st century? Will it continue with 'modernization' under authoritarian rule, or will it embrace universal human values, join the mainstream of civilized nations, and build a democratic system? There can be no avoiding these questions".[57] In outlining a different blueprint for China's future, Liu drew on six fundamental principles: freedom, human rights, equality, republicanism, democracy, and constitutional rule. Flowing from these, were 19 specific demands:

- A new constitution
- Separation of powers
- Legislative democracy
- An independent judiciary
- Public control of public servants
- Guarantee of human rights
- Election of public officials
- Greater rural-urban equality
- Freedom to form groups
- Freedom to assemble
- Freedom of expression
- Freedom of religion
- Civic education
- Protection of private property
- Financial and tax reform
- Social security
- Protection of the environment
- A federated republic
- Truth and reconciliation

Liu and his fellow writers ended their open letter with the stirring conclusion: "Together we can work for major changes in Chinese

---

[57] Xiaobo Liu et al., 'China's Charter 08', translated by Perry Link, New York Review of Books, December 18, 2008, at http://www.nybooks.com/articles/archives/2009/jan/15/chinas-charter-08/ [22 December 2011].

society and for the rapid establishment of a free, democratic, and constitutional country. We can bring to reality the goals and ideals that our people have incessantly been seeking for more than a hundred years, and can bring a brilliant new chapter to Chinese civilization".

Before December 10th had even dawned, Liu and a number of others most closely related to the Charter were taken into detention by the police. Liu was to end up being held incommunicado in hotels in the suburbs of Beijing for most of the next year, before being put on trial and sentenced for state subversion on Christmas Day 2009. His being awarded the Nobel Peace Prize in 2010 will be covered later.

Comparing the book by the authors at the Party School, and the text of Charter 08 is instructive. While one work was by trusted, high ranking Party ideologues, and the other by peripheral and in some cases soon imprisoned dissidents and activists, in fact, the substance of their proposals was surprisingly similar. For Zhou Tianyong and his fellow authors, reform of the courts, strengthening of the legal system, clarifying the division of powers between the executive, the judiciary and the legislators, and reforming the congress system by allowing a greater role for voting were all high on the 'must do' list.[58] The two areas where they differed from Charter 08 strongly were simply about the role of multi-party competition and (as quoted above) the fundamental right of the Party to maintain its monopoly on power.

The key priority of the Cultural Revolution generation in power had been stability. According to one commentator:

> This generation not only bore the burden of the cost of the CR, but also has to bear the cost of the reform. They lost much during the CR, but did not receive any compensation in the reform era... This

---

[58] Storming the Fortress' and its political programme are discussed in some length in Kerry Brown, *Ballot Box China: Grass Roots Democracy and the Final Major One-Party State*, Zed Books, London, 2011, p 151 onwards.

generation has been extremely unlucky; during their childhood, they experienced 'three bad years'; during the normal years of schooling, they were sent to the countryside to do manual labour; when they became adults, they lived in a time of sexual restraint; when they wanted to have children, they could have only one child. Then they became experienced workers, they were unemployed, they needed to care for their elderly and paid a great deal for their children's education.[59]

Perhaps this overstates it; the generation from the 1920s to the 1940s also experienced extreme hardship and the devastating wars then. But the generation after them, from which Hu and the most influential elite leaders around him from 2002 onwards came, would have been deeply influenced both by their memories of instability and disruption at that time, and by their first hand encounter with massive dislocation from 1966 onwards. The impact of that was to create deep divisions in society, as was seen in Chapter One, and to create conflict, some of it leading to tragic fatalities. Marked by these experiences, stability at all costs is the central premise of the Hu era leaders, with economic development as the key mechanism by which to deliver this.

As if to prove how close by instability was, in July of 2009, while fighting the global economic crisis which had started a few months earlier, the Xinjiang region of China was convulsed with the same kinds of street violence that had occurred in Lhasa, Tibet, in early 2008. This unrest was largely blamed by the reaction in Xinjiang to chips, posted in early July on the video sharing website YouTube, of Uyghur workers being beaten up in Guangzhou, southern China, by local Han, after accusations of theft had been made against them. On July 9th, protests erupted in Urumqi, with over 200 killed, the majority of them Han. The disturbances were so serious that Hu suffered the indignity of having to make an early exit from a meeting of the G8 in Italy, at which China was an observer,

---

[59] Quoted in Cheng Li, *China's Leaders*, p 12–13.

delegating responsibility to State Councillor Dai Bingguo, while he returned to Beijing to deal with the situation.

Governance in Xinjiang had posed challenges for generations of central PRC leaders. In his history of the region, American scholar James Millward stated that the "'autonomy system' [in Xinjiang] leaves real power in the hands of Han Party secretaries". As in Tibet, "rapid economic developments... seemingly benefit Han migrants more than Uyghur residents".[60] Relations between Han and the majority Muslim Uyghur had been difficult for years, exacerbated by heavier migration into the region from the 1990s onwards. By 2009, relations had deteriorated again. But once more, in a repeat of the sequence of events in Tibet a year before, the central authorities and the security agents seemed to be taken aback by the strength of the local protests. Massive numbers of armed police and security officers were sent into the region, pacifying it within a few days. A curfew was imposed, and a form of eerie stability returned by mid July. But the shock created by what had happened was not so easy to dispel.

A few weeks after the protests, Hu made a visit to the region. While touring factories and talking to local people, he was reported in the Chinese state press as saying, "The victory of this struggle fully showed the power of the Party and the people... The [separatist] forces are doomed to fail and their sabotage activities will not shake the overall situation of the stable development of the reform in Xinjiang".[61] But the removal of the Urumqi City Party Secretary and the Police Chief in early September was an indication of how rattled the central leadership had been. And despite Hu's categorical words, Xinjiang in fact posed massive challenges to Beijing, and ones where it needed to think about things differently.

---

[60] James A Millward, *Eurasian Crossroads: A History of Xinjiang*, Columbia University Press, New York, 2007, p 350.
[61] Quoted in China Economic Review, August 26, 2009, 'Hu Jintao Visits Xinjiang', http://www.chinaeconomicreview.com/dailybriefing/2009_08_26/Hu_Jintao_visits_Xinjiang.html [16 February 2011].

Those arriving in Urumqi after three days in the train in the 1990s would have seen an immense sign across the square from the central station proclaiming unity amongst China's ethnic minorities (similar signs were daubed in Hohhot, Inner Mongolia, and Lhasa, other so-called border 'autonomous' regions). The Chinese 1982 Constitution described the People's Republic as a multi-ethnic state where "all nationalities… are equal". It continues, in Article Four: "The state helps the areas inhabited by minority nationalities speed up their economic and cultural development in accordance with the peculiarities and needs of the different minority nationalities. Regional autonomy is practised in areas where people of minority nationalities live in compact communities; in these areas organs of self-government are established for the exercise of the right of autonomy. All the national autonomous areas are inalienable parts of the People's Republic of China. The people of all nationalities have the freedom to use and develop their own spoken and written languages, and to preserve or reform their own ways and customs".[62] That at least was the theoretical promise in the ruling rhetoric.

Whatever the Constitution might say, the position of at least three of the five autonomous regions (the other two being Guangxi and Ningxia) remained highly contentious. A great part of the legitimacy of the CCP when it came to power in 1949 was the promise to provide unity, equality and stability over a vastly complex social, political and ethnic entity. As one study of the early years of the PRC has pointed out, the 'liberation' of Tibet from 1949 to 1951 raised a number of deep issues: "As later development would reveal, Mao and his comrades were far from ready to deal with these challenges. The 'new China' with Tibet incorporated into it became a country more complicated and difficult for Mao and the Party leadership to manage… More than half a century after the Communists occupied Tibet, two fundamental — and

---

[62] 'Constitution of the People's Republic of China', at http://english.peopledaily.com.cn/constitution/constitution.html [22 December 2011].

closely interrelated — challenges continue to face the Communist state: how to define Tibet's position in China, and how to define 'China'."[63] Exactly the same challenges were posed by Xinjiang, which had partially been an independent state from 1945 to 1949. Occupying 18 percent of the Chinese landmass, and sharing some of the most sensitive and contentious borders, with Pakistan, Afghanistan, Russia and Mongolia, Xinjiang's position was made even more difficult by the fact that it was a potential source of greatly needed resources for the rest of China, including gas and oil (though these remained hard to exploit) and that its main occupants, the Uyghur, had little in common with the dominant Han from the main part of China — neither religion, language, culture, nor even appearance. During the Cultural Revolution, from 1966, these ethnic tensions had exploded, with mosques attacked, a large contingent of youths from the rest of China sent to the area to 'cultivate it', and the start of a major new influx of settlers. Resentments starting from this era were never wholly dispelled.

Even during the good times, in the relatively liberal era of the 1980s, tensions were not far from the surface. In the 1990s, there were massive protests in some Xinjiang cities, culminating in a bomb attack in Beijing on a bus in 1997. By 2001, and the September 11th attacks, in return for their support for military action against Afghanistan and eventually Iraq, the Chinese government under Jiang Zemin felt emboldened enough to ask the Americans to place two Xinjiang groups on the international terrorist list. The USA complied.

It was true that some things in the region changed for the better. Those who had visited Xinjiang in the mid 1990s, and then returned there in 2003, could see the impact of the many millions of dollars of central funds going into developing the infrastructure of the

---

[63] Jian Chen, 'The Chinese Communist "Liberation" of Tibet, 1949–1951', in Jeremy Brown and Paul G Pickowicz (Eds), *Dilemmas of Victory: The Early Years of the People's Republic of China*, Harvard University Press, Cambridge, MA, 2007, p 158–159.

area and rehousing people. The same development model used in the rest of the country was now transforming urban Xinjiang. The remote city of Kashgar, once requiring a three-day bus ride from Urumqi, became accessible by train. What airports that existed were expanded, with many others built from scratch. The man who was in charge of the region while most of this was happening was a native of the coastal province of Shandong. Wang Lequan was to prove one of the most controversial of China's provincial leaders. He was also one of the most powerful, with a seat on the full Politburo, and perhaps most unusually, an extension of his period in power over not just two (the norm), but well into three terms. By the time of the 2009 riots, he had been Party Secretary since 1997. Rumours circulated locally of him favouring natives of his own province in the lucrative energy and infrastructure projects. He was said to be complicit in corruption, and to give the security services a free hand to wage massive clampdowns on the religious practices of local Uyghurs from time to time, violating what many felt was their constitutional right to freedom of religious belief. In the aftermath of 2009, Wang was to be a prime target of anger not just by Uyghurs in 2009 who had always detested him, but the local Han, who felt that he had failed to protect them when the attacks happened.

While Wang survived into 2010, his age (he was 68, near the unwritten but now largely recognised retirement age for cadres), his controversy, and accusations of his mismanagement of the region meant that a changeover to a new leader became almost inevitable. The coup de grâce was delivered by Vice Premier Xi Jinping who visited Urumqi on April 26th, and discreetly declared a 'routine' change of local leadership. Wang was sent back to Beijing to a largely ceremonial retirement slot, and Zhang Chunxian replaced him.

Despite the strong statements about preserving stability in the area and maintaining the unity of the country, the central leadership must have known that having two large, visible and damaging uprisings in the space of less than 14 months was highly problematic. Its initial strategy was to be defensive and increase control and repression. Blaming the internet for spreading rumours and assisting 'black separatist elements' the government simply restricted access to the web for all 18 million citizens of the area for almost a year (only government sites were accessible). There were also dark hints of foreign involvement. A security clampdown was instigated against those accused of being activists, with the Public Security Bureau and the People's Armed Police in control of a roundup which led to a large number of executions and long prison sentences in the following year. But what to do about the long-term stability of the region so that the kind of flare ups that erupted in 2009 never happened again remained a problem.

Throughout the first half of 2010, the central government convened a series of meetings addressing this issue, culminating in two conferences personally chaired by Hu. The one on Xinjiang, held from May 17th–19th, resulted in announcements of millions of dollars of new support. Hu was reported at the meeting to have called for "a prosperous, harmonious and stable socialist Xinjiang", one where "[b]y 2015, per capita GDP in Xinjiang should catch up with the country's average level and the residents' income and their access to basic public services should reach the average level of the country's western regions". Within the coming decade by 2020, Hu was quoted as saying that "Xinjiang should fulfil the goal of achieving a moderately prosperous society in all aspects... by promoting coordinated regional development. It should also improve people's living standards and build an eco-friendly environment, as well as ensure ethnic unity, social stability and security".[64]

Similar bold predictions had been made about Tibet only a few months earlier, during a conference in Beijing from January 18th–20th, 2010. There Hu had declared that the key objective was

---

[64] Xinhua, 'Chinese central authorities outline roadmap for Xinjiang's leapfrog development, lasting stability', May 20, 2010, at http://news.xinhuanet.com/english2010/china/2010-05/20/c_13306534.htm [22 December 2011].

"to substantially prevent and strike 'penetration and sabotage' by 'Tibet independence' separatists, in order to safeguard social stability, socialist legal system, the fundamental interests of the public, national unity, and ethnic solidarity". But he had also promised that the "leapfrog development of Tibet actually means the combination of economic growth, well-off life, a healthy eco-environment, and social stability and progress".[65] With both Xinjiang and Tibet, the vision of the central leadership was that economic development was the key to ensuring that these two difficult, contentious regions would remain stable. Billions of Chinese yuan were promised. Perhaps the most visible symbol of this was the all-out attempt to rebuild and renovate Kashgar. Huge areas of the old city were deemed unsanitary and bulldozed down, with little if any attempt to listen to local people. The principle vision of modernity and progress belonged to the 'enlightened leaders' in Beijing, of which Hu was the chief. But local voices were less harmonious. "By some accounts" a *Time* report from July 2009 stated, "at least 85% of Old Kashgar will be knocked down. Many expect the ancient quarter, considered one of Central Asia's best preserved sites of Islamic architecture, to disappear almost entirely before the end of the year. 'This is the Uighurs' Jerusalem,' says Henryk Szadziewski of the Washington-based Uyghur Human Rights Project. 'By destroying it, you rip the soul out of a people'."[66]

Critics of the Hu–Wen leadership pointed out that the fundamental problem was not economic development. What created the most anger was the very unequal way in which the benefits of growth had been spread amongst different groups, with the Han perceived as getting the main share. The inability of ethnic minority groups to use their own languages in university

---

[65] Xinhua, 'China to achieve fast-paced development, lasting stability in Tibet,' January 23, 2010, at http://news.xinhuanet.com/english/2010–01/23/content_12859870_1.htm [22 December 2011].
[66] Ishaan Thardoor, 'Tearing Down Old Kashgar: Another Blow to the Uighurs', *Time*, July 29, 2009, at http://www.time.com/time/world/article/0,8599,1913166,00.html [22 December 2011].

and very high unemployment rate amongst young male Uyghurs (these had, after all, been the main participants in the July 9th riots) worsened things. Ilham Tohti, a Beijing-based Uyghur scholar, stated in an interview just before the riots in early March 2009 that "[u]nemployment among Uyghurs is among the highest in the world". He went on, "In the 1990s, I participated in the central government's 9th five-year research plan, and I was responsible for research on Xinjiang. At that time I wrote that there were 1.5 million unemployed workers in Xinjiang, but the Xinjiang government rejected this. Two years ago they finally acknowledged that there is surplus labour in the Xinjiang Uyghur Autonomous Region. Other provinces in China have had some improvements with regard to democracy. But in Xinjiang, the situation has worsened".[67]

The two meetings held in Beijing in 2010 gave little sense that the central leadership was considering these problems, or thinking about any long-term solutions to the regions which were not ultimately tied to economic development. The overwhelming impression was of them merely buying time as they hoped that further inward migration, and the recruitment of more amenable local citizens (through the deployment of incentives and benefits that had partially worked in the past) would appease enough people to avoid a repetition of the explosion of anger that had marred 2008–9. As of spring 2011, however, the government was insufficiently relaxed about the initial success of its strategy to reopen up Tibet to international travellers. The breakneck reconstruction of Kashgar continueds apace.

## Political Succession

Just as it had dominated the end of Jiang's era in office, from 2009, excitement has been growing over how the succession process scheduled to take place in late 2012 is going to happen. The greatest

---

[67] Radio Free Asia, 'Uyghur Scholar Calls for Jobs,' March 6, 2009, at http://www.rfa.org/english/news/uyghur/tohti-03062009130647.html [22 December 2011].

clue to who would replace Hu came when the new leadership line-up walked out from behind the red curtains at the Party Congress in October 2007. From that moment, the suspicion that Xi was a front runner for General Secretary converted into something approaching certainty. All that was needed now was for him to be given the Vice Chair spot on the Central Military Commission at the Plenum in late 2009, and it would all pretty much be a done deal. When it was clear as this meeting ended that he had not been promoted, rumours started flying around in some quarters that he had somehow fallen from favour. In the end, however, his elevation was delayed by only a year. His success in October 2010 at the Plenum that year in securing the CMC position meant that, barring disaster or calamity, the number one spot in 2012 would be his.

That still left plenty of uncertainty. Unlike the Politburos under Jiang, those under Hu, because of their stress on collective leadership, have been watertight. There have been no leaks to either the press or other influential opinion formers. The barrenness of information about what was happening inside the deepest recesses of the Party has only inflamed speculation further with constant rumours that Hu is still battling against vestiges of the influence of Jiang. What is clear is that the Party knows that a messy, unclear transition is not in its favour. The lack of a political godfather figure's influence, like that of former paramount leader Deng Xiaoping in the 1980s and 1990s, complicates matters. In many areas the Party has to create new rules and procedures to handle the transition, ones which can succeed in balancing many different interests, areas and factions.

From 2010 onwards Hu Jintao has been living in a tricky period in which the atmosphere in Beijing, always heavy with rumours of elitist division and subterfuge, became even more so. This means that all sorts of ruptures have been imputed between him and Premier Wen about the need for accelerated political reform. From 2009, a period of marked repression dawned, something which will be looked at later. Such edginess reached into the way China related to the outside world, with some of its actions being interpreted as assertive and aggressive, and others as unsure and immature (this will be covered in Chapter Four). At the heart of this, however, is the simple fact that whoever rules China from 2012 is going to be in charge of the world's second largest economy, and one of its fastest emerging markets. It is a position worth fighting for, carrying immense power and authority.

And whatever even its fiercest critics might say, China is a powerful country, despite its enormous internal vulnerabilities, for one predominant reason — the extraordinary success of its economy. It is to that that we now turn.

Chapter Three

# A STRONG RICH COUNTRY: THE CHINESE ECONOMY UNDER HU

When China entered the WTO in late 2001, after a gruelling 15-year process of negotiations, it was a moment of bittersweet reflection. Assessments at the time looked at the challenges that entry to the global system would pose for China's indigenous industries. One analysis by Wang Shaoguang, writing in 2000 in Hong Kong, looked at the likely social impact:

> Even if the WTO membership is potentially a productivity-enhancing move for China, the benefits and costs of such a change will not be evenly distributed. Unless there is a mechanism that can induce or force the winners to compensate the losers, distributive conflicts between the two groups will be inevitable.

Wang continued, looking at the sectoral impact of WTO entry:

> Whereas China gains no new access to the US market, the United States, and for that matter, other countries, will secure market access to whole areas of the Chinese economy to which they were previously denied, once China becomes a WTO member state… Who stand to lose once China becomes a WTO member? Farmers and workers are most likely to suffer negative consequences from the deal in the form of lost jobs and downward pressure on wages. The WTO membership requires China to dismantle its remaining import barriers. This will entail painful domestic restructuring and adjustment because these barriers have been used primarily to protect state owned industries and farmers.[1]

---

[1] Shaoguang Wang, 'Openness, Distributive Conflict, and Social Insurance: The Social and Political Implications of China's WTO Membership', at http://www.gateway2china.com/report/CUHK_paper.htm [22 December 2011].

A report in *The Economist* in September 2001, just before China's final signing of the deal, was similarly wary:

> It has been 15 years since China first applied to join the multilateral trading system then called the GATT and now known as the World Trade Organisation (WTO). But with the talks at last drawing to a conclusion, the next task for China's leaders will be to make sure that public opinion remains favourable. Although some of the economic change necessary to prepare China for membership has already taken place, much painful restructuring still remains to be carried out, and with it the risk of growing public resentment.[2]

The assessment continued by highlighting how the commitment to decrease tariffs was likely to expose China's agricultural sector in particular to massive foreign competition and open up some of its most sensitive, state dominated sectors to fierce international competition. As Vice President, in February 2002, according to the People's Daily, Hu spoke at the Party School only a few weeks after China had joined the organisation, stressing to provincial and central leaders in training that China needed to study both the 'opportunities and challenges' that came from WTO entry. The report continued,

> Hu said that though officials at all levels have achieved progress in improving their ability to lead the modernization drive after years of study and practice, they still need to re-study to meet the new situation, especially new issues the country faces as a member of the WTO.[3]

In fact, not only was China able to fulfil the commitments it had made in order to enter the WTO, and to comply on time with those over

---

[2] China and the WTO: Ready for the Competition', *The Economist*, September 13, 2001, at http://www.economist.com/node/780479 [22 December 2011].
[3] People's Daily Online, 'Hu Jintao on Study of International Situation Following WTO Entry', February 22, 2002, at http://english.peopledaily.com.cn/200202/22/eng20020222_90796.shtml [22 December 2011].

the coming five-year transition period, it was also able to continue protecting key strategic sectors like telecommunications, financial services and the defence industries, as well as repel a number of attempts by the US and others to take it to WTO arbitration over its compliance with regulations. More remarkably, WTO entry can be seen as a moment when the Chinese economy entered a phase of remarkable expansion and dynamism — something that continues to this day — more than tripling its size, and leaping from below tenth in the list of major world economies to second. Looking at foreign trade in particular, economist Barry Naughton was able to comment that

> we can see how dramatic the change associated with WTO membership has been... It is the surge of overseas trade (OT) imports that is most directly attributable to WTO-induced trade liberalisation... The huge surge in China's foreign trade after 2002 can be directly associated with very recent [as of 2007] liberalisation of the import regime, drive by WTO membership.[4]

Hu positioned himself in the same CCP tradition as Deng Xiaoping in terms of replacing an ideological commitment to class struggle, which Mao had taken with a total focus on producing economic growth and prosperity. This was clear from his comments in December 2008 to commemorate the 30th anniversary of the opening up and reform process. "The slogan 'The class struggle is the key link', which we used to guide our work during the 'Cultural Revolution'," he said, "was thoroughly repudiated. A historic decision was adopted at the Session to make economic development the central task of the Party and the government and to adopt reform and opening up".[5] He had made similar comments at the work report he had presented to the 17th Party Congress over a year before.

---

[4] Barry Naughton, *The Chinese Economy: Transitions and Growth*, MIT Press, Cambridge, MA, 2007, p 392.
[5] Jintao Hu, 'Hu Jintao's Speech at the Meeting Marking the 30th Anniversary of Reform and Opening Up,' December 18, 2008, at http://www.china.org.cn/archive/2009-05/11/content_17753659.htm [22 December 2011].

The pattern of economic development under Hu can be divided into three key areas: the first is the opening up of the Chinese economy, under WTO, and the explosion of manufacturing and exports which are ongoing; the second was the start of a process of Chinese international investment, and the third was deeper integration into the global economic system, partly as a result of the 2008 economic crisis, and partly through the natural impact of the increase in the size of China's own economy. The final part of this chapter will look at some of the challenges that economic policy under Hu had created.

## China as the Factory of the World

Zhu Rongji when he was Premier had famously promised that China would become the factory of the world, but the time when this can be said to have really happened was after 2002. The complex factors that led to a massive surge in foreign investment into China, particularly the coastal areas, have been closely studied. While there may be debate about the ways in which China achieved this, there can be no dispute about its success. By 2007, China was the world's main manufacturer, and by 2009, it had succeeded in ousting Germany from the position of number one exporter. In terms of raw statistics, there were few indicators in which it was not either in top slot, or close to it. From 2002, China became a country of big statistics, and they seemed to get bigger every year.

The Organisation for Economic Co-operation and Development (OECD) produced a report in 2005 which assessed the stage that the Chinese economy had arrived at, close to the end of its implementation period for WTO commitments. Recognising the large increases in GDP over the last two and a half decades, the report attributed these to two powerful factors. The first was the willingness of central and provincial policy makers to embrace the market. The second was the cultivation of a non-state sector.[6]

---

[6] In the report, this is called a private sector, but because of the continuing strong role of the state in the operations of the private sector in China, it is perhaps more accurate to call it 'non-state.'

> The government... rigorously enforced a number of competition laws in order to unify the internal market, while the business environment was further sharpened by allowing foreign direct investment in the country, reducing tariffs, abolishing the state export trading monopoly and ending multiple exchange rates.

The report also stated:

> In addition, fundamental changes were made to the constitution in 2004, stressing the role of the non-state sector in supporting economic activity in the country and protecting private property from arbitrary seizure. In 2005, regulations that prevented privately owned companies entering a number of sectors of the economy, such as infrastructure, public utilities and financial services were abolished. Overall, these changes have permitted the emergence of a powerful private sector in the economy.[7]

Despite this, there was still clear political risk in the deeper embrace of marketisation. This lay behind Hu's opening words of his work report during the Party Congress in 2007 where he had said that it was important to "persist in reform and opening up". Just as leftists around Deng Liqun in the 1990s had mounted a campaign against what they saw as over-liberal reforms under Jiang, which exposed Chinese workers to aggressive foreign competition and the vagaries of a market economy manipulated to the capitalist west's advantage, so did many around Hu and Wen criticise the adventure of entry into WTO and the way in which the Chinese government was not only maintaining, but in many areas deepening, marketisation of the Chinese economy. Reports of almost all the factors of production, from power to water supply having a market created around them must have bought back the darkest fears of more staid state-supporters as the impact of WTO membership unfolded from 2002.

---

[7] OECD, 'Economic Survey of China 2005', September 15, 2005, available at http://www.oecd.org/document/12/0,3343,en_2649_34111_35331797_1_1_1_1,00.html [22 December 2011].

These arguments reached deep into the heart of the Party elite. No one, not least the OECD report quoted above, doubted that the private sector had energised large sections of the economy. Many were now employed by non-state owned enterprises. Even so (and this will be dealt with in the chapter on ideology later) observers like Yasheng Huang could claim that there was, in fact, a political pecking order, and that state owned enterprises, despite their being rationalised and reduced in number, still enjoyed massive advantages. "Amongst all the constraints on the growth of private firms", Huang argues, "the low political and legal statuses of private firms are most fundamental and most blatant".[8] Political interference in the operations of the private sector was not remotely cured by acceptance of entrepreneurs into the CCP in 2001, one of Jiang Zemin's great achievements. That, at best, represented a pragmatic accommodation or compact with a force in society that was delivering most of the growth and much needed job creation. But there were plenty of examples of business people who ran afoul of the central government and ended up being silenced, imprisoned and, more often than not, placed in jail.

One of the most eminent of these was retailer Huang Guangyu, reportedly China's richest man in 2006. Described by a *Time* Magazine report in 2006 as "a classic Chinese rag to riches tale", Huang had left school at 16 and made his first money by selling goods by the roadside. By the mid 2000s he was reportedly worth USD 1.7 billion.[9] His Gome brand was one of the best known for selling appliances and household goods in China. But a mere two years later, just after the Beijing Olympics, Huang disappeared. The man popularly known as 'the price butcher' was subsequently charged formally with insider trading. In May 2010, he was jailed for 14 years for bribery. Huang's case raised a number of issues about the security of entrepreneurs in Hu's China. Was it really possible

---

[8]Yasheng Huang, *Selling China: Foreign Direct Investment During the Reform Era*, Cambridge University Press, Cambridge, 2003, p 122–123.
[9]James McGregor, 'Huang Guangyu,' *Time Magazine*, May 8, 2006, at http://www.time.com/time/magazine/article/0,9171,1187472,00. html [22 December 2011].

to operate in this environment without having to do deals which invaded the area of illegality? Had Huang angered some powerful political former patron? He had never expressed any political views which the CCP might object to. But the felling of such a prominent figure, following on from a number of other high profile corporate downfalls, underlined the point that Yasheng Huang had made — in China, there was a political pecking order, and the non-state sector, however much it prospered, did so only with the blessing, and the tolerance, of the Party.

The role of the non-state/private sector and of the embrace of the market remained a live one. At the National People's Congress in 2011, the Politburo's most representative hardliner, Wu Bangguo, issued a rallying call to not concede to western political models and to oppose the kind of wholesale marketisation of the economy that was seen as having led to the economic crisis in the west.

Hu himself maintained a bland orthodoxy on the issue of the non-state sector. His speeches stressed the need to maintain the Dengist line, to take economic delivery as the key, and to continue with the mantra of socialism with Chinese characteristics. The Party (as opposed to Country) constitution was revised at the end of the 17th National Congress to include language which showed that it encouraged, supported and guided the development of the non-state sector. But business people lived in a vulnerable position, and their need to cultivate political links was crucial to their prosperity and survival, just as much as the Party needed their productivity to deliver its economic targets.

This ambiguity about the place of business in a new China that was thriving but remained under CCP rule was best seen in Hu's attitude to foreign business leaders. In the 1990s, the heads of companies like BP, Shell, General Motors, News International, and others were able to pass through Beijing, lobbying for their interests. Jiang frequently made time to meet them, earning some consultancies, Chinese and non-Chinese, handsome fees for arranging such visits (an unofficial estimate in 2001 put a value of about USD 50 thousand to meet the President, with a sliding scale for those lower in the Politburo). But from 2002, much of that stopped. Hu was rarely seen mingling with multinational company leaders. It is true that he spoke at events arranged by Forbes, but largely on political issues. And during his visits abroad (see the next chapter) his engagement with business people was usually during mass meetings. A senior executive for a foreign corporation with major investment in China complained to me in 2008 that getting meetings with Hu had proved impossible.

## Behind the Factory Doors

As the world's leading manufacturer, how did China look? Paul Midler, an American helping foreign companies enter the PRC's manufacturing sector, detailed some of the results in an account written towards the end of the decade. Theoretically, it had been expected that WTO entry would make China an even more attractive place to invest than before, and that it would allow foreign companies to enjoy the benefits of the seemingly endless cheap labour that the country had to offer. Companies like Wal Mart and Tesco outsourced vast amounts of goods, in immense factories around the Pearl River Delta and elsewhere on the coastal areas of China. Foxconn, the Taiwan owned electrical appliance company, was perhaps the most infamous, based in the original special economic zone in Shenzhen, with over 480 thousand people. A spate of suicides there in 2010 gave the company unwelcome prominence. Foxconn manufactured Apple products and a range of other technical goods. Another factory made 90 percent of the world's microwaves. But for Midler, the untrammelled success of outsourcing to China, as his book title shows, was a myth. "China manufacturing operated in a world where principles were in short supply and the court system could not be counted on to keep operators honest". he wrote. But the final conclusion was a far more sobering one. After years of dealing with ill made goods, some of them actually harmfully so, and with increasingly powerful Chinese factories turning the tables on their foreign customers because of the monopoly they were eventually able to exercise, Midler came to question the whole system. "This decision to fling open wide the doors of trade with China — before we were ready, before China was ready, before we understood what we were getting into; an action motivated by our own greed — this decision more than anything else was the one thing related to China that was truly poorly made."[10]

The idea that in the space of a few years China had become what was in effect the factory of the world was not lost on the popularist and polemical authors of 'China is Unhappy.' Part of the shock of reading this work is that its main complaint is often levelled at the very elites amongst whom Hu took centre stage — although the authors were smart enough to work out that directly blaming the political leaders would have landed them in the same mess as imprisoned Chinese academic and dissident Liu Xiaobo. In many ways, their argument was underpinned by the same cynicism which many claimed dominated contemporary China, angrily denouncing the exploitation of workers, and yet also appreciating many of the things the west had brought which were now serving to make China more powerful, more assertive, and more capable of addressing some of its profound historic grievances. As one of the lead authors, Wang Xiaodong wrote in his contributions, referring to the baby milk powder scandal of 2008 that led to a number of tragic deaths, China was a superpower that could not even sort out the quality of its own food.[11] The question which was implied but never directly stated was 'Whose fault was this?' The business people, greedily ripping people off as a way of life or the politicians who allowed them to do this? For Wang and his co-authors there was a powerful sense of implication that they were both as bad as one another.

---

[10] Paul Midler, *Poorly Made in China: An Insider's Account of the Tactics Behind China's Production Game*, John Wiley and Sons, New Jersey, 2009, p 240.
[11] Xiaodong Wang et al., *Zhongguo Bu Gaoxing*, ('China is Unhappy'), Phoenix Media Publishing and Jiangsu Publishing House, 2009, p 18 (Author's translation).

The one wholly accepted statement about China's economy from 2002 onwards was that it had been an immense factory for GDP growth, putting in double digit figures from 2003 to 2007, and even in the very worst period of the economic crisis after 2007, managing 9 percent while the rest of the world was mostly contracting. Goldman Sachs economist and creator of the BRIC (Brazil, Russia, India, China) acronym Jim O'Neil breathlessly recounted the scale of this growth in 2011, a decade after China had entered the WTO:

> There is nothing quite like this China phenomenon in modern history. Since 2001, China's economy has grown by $4.3 trillion, in the process effectively creating more than another two of itself than existed in 2001. That growth is equivalent to creating more than two new United Kingdoms.[12]

But the cogitations and drafting, and final passing of the 12th Five Year Plan over 2010 to 2011 made clear that growth and growth alone was no longer enough. China's economic success on one level had created a number of imbalances. Inequality has already been referred to. The environment had suffered terribly under the impact of rapid industrialisation. Chinese workers' wages had remained stagnant, sometimes even falling, with discontent amongst migrant workers rising as the decade wore on. Domestic consumption had fallen, even as the 12th Five Year Plan covering 2011 to 2015 made clear that there needed to be more reliance on the internal, rather than the external market. And levels of unhappiness and dissatisfaction, at least according to some surveys, were sky-high — despite the fact that China had never been richer. Per capita, as many pointed out, China remained a poor country, ranking 127th in the world between Turkmenistan and

---

[12] Jim O'Neill, 'We need to be part of the great Chinese march,' *Evening Standard*, February 15, 2011, at http://www.thisislondon.co.uk/standard/article-23923374-we-need-to-be-part-of-the-great-chinese-march.do [22 December 2011].

Albania in 2010, according to the Central Intelligence Agency.[13] As Wen Jiabao stated at the National People's Congress the same year, 150 million people still lived below the poverty line of USD 2 a day, despite the World Bank praising the government for lifting more people out of poverty than any other over the last decade. One report in 2006 called China the world's first "rich poor country".[14] The political dimension of these challenges will be discussed in the third and fourth chapters.

## China's Overseas Investment

Beyond the leadership transition, the 16th Party Congress of 2002 was important for another reason, and one which may well have a far deeper and longer impact. Since the reform and opening up process started, China had been accumulating capital in its central reserves through the receipts of heavy exporting. With a non-convertible currency, it had managed to create a powerful firewall between its internal market and the rest of the world, something which was widely seen as protecting it from the worst vagaries of the Asian Financial Crisis in 1998–1999. The opening of the Chinese economy meant not only that increasing volumes of foreign direct investment came into China, but that Chinese enterprises themselves were much more aware of their need to internationalise. So alongside a process of privatisation and marketisation, reaching its culmination during the premiership of Zhu Rongji, there was also a small sign that Chinese enterprises, mostly state ones, were investing abroad.

The leadership around Jiang was aware of the need to allow enterprises, state or non-state, to start becoming active

---

[13] https://www.cia.gov/library/publications/the-world-factbook/rankorder/ 2004rank.html?countryName=China&countryCode=ch&regionCode=eas&rank= 127#ch [22 December 2011].
[14] C Fred Bergsten et al., *China, the Balance Sheet: What the World Needs to Know about the Emerging Superpower*, Peterson Institute of International Economics, New York, 2006.

internationally. But the PRC had very limited knowledge of this. According to one study of the evolution of Chinese multinational enterprises, there had been five stages of Chinese outward investment up to entry to the WTO. The first, from 1949 to the mid 1950s, had merely allowed the creation of some overseas enterprises by the new PRC in Hong Kong; the second, over the two decades from the mid 1950s to the mid 1970s, had seen Chinese overseas efforts mostly focused on giving aid assistance to third world (as they were called then) countries viewed as being engaged in a similar revolutionary struggle as the PRC against the hegemony and oppression of developed countries; the third involved construction projects, again largely active in developing countries, and lasted till the late 1970s; stage four was marked by the passing of formal 'Go Abroad' policies on August 13th, 1979; the final stage before WTO was when "a large group of enterprises established after the 1978 economic reforms sought to internationalise their business", and created foreign enterprises abroad.[15]

In order to take things to the final sixth level, the 2002 Congress passed what was called a 'Going Out' policy. This built on the decision made five years before at the previous Congress to support the globalisation of Chinese enterprises, but was presented more formally, with the selection of 50 major enterprises in 2002. Policies were put in place to support their entry into the international market. One of these, D'Long, was to become a famous failure. A property company based in the north west of China, it was to expand rapidly after government encouragement, only to collapse with enormous debts.[16] Many wryly noted that government support for outward

---

[15] Xiaohua Yang and Clyde Stoltenberg, 'Growth of Made-in-China Multinationals: An Institutional and Historical Perspective', in Ilan Alon and John R McIntyre (Eds), *Globalization of Chinese Enterprises*, Palgrave Macmillan, Basingstoke, Hampshire, 2008, p 63–66.

[16] Kerry Brown, 'No Reverse Gear: Chinese Sovereign Wealth Funds and Overseas Direct Investment', CLSA September 2008, p 6–8, at http://www.kerry-brown.co.uk/files/clsa_paper_final.pdf [22 December 2011].

enterprises was sometimes a kiss of death, giving them almost limitless financial support no matter how reckless or unwise their investment decisions might be. But Jiang stated clearly in 2002 that "[n]ot only should we attract the foreign firms to actively invest in China, but also we should direct domestic firms to go out, invest abroad and exploit the local market and resources. We should not only target the markets of European Union and the US, but the markets in developing countries..."[17]

A look at the Chinese government statistics from 2002 shows a big increase in the deployment of capital abroad, although much of it was filtered through financial entrepots: Hong Kong or offshore destinations like the British Virgin Islands and the Cayman Islands. Central government policy was relaxed, allowing Chinese enterprises at provincial level, along with provinces themselves, to invest abroad.[18] One of the most significant moments came in September 2007, when, after a great deal of discussion, a sovereign wealth fund was also set up, the Chinese Investment Corporation (CIC), with USD 200 billion of central funds.

It is still possible today to feel some of the excitement of anticipation about the impact of the CIC. China had, after all, accrued over USD 700 billion by 2006 in foreign exchange reserves, overtaking Japan that year.[19] This had been a highly symbolic moment in China's development after entry to WTO, showing the success of the implementation, but also throwing up a number of challenges.

---

[17] Quoted in Fang-Cheng Tang et al., 'Knowledge Acquisition and Learning Strategies in Globalization of China's Enterprises', in Alon and McIntyre (Eds), p 37.
[18] This is dealt with in Kerry Brown, *The Rise of the Dragon: Inward and Outward Investment in China in the Reform Period 1978–2007*, Chandos Publishing, Oxford, 2008, p 150–151.
[19] China Business News, "China's Currency Reserves Top Japan's", March 28, 2006, quoted in Jingtao Yi, 'China's Rapid Accumulation of Foreign Exchange Reserves and its Policy Implications', China Policy Institution, Nottingham, Briefing Series No 10, p 3.

One analyst stated:

> Recent heavy foreign exchange accumulation including rapidly increased speculative capital flows have increased the risk to the financial system, exacerbated inflationary pressure, incurred huge opportunity costs, resulted in large wealth losses with a weakening dollar, intensified pressure for RMB appreciation and increased the complexity of macroeconomic adjustment and foreign exchange reserve management.

One option was therefore to increase investment abroad:

> Chinese economists have suggested that its huge foreign exchange reserves could be used to import petroleum and other essential raw materials, as well as high technology and to invest in key sectors abroad.[20]

Before Hu Jintao visited Japan in 2008, one report stated:

> China's increasingly aggressive sovereign wealth fund is poised to unleash a USD 10 billion (£5.14 billion) investment spree in Japan and is initially expected to set its sights on the energy sector... Analysts speculated that the discussion of a possible CIC stake in [Japanese energy company] Inpex might portend a 'friendship' investment ahead of the visit to Tokyo later this year of the Chinese President, Hu Jintao.[21]

But it soon became clear that there was a problem, one which had raised its head when China had first become more visible as a potential outward investor in 2005. It was already obvious that the country was suffering from a very severe energy and resource hunger, something that journalist James Kynge had written about

---

[20] Jingtao Yi, 'China's Rapid Accumulation of Foreign Reserves', p 11.
[21] Leo Lewis, 'China Investment Corporation poised for a $10 bn spree in Japan', *The Times*, February 22, 2008, at http://business.timesonline.co.uk/tol/business/industry_sectors/banking_and_finance/article3414693.ece [22 December 2011].

first in the *Financial Times* and then, in 2006, in a book simply entitled *China Shakes the World: The Rise of a Hungry Nation*.[22] China's need for increasing amounts of energy had been noted from the early 2000s, but the explosion of its productivity only enflamed this, meaning that by 2005 it was well on its way to becoming the biggest user of all energy sources except oil. With its relative lack of easily exploitable natural resources, foreign markets became a key target, with outward investment as the means of achieving this. China's outward investment statistics started to bear that out, despite the various other drivers of this new phenomenon (servicing export markets, creating sales networks, securing intellectual property) .

Over 2005, a leading Chinese state owned energy company, the China National Overseas Oil Corporation (CNOOC) started to express interest in purchasing a small-sized US energy company based in Texas. The tale of the pursuit by the Chinese of Unocal became one of the most closely followed business stories of 2005, but also marked a watershed in China's evolution as an outward investor, and the ways in which the outside world embraced this. While never making a formal bid, the executives of CNOOC, through its Hong Kong subsidiary, made it clear they were interested in pursuing a deal for up to USD 16 billion. But it was when the Congressional Committee which scrutinises major investments into the US became involved that the Chinese started to get cold feet. By mid 2005 they dropped their interest, stating that the highly political nature of the attacks on them from the US meant that the commercial merits of their proposal were never likely to get a fair hearing. One executive simply stated that CNOOC had been willing to observe all the local rules and regulations if the deal had gone ahead and that simple prejudice had prevented this.

The Unocal saga captured something about the ways in which China in the mid-Hu period was seen. While Hu was on his first

---

[22] James Kynge, *China Shakes The World: The Rise of a Hungry Nation*, Weidenfield and Nicholson, London, 2006.

state visit to the UK, meeting business people and talking up the immense economic power that China now had, there was still a large suspicion about the role of the state in any Chinese corporation, and just how transparent these entities could be. Huawei, the dynamic telecoms company was a test case in this — a company which by 2007 was the largest Chinese investor in the UK, one of the largest in Africa, and building up over 70 percent of its business abroad, but a company that was also dogged by claims that it had links with the PLA through the fact that its founder, Ren Zhengfei, was once a serving soldier in the Chinese army. Signing significant deals with British Telecom and being one of the key sponsors of the 2008 Olympics still did not dispel suspicions that Huawei's involvement in a sensitive strategic sector was a big problem. The London Sunday Times reported in March 2009 that there was a clear glass ceiling to the kind of deals that Huawei could bid for in the UK, simply because of this suspicion about so-called private company links with the state.[23] And Yasheng Huang was able to spell out clearly that while the tip of the Huawei iceberg was a company domiciled in Hong Kong, once one went over the border from the Special Administrative Region (which Hong Kong had been since 1997) into the PRC, things became much murkier, and it was in the head office in Shenzhen the shots for the company, wherever it operated, were really called.[24]

Huawei's case, and that of the other major Chinese telecoms company ZTE, was not helped by the huge interest in Chinese cyber espionage that occurred from 2006 onwards. The German government, and then the US and Canadian and finally Australian governments, all claimed they had found evidence of hostile electronic attacks against their secure systems. The man popularly known as the father of the Great Firewall of China Fang Binxing was

---

[23] Michael Smith, 'Spy chief fears Chinese cyber attack', *Sunday Times*, March 29, 2009, at http://www.timesonline.co.uk/tol/news/uk/article5993156.ece [22 December 2011].
[24] Yasheng Huang, *Capitalism with Chinese Characteristics: Entrepreneurship and the State*, Cambridge University Press, Cambridge, 2008, p 11.

accused of setting up an informal infrastructure which saw Chinese cyber attacks, some of them guided from small universities in the hinterland of China, and many of them with surprisingly penetrating capacity, launched against foreign targets. The PLA had, after all, talked of the need to concentrate on informationisation, perhaps realising that it was many decades away from ever truly being able to challenge the hegemony of the US in hard military power (this will be dealt with in more detail in the next chapter). Even so, those who looked hard could join the links and see a China under a leader who was evidently a keen supporter of security. It was therefore perfectly reasonable to strengthen China's capacity in this area. If the central government was content to shut off most of the internet except for government sites in Xinjiang for almost a year after July 2009, why would it not also tolerate support for attacks on the systems of other countries, especially as it had so many talented young software engineers and programmers.

One of the most contentious areas in which Huawei was active was Africa. It was Chinese investments here, as discussion of the Beijing 2008 Olympics has made clear, that caused most problems. Hu Jintao had hosted several high level meetings with African leaders in Beijing and visited a large number of countries with his fellow Politburo leaders since 2002. The meat at the heart of the new, burgeoning China-Africa relationship however was the large amount of trade and investment China was sending to various countries, capped in 2008 by a USD 5 billion stake in the South African Standard Bank. By 2011, the state owned China Development Bank was acknowledged as the largest supporter of aid projects, soft loans and large investments of any international banks on the continent. Chinese investment was used to exploit energy and mineral resources, build roads and factories, and develop infrastructure. Figures like the President of Senegal were able to say that Chinese investment was quicker, more effective and less tied to moralising lectures from old colonialists in the West. He stated in early 2008,

> China's approach to our needs, is simply better adapted than the slow and sometimes patronising post-colonial approach of

European investors, donor organisations and non-governmental organisations. In fact, the Chinese model for stimulating rapid economic development has much to teach Africa... I achieved more in my one hour meeting with President Hu Jintao in an executive suite at my hotel in Berlin during the recent G8 meeting in Heiligendamm than I did during the entire, orchestrated meeting of world leaders at the summit — where African leaders were told little more than that G8 nations would respect existing commitments.[25]

That did not prevent the same intense scrutiny that fell upon the head of CNOOC in the US, also working against Chinese investments in certain problem countries in Africa. In the Zambian election in 2005, in particular, the opposition mounted a campaign against what was perceived as Chinese investment creating jobs that were then taken by Chinese and creating little value for locals. Stories of the Chinese ambassador calling in the head of the government and warning that if this issue was not dealt with China would simply withdraw its money only reinforced the impression that the PRC was becoming a kind of 'new colonialist.' Even so, by the end of the decade, Chinese investment was still pouring into countries like Nigeria, Tanzania, South Africa, and Libya — the latter a particular problem when massive unrest in early 2011 led to the withdrawal of over 35 thousand Chinese nationals who were working there.

When the 2008 economic crisis hit, therefore, China seemed to be in an excellent position to exploit investment opportunities abroad. But the activities of the CIC in purchasing small stakes in Blackstone, JP Morgan and others, and the China Development Bank's purchase of a 3.6 percent share in Barclays Bank, had all created intense interest not just abroad, but in China itself — and in the view of many Chinese, the government was becoming very

---

[25] Abdoulaye Wade, 'Time for the west to practise what it preaches', *Financial Time*, January 23, 2008, at http://www.ft.com/cms/s/0/5d347f88-c897-11dc-94a6-0000779fd2ac.html#axzz1MFsMHg36 [22 December 2011].

good at wasting state money on investments that performed very poorly. One blogger complained about the government throwing away cash earned by the sweat and blood of Chinese workers on western companies that immediately lost value.[26] Bad timing meant that at almost the exact moment the CIC was set up, its initial deals lost money. From 2008, therefore, extreme caution set in. Despite the fact that assets aplenty became available in late 2008 when the crisis in banks and investment companies really hit, the Chinese did little. Rumours swirled around of the head of the CIC Luo Jiwei visiting the US to talk to Morgan Stanley about a major purchase of shares there. But nothing happened. Excited news at the same period that the State Administration for Foreign Exchange (SAFE) was purchasing small shareholdings on the London Stock Exchange of major FTSE companies like Tesco and BP was taken as a sign that the great wave of Chinese investment was about to happen. By 2011, however, the largest investments were still predominantly in resources and energy, with some of the highest profile ones still in Central Asia, Australia and Latin America. In Europe, despite the constant talk by Chinese business people of their liking of the stable business environment there, and the security in their likely returns, the largest investment was the USD 1.6 billion for Volvo by the non-state automotive company Geely, still small by standards elsewhere in the world. Other automotive investments like the purchase by Nanjing Auto of MG Rover in the UK, despite immense government lobbying and effort, did not lead to the kinds of job creation that had been expected. The Chinese leadership under Hu sat on a larger and larger mountain of capital, but exercised the same restraint and caution as they did in internal politics. The opportunity offered by the economic crisis came and went with little significant activity. The Chinese spending spree, if it ever happens, is for the future.

---

[26] A fairly typical example appeared on sina.com. "O senior officials of the Chinese government please do not be fooled by sweet-talking wolves dressed in human skin. The foreign reserves are the product of the sweat and blood of the people of China, please invest them with more care!" Quoted in the *International Herald Tribune*, August 2, 2007.

## The Global Economic Crisis

Indeed, the economic crisis from 2008 onwards raised a number of questions about how China's economy was integrated into the world, and who, almost a decade after entry to the WTO, was now calling the shots. When Lehmann Brothers collapsed in September 2008, the shock sent through the global finance system started a run on banks in the UK, the sharp fall of share prices for companies as mighty as Goldman Sachs, and an international contagion that nearly felled the global banking system. Just as in 1998 during the Asian economic crisis, China remained insulated because of its controls on capital flows and the protected currency. But the collapse of export markets meant that from late 2008 there was worried talk of as many as 20 million laid off workers in the PRC, creating problems of instability and possible social unrest. Large numbers of foreign companies reduced their exports. The ever rising deficit between the PRC and, in particular, the US and the EU became a major political issue, with politicians in much of the developed world complaining about unfair trade barriers to exporting to China at the same time as they were asking for more Chinese investment.

The Chinese government's response to the sharp decline in growth rates in the rest of the world was to support a massive fiscal stimulus package from 2009 onwards, pumping USD 600 billion into the economy. Here the Hu–Wen leadership practised exactly what it preached, with Wen Jiabao being the public face of the government's response to the global crisis, speaking within and outside China about the need for the central and local governments to support enterprises and individuals in restoring confidence in the global system. Those that looked at the details of the stimulus package, however, could see that many of the things promised had already appeared before. Bridges, roads, airports, and railways were all set down, along with increased spending on schools and hospitals. Wen Jiabao at the National People's Congress in 2008 had promised that education would be receiving more support and that there would be an increase in the numbers who were able to go to school beyond the age of 12. Even so, scepticism remained about just how capable provincial governments would be in disbursing these funds. The hardest problem to tackle remained the fact that while the government could take the Chinese consumers to the vast new shopping malls being built throughout China (the world's largest Louis Vuitton shop was in the city of Taiyuan in Shanxi province, previously a sleepy, polluted Central-China backwater, but now populated with a new generation of business people who have grown mega-wealthy on the rich coal reserves in the area) they could not force them to buy, and certainly not on credit cards. The Chinese people remained inveterate savers, amassing something like USD 2 trillion in deposit accounts, despite low levels of interest. Enterprises were little better, with an abiding dislike of being in debt. Companies ran on tiny amounts of investment. Those that sought loans did so from their friends or families. The Chinese saved while most of the developed world ran up enormous credit card bills and was swamped in personal debt.

In the China of Hu Jintao, there were plenty of things for the average urban citizen to be anxious about despite the signs of a booming economy all around. Healthcare was largely something individuals had to pay for, with bills for operations capable of crippling the finances of whole families. Stories abounded of very ill people simply being left to die because they could not afford care. Middle class parents, however large this sector was in the PRC, were also saddled with new mortgage debt after buying properties on a booming market, a market which was beset by stories of an imminent bubble. Only in 2011 did the government pass regulations reining in the excesses of speculative buyers, restricting house purchases. Despite the vast majority from this generation having only one child, they still had to think of the future costs of putting their children through university, either in China or abroad, both of which were fiercely competitive, and both of which involved whole families clubbing together to support one individual. They were also restricted in how they might use whatever capital they had, reliant either on the highly volatile stock exchanges in Shanghai or Shenzhen, or investments in property, with little opportunity for individual investments abroad.

This must have been the cause of the ambiguous messages that came from surveys conducted by organisations like the Pew Foundation which showed the Chinese being largely supportive and admiring of their government, while others showed high levels of dissatisfaction and anxiety. These pressures became all too clear in the spate of suicides at the immense Foxconn factory in Shenzhen in 2010, where workers in what seemed like a model environment with state-of-the-art facilities threw themselves off the top of one of the taller buildings on the site. International coverage of this issue forced the owner, Taiwanese Terry Guo, to mount a campaign to improve conditions in the factory. One of the first measures was a pay rise.

With all these internal issues, China's leaders clearly regarded the international crisis raging around in the outside world with great irritation. But it did bring some unexpected benefits. Not the least of these was a sharp appreciation by other major economic powers that in a world where China ranked either first or second for most economic indicators, not having it centrally embedded in international forums for decision making made little sense. At the G20 in April 2009, Hu got the most exposure he ever had internationally. His attendance was seen as critical for the success of the event. Over April 1st and 2nd, most of London was shut down as the cavalcades of leaders swept in and out of the conference venue. But the movements of Hu, and his sanction for the Chinese supporting a fund set up to help ailing economies by the International Monetary Fund (IMF) was greeted with relief. This was, after all, an organisation the Chinese had previously regarded with deep suspicion because of accusations that it was simply a mechanism to promote western style laissez faire capitalism.

The G20 meeting was the moment at which China decided at which the economic crisis offered an opportunity for the country to seek better, more proportionate representation within international entities. The rest of the world could no longer just pretend that China was a marginal economy. That had implications for its international and geopolitical role, though here the country had a far more ambiguous and complex message to forge, within itself, and then outwards to the rest of the world.

# Chapter Four

# CHINA'S INTERNATIONAL FACE UNDER HU

Whatever their differences in terms of educational, cultural and linguistic background, politicians in China and in much of the rest of the world have one thing in common, and that is a very contradictory function. While their primary objective is to serve as domestic actors, no matter how much they try to stay focused on this, they tend to end up spending huge amounts of time and effort dealing with issues way beyond their border.

Hu is no exception. His first visit abroad was probably in 1985, when he was already in his early forties. But as he took on greater responsibilities, he has had to travel to more and more countries. A man who spent the first decade of his political career in the highly provincial atmosphere of Gansu has, since 2002, been the face of China at major international fora, and the most powerful person to speak to for world leaders like the President of the US, the Chancellor of Germany or the Prime Minister of India. Just as with politicians from developed countries, Hu had little training for this representational function, yet he has become China's most significant modern diplomat through rising up the levels of the Communist Party, itself an often highly introspective environment.

While Hu may therefore have started off, much like elected politicians in the west, with the objective of focusing on internal issues, like inequality, environmental challenges, and economic development, he has almost inevitably been drawn into a workload increasingly dominated by China's international position. He has been drawn in at a time when China has never before been so scrutinised and so prominent in international affairs. A politician, therefore, whose overwhelming experience was as a domestic operator in a highly controlled, opaque political organisation, has needed to work internationally in the very different environments and under the radically different dynamics of the international political and news agenda.

The challenges, that China's rising international profile have raised, have been as much ideological as they are political. Hu has attempted to craft a coherent narrative of what China is in the 21$^{st}$ century, and how its careering economic influence is, in fact, a 'win win' for the rest of the world. He has presided over a China which has political and economic influence in the Middle East, Central Asia, South East Asia, Africa and Latin America, but also regions and territories which it long thought were remote and unreachable for its diplomatic scope — North America, Europe, and Australia. It is a country which is now involved in the issues it wants to be involved in — those that relate to its strategic interests in terms of resources, its maritime and land borders, and its disputed claims over islands in the South China Sea — but also in those for which it is a reluctant participant, and which it has wished to steer clear of before — the endlessly complex politics of the Middle East where China gets so much of its energy, or the relations between states in Africa and their domestic issues.

## The Legacy of History

Hu Jintao may have been guiding a country with a renewed sense of economic purpose, much of it linked to the global economy. But the dominant motifs of his time in power for foreign affairs were set down many decades before. The first of these was the powerful insistence on sovereignty and non-interference in the internal affairs of others (and conversely by others in its own); the second was to build cooperative, close relations with the US. Both these postulates were inherited from leadership periods under Mao and then Deng when the international role of China was utterly different from what it became in the years after 2002. But both cast a powerful shadow, even as they seemed to be daily proved wrong by events which were planned and unplanned.

The fundamental parameters of Chinese foreign policy were set down in the 1950s just after the establishment of the PRC as a sovereign state, and, not surprisingly, were heavily influenced by the traumatic wars, international and internal, by which the PRC had been created. The famous Five Principles of Peaceful Co-Existence were set out in 1955 by the then Premier Zhou Enlai at the Bandung Conference in Indonesia. They were: peaceful co-existence; mutual respect for territorial integrity and sovereignty; non-aggression; non-interference in others' affairs, and equality and mutual benefit. As Sophie Richardson has shown, China maintained faith in these principles throughout the decades from their first announcement, even managing to engage with radically different regimes like those that ruled Cambodia from 1960 to 1980.[1] China was able to determine its own borders, over 14 of which were in dispute, from 1949 onwards, through a series of careful negotiations, perhaps the most dramatic of which was with the Russians, finally resolved in the 1990s. Of the land border issues, only the two disputes with India remain unresolved.[2] On the issue of Xinjiang, Tibet, and Taiwan, the PRC asserted the uniform line that these were internal issues, and that they were ones which were relevant to China and China alone. This tied well with the narrative of the CCP that they had finally restored self mastery and respect to the country after decades of weakness, exploitation and abuse. Careful definition of national self-interest through the Five Principles meant that Chinese foreign policy had an introspective feel, largely limiting any comments or interventions on other countries with the statement that interference was wrong. This in particular guided their response to the disastrous Democratic People's Republic of Kampuchea

---

[1] Sophie Richardson, *China, Cambodia, and the Five Principles of Peaceful Co-existence*, Columbia University Press, New York, 2010, p 9–11.
[2] M Taylor Fravel, *Strong Borders, Secure Nation: Co-operation and Conflict in China's Territorial Disputes*, Princeton University Press, New Jersey, 2008, has full background for this in Chapter Three, p 126 onward.

in Cambodia from 1975 to 1978 which they still regarded as the legitimate government of the country even after it had been swept away by Vietnamese invasion in late 1978.

China's reluctance to become involved in any activity beyond its borders was a cause of as much relief as frustration for most of the early existence of the PRC, despite the fact that it was sometimes pulled into events where it could define a direct impact on its own interests — the war in Vietnam, for instance, or events on the Korean Peninsula. After formally taking up its position on the UN Security Council Permanent Five representatives in 1972, in cases where it was placed under pressure to take a stand on issues which involved the affairs of other sovereign states, like the first Iraq War in 1990, it largely abstained. It has only used its power of veto five times since taking its seat on the UN in 1971.

China's position on non-interference somewhat cut against the increasing drift of globalisation and the language used by leaders like then British Prime Minister Tony Blair during the NATO-led intervention in Yugoslavia in the late 1990s. Their seeking of principles by which intervention could be seen as legal, correct and proper meant that China was slowly pulled into a system where it was less and less easy to assert non-interference as a final statement, and ask all countries to observe that. Examples abound of pragmatism trumping principle in recent years.[3] On issues which it had never felt involved and which it could see only limited or very tangential interests for itself, China was increasingly expected to take a position, or stand the risk of being isolated, accused of being non-cooperative, and diplomatically exposed. To

---

[3] For examples of this see the International Crisis Group report, 'China's growing role in UN peacekeeping', April 2009 (http://www.crisisgroup.org/en/regions/asia/north-east-asia/china/166-chinas-growing-role-in-un-peacekeeping.aspx [22 December 2011]) which documents the evolution of China's approach to peacekeeping in the last 30 years — from rejecting the entire concept to adopting a case-by-case approach that balances its interests against adherence to non-intervention (leading it to becoming the top contributor of troops in the P5).

avoid being diplomatically exposed, China has frequently taken complementary positions with Russia.[4]

Running alongside this was the second issue mentioned above of the importance of relations with the US. Mao had made his final great strategic decision, just as the Cultural Revolution was ending its most violent, disruptive period, of re-engaging with the Americans, something which culminated in the visit of US President Nixon to China in 1972. He did so at the risk of deep and acrimonious opposition from the radicals who had become increasingly important in the Party from 1967 onwards — figures like Jiang Qing, his wife, and Kang Sheng, who regarded the US as the great imperialist enemy, and any rapprochement with it as heresy. But Mao's decision was to clarify one thing, years before Deng launched the economic reforms: that diplomatically, sticking close to the US made sense, and that it outranked relations with any other power.

Mao pushed for rapprochement between the two countries despite their stark political and social differences. Mao understood one thing, and that was power. It was this, more than anything else, which the US had and which Mao wanted to keep close to. Even over the transition from his leadership to that of Deng, the importance of keeping the US close by was maintained, with the US finally shifting formal diplomatic recognition from the Republic of China on Taiwan to the PRC in 1979. Even during the biggest shock to their relationship, the impact of the repression of student demonstrators in Tiananmen Square and other centres in China in 1989, the US and China maintained a relationship which was strong enough to see them return to relative normalcy within only a few years. "Between June 1989 and mid-1991," argues Robert Ross,

---

[4] Three of China's UNSC vetoes have been in tandem with Russia: on a US-UK sponsored SC draft Myanmar resolution (2007); on a draft Zimbabwe sanctions resolution (2008); and on a Middle East Ceasefire Violation (1972). (See International Crisis Group report, China and Inter-Korean Clashes in the Yellow Sea, January 27, 2011, p 20, at http://www.crisisgroup.org).

"American policy makers perceived the inability of Chinese leaders to help maintain US-China cooperation. Chinese leaders, embroiled in succession politics, depended on an able and willing [George HW] Bush administration to maintain US-China cooperation."[5] Despite Bill Clinton talking about getting tougher on Beijing during his election campaign in 1992, in the end when he became President, he pursued a relationship broadly consistent with that of his predecessors, looking for areas of deeper cooperation, and culminating in China's entry into the WTO in 2001.

Hu was deeply aware of the importance of keeping the relationship with the US on an even keel. It was, after all, China's largest export market (only to be overtaken a little later in the 2000s by the EU) and one of its largest sources of foreign direct investment. It was the place where many of its top students went for graduate study and a place whose culture was appealing to many of the young, emerging middle class. On his visit to the US as Vice President in 2002, Hu had, according to a senior US official who had been charged with meeting him then, been very nervous before being taken to the White House to see President Bush.[6] His need to talk with a US leadership authoritatively was underscored when he spearheaded the Chinese government response in 1999 when the Chinese embassy in Belgrade was 'accidentally' bombed. But in ways in which Hu could never have expected, relations with the US were to become particularly complicated and challenging over the coming decade when he was in power.

The portents in early 2001, under the new US President George W Bush and in Jiang Zemin's final period as Party leader, were not good. The Hainan spy plane incident, in which a US air force pilot was shot down over the southern island, had put the relationship in its worst state since the 1999 Belgrade bombing. As the Chinese government discussed the incident internally and

---

[5] Robert R Ross, *Chinese Security Policy: Structure, Power and Politics*, Routledge, London, 2009, p 246.
[6] Personal correspondence.

formulated its response, for several days, senior members of the Bush administration were unable to reach leaders in China to discuss how to sort the mess of the pilot's downed plane and the death of the Chinese pilot who had been struck during the accident. The leadership transition atmosphere on the Chinese side did not help matters, despite talk afterwards of setting up a more effective 'red phone line' between the two countries.

All this however was changed by the September 11th attacks in 2001, in which China's initial sympathetic response led to deeper talk and substantive action in the months afterwards of greater cooperation on counter-terrorism. The results of this were covered in the section on Xinjiang in Chapter Two. By the time of Hu's ascension, the Bush presidency had already made its key foreign policy focus the so-called 'war on terror', something which initially began with greater pressure on Iraq and Saddam Hussein's leadership. The relative Chinese compliance on allowing the US-led attack on Iraq to proceed in the spring of 2003, at about the same time that China was preoccupied with combating its SARS outbreak, was one of the strongest signs that the PRC was starting to find it increasingly difficult to maintain a line of 'non-interference' when it was pulled more into international diplomatic issues beyond the purview of its national interests.

## Creating the Narrative — Peaceful Rise

Theorists at the Party School in Beijing, which Hu led as President in the 1990s and which was subsequently headed by Zeng Qinghong, began to take up the issue of crafting a more appropriate message of what China meant in the international system. In 2005, the then Executive Vice President of the Central Party school, Zheng Bijian, a veteran academic with a long background in advising and researching for the central government, published an article in the US journal *Foreign Affairs* in which he argued that China's "contribution to the world as an engine of growth will be unprecedented". However, as he went on, "[i]n per capita terms,

China remains a low-income developing country, ranked roughly 100th in the world. Its impact on the world economy is still limited".[7] China would need "another 45 years — until 2050 — before it can be called a modernised, medium-level developed country".[8] Zheng outlined the immense challenges the country faced in trying to modernise its economy over the coming four decades, before concluding with remarks on the role of the PRC in the world:

> China does not seek hegemony or predominance in world affairs. It advocates a new international political and economic order, one that can be achieved through incremental reforms and the democratization of international relations. China's development depends on world peace — a peace that its development will in turn reinforce.[9]

Many elite statements in Beijing over this period echoed what Zheng had written. This was not surprising. Zheng was an establishment thinker linked to the key institutional producers of ideology (see Chapter Five for the role of ideology in contemporary China). His voice can therefore be taken as a representative expression of leadership thinking. The criticism he made in his article about 'hegemony' reflected the shrill assertion in the 1970s and 1980s by China while it was opposing US domination in the world, all the while stating that it itself never sought 'great power hegemony'. Under Jiang Zemin this had become 'multipolarity', with China seen as supporting the voices of all those powers outside the great power system, the most visible of which was the US, to be given more international space. The reference to China rising in a 'harmonious world' that Zheng used was linked directly to the newer talk, which will be looked at in greater detail in the

---

[7] Bijian Zheng, 'China's "Peaceful Rise" to Great-Power Status', *Foreign Affairs*, 2005, 84(5), p 18.
[8] *Ibid.*, p 21.
[9] *Ibid.*, p 24.

next chapter, of a harmonious society, where numerous different interests and power centres could be balanced.

Zheng's statements attracted a great deal of attention, with the Chinese and English phrases for 'peaceful rise of China' (*zhongguo jueqi*) becoming akin to a kind of mantra as the year wore on. Part of the rationale behind them may have been the big 'soft power' campaign that observers started to see in the build up to the 2008 Olympics, with Confucius institutes and the Chinese Language Council International (*Han Ban*), promoting the study of Chinese language and culture increasing in number around the world,[10] and a range of other instruments and activities being utilised, from advertising abroad to becoming more active in foreign media. But part of it was also linked to the need to modernise the image of a China that was rapidly changing and developing, and increasingly linked to the outside world, yet which still felt that it was poorly understood.

Around the same time that Zheng's essay was published, Joshua Cooper Ramo, an American writer and consultant partly based in Beijing, set out China's new development model implied by Zheng more systematically. His paper entitled 'The Beijing Consensus', published in 2004, asserted that China offered an authentic alternative to the western, liberal democratic, laissez faire model which had been promoted most actively by the US and was encapsulated in the theory from the 1980s of a 'Washington Consensus'. "China's rise is already reshaping the international order by introducing a new physics of development and power," he argued.[11] The 'Beijing Consensus' he was offering in essence was

---

[10] Between 2004 and 2009, 282 Confucian Institutes were set up, in 87 countries. See Victoria Tuke, 'China's Soft Power Development by 2020', in Kerry Brown (Ed), *China 2020: The Next Decade of the People's Republic of China*, Chandos, Oxford, 2011, p 206.
[11] Joshua Cooper Ramo, *The Beijing Consensus*, The Foreign Policy Centre, London, 2004, p 2.

simply three theorems about how to organise the place of a developing country in the world, along with a couple of axioms about why the physics is attracting students in places like New Delhi and Brasilia. [It involved] the use of bleeding edge, rather than cutting edge innovation, focusing on not just GDP growth but quality of life indicators, and finally a theory of self-determination, one that stresses using leverage to move big, hegemonic powers that may be tempted to tread on your toes.[12]

Throughout the middle years of the Hu–Wen decade, there was much talk of China presenting a new alternative for the developing world. It was one where the operations of what some commentators called state capitalism offered more stability and better quality growth. The rise of China on these terms was not a threat, not a source of disruption but on the contrary something to emulate, something positive, which needed to be embraced. In the terminology favoured by Chinese officials, it offered 'win win' outcomes. This was the phrase Hu used when he spoke at the 2007 Party Congress:

China will unswervingly follow the path of peaceful development. The Chinese nation is a peace-loving people and China is always a staunch force for safeguarding world peace… We will never interfere in the internal affairs of other countries or impose our own will on them. China works for the peaceful settlement of international disputes… [and] opposes all forms of hegemonism and power politics.[13]

## Modern China: Not An Easy Sell

The words were nice. But there was a problem. In many areas, 'peacefully rising China' was getting increasingly discordant

---

[12] *Ibid.*, p 12–13.
[13] Jintao Hu, 'Hold High the Great Banner of Socialism with Chinese Characteristics and Strive for New Victories in Building a Moderately Prosperous Society in All Respects', Speech at the 17th Party Congress, October 15, 2007.

responses outside its own borders. As the previous chapter showed, China's investments abroad strongly divided opinions. Its internal issues, particularly Xinjiang and Tibet, continued to attract criticism and scrutiny. And its attempts to convey a reassuring message about what the country and its development meant for the rest of the world in the lead up to the Olympics, exposed the division of global public opinion into those who were strong supporters of its new-found prominence, and those who were equally fervently against it. While China was led by one of the world's most deliberately self-effacing and cautious leaders, it was a place towards which studied neutrality was not an easy option. This ambiguous position occupied by China is reflected in the record of its foreign affairs from 2002 onwards. Relations with the US, after going through a number of negative and positive phases, deteriorated markedly from the inauguration of President Obama in January 2009. North Korea in particular posed increasingly complex problems for the Chinese leadership from the testing of its first nuclear device in 2007, forcing it into the sort of prominent international role which many accused it of craving, but which its actions and words showed it regarded as unwelcome and irritating. Recent history with Japan remained a constant source of bad blood and fractiousness. On the positive side, with Taiwan, Hu had, in the signing of the Economic Cooperation Framework Agreement (ECFA) in 2010, one of his most powerful foreign policy triumphs, albeit about an issue which he and his co-leaders regarded as purely internal (see section 'Hu's Big Gamble: A Deal with Taiwan' below).

For the US, China had to place its self-interest and huge trade links against an increasing articulated awareness that there was an influential bloc in America which felt that the country was moving from a strategic partner (a term beloved by President George W Bush) to a competitor. Under the second Bush term in 2004–2008, a number of new bilateral dialogues had been set up, the most significant of which was the Strategic Economic Dialogue in 2006. These had, in the words of one senior official involved in them, "been a way to address key concerns and show that our main interests were complimentary, not antagonistic".[14] The dialogue had been particularly important to both sides during the fallout from the global economic crisis in 2008. It was expanded in 2009 under President Barack Obama to become the 'Strategic and Economic Dialogue' and include greater discussion of foreign policy in addition to economic issues.

There was increasingly ambitious talk as 2008 wore into 2009, of a 'G2' to replace the other iterations of the 'G' combination of leading countries — one that consisted of only the US and China, in recognition that they were the key countries that mattered. Such talk made the leadership around Hu particularly jumpy, even while it may have played up their increasing sense of importance. Wen Jiabao in particular protested that China was neither ready, nor willing for such a combination. "Some say that world affairs will be managed solely by China and the United States," he stated in front of a group of reporters at the China EU summit, "I think that view is baseless and wrong. It is impossible for a couple of countries or a group of big powers to resolve all global issues. Multipolarization and multilateralism represent the larger trend and the will of people."[15] Talk of G2 was even viewed in some quarters in China as an attempt by hostile elements in the developed world to draw the country into a position of responsibility long before it was willing and ready, impeding its development and making it more unstable.

Most of the Chinese leadership agreed that after a patchy start, George W Bush had left relations with China in 2008 in good stead. He had hosted Hu Jintao to a summit in the US in 2006, a visit dominated by demands that China become a better stakeholder in the international community and work more cooperatively on

---

[14] Personal communication.
[15] Xinhua, 'Chinese premier rejects allegations of China/US monopolizing world affairs in future,' May 21, 2009, at http://www.china-embassy.org/eng/zmgx/t563619.htm [22 December 2011].

access to oil.[16] He himself had also visited China, going first in 2002, again in 2005 and finally in 2008 (the latter to attend the Olympics). To the surprise of some, despite gloomy predictions beforehand, the US election campaign in 2008 had been largely devoid of comment on China, despite the issue of increasing deficits and arguments over what was regarded as the artificially low exchange rate of the Chinese currency. By Obama's inauguration, all looked set for one of the best periods of US-China cooperation for many years, bucking the two trends that on the whole, Chinese leaders got along better with Republican than Democrat Presidents, and that the opening months of a new presidency were always a time when China tested out the new incumbent. For the first few months, commentators were astonished at how smoothly things seemed to be going. Maybe, some asked, a new phase of deeper cooperation and understanding had dawned between the two.

## The Mystery of Obama's Handling in China in 2009

All this was to be blown away by Obama's visit to China in November 2009. The portents to the visit boded well. The new President himself had selected China as a place to visit during his first year in office, something no other American President had ever done. But when the time came for him to visit Beijing and Shanghai in 2009, 30 years after the two countries had formalised their diplomatic ties, something out of the ordinary seemed to happen. Unlike Clinton or Bush, as the visit wore on, there were accusations that Obama was being treated laxly, and that there were far too many constraints being placed on his movements and activities. He was allowed very little contact with the Chinese public, unlike President Clinton who had been accorded a public walkabout when visiting in 1998. No questions from journalists were permitted at the joint press conference held towards the

---

[16] David E Sanger, 'China's Oil Needs Are High on US Agenda', *New York Times*, April 19, 2006, at http://www.nytimes.com/2006/04/19/world/asia/19china.html [22 December 2011].

end of Obama's time in Beijing. The strenuous management of his entourage and of his interaction with people puzzled those who looked at the very lengthy joint statement put out by both sides at the end of the visit, which seemed to imply from its detail that things had never looked better between the two countries. While the joint statement listed impressive areas of common endeavour and interest, the heavy controls over Obama while physically in China evidently displeased the US side. Many watching from America interpreted this as strong evidence for an increasingly assertive PRC.

For those that had originally promoted the idea of a Beijing Consensus like Ramo, the first time that a viable alternative of development to that presented by the industrialised West was coming into existence was predominantly something to be welcomed. But there was another sense of 'Beijing Consensus' used from 2008 which was much more negative and critical — one where the 'peaceful rise' of China was taken as meaning the exact opposite. In this secondary meaning, China figured as a country with radically different political values, whose rise presented significant threats to western interests, and whose example was emboldening countries that were heedless of human rights and disruptive to the global order. For those who believed in this meaning, the 'harmony' so often preached by leaders like Hu was only duplicitous cover for something much more ominous and unwelcome — a form of resource hungry, lawless, self-centred nationalism which was there to promote the CCP's interests in remaining in power above all else. A muscular presentation of this view of China is presented in American academic Stefan Halper's 'Beijing Consensus'[17] of 2009, where China's rise is taken as posing a whole number of challenges and problems for western leaders, and where the real endgame for western powers is a form of containment before it gets too late.

For the new US President, worse was to follow. The Copenhagen Climate Change Summit which occurred only a few weeks later

---

[17] See Stefan Halper, *The Beijing Consensus*, Basic Books, New York and London, 2010.

did much to reaffirm the view of China operating solely on the grounds of pursuing its own narrow self-interest at the expense of everything else. China was accused by some of scuppering a 'last chance' solution for controlling carbon emission, watering down the already weak deal that was on the table, and sticking by its negotiating point that as China's per capita usage was way lower than any country in the EU and US it would sign up to nothing that might impede its own rapid economic growth. Its attitude to the rest of the world was symbolised most pointedly for some critics by Premier Wen Jiabao sending a relatively junior official to speak to President Obama during one negotiating session. On another occasion, at least according to US negotiators, Wen failed to invite Obama to an important meeting to discuss terms for a final deal, causing the President to simply present himself at the door to the meeting room and ask if he could now come in and join the discussion.

All the ambiguity which the US, EU and other powers felt about China, and which China projected from itself, was on display in Copenhagen. For climate change negotiations, it was clearly a country too important to ignore, yet tiresomely rigid and stubborn as a negotiating partner. Supporters of China felt that the developed world's complaints were hypocritical, in view of the many decades in which it had itself been polluting the world first, given its earlier stage of industrialisation, then relocating its most damaging industries to China and other developing countries, adding insult to injury by now demanding they pay the costs to clean this up.

Just what Hu's role had been in all of these was unclear. According to some unsubstantiated reports, he had summoned a meeting of the Politburo only a few weeks before the Summit and had asked three Chinese experts on climate change to speak about the subject. He had reportedly also gone through the figures which he had been given in great detail, asking for more information and data. The political sensitivity of any final binding deal committing China to targets which might then hamper its own needs and be against its national interest meant that the leadership were in an unenviable position. They evidently knew the potentially devastating impact of climate change on the Chinese environment, and on its people, if nothing was done. But they could not risk accusations of being a government that was soft in protecting China's own development and defending the interests and rights of the country, and especially of being seen as too conciliatory towards the US. It was symbolic too, that Hu did not attend, despite other countries sending their most senior leaders to the Summit. Once more he had been absent at a time when there was a real danger he might be exposed to anger and criticism had the negotiations turned out badly for the PRC.

The fallout from Copenhagen was still being absorbed when British citizen Akmal Shaikh became the first European to be executed in China since 1954. Charged with drug trafficking, he was executed by lethal injection on December 27th, 2009 in a prison near Urumqi, Xinjiang. Coming only a few days after the imprisonment of Liu Xiaobo, it was an event that marked a deepening of the deterioration of China's international image. Over 26 separate representations from the UK government on behalf of Mr. Shaikh made in the months before his death had failed to win him clemency. There was little doubt that he had been caught with four kilos of heroin while entering Xinjiang from Pakistan. But his defence had stressed his history of bipolarity and mental health issues, and argued that he had been abused by dealers who had planted the drugs on him. The Chinese government said this was a matter for the country's legal system and that all due process had been followed. Lurking in the background, and something which figured in the blogs and internet coverage of this event in China, was the relationship between this event and the memory of foreign exploitation in narratives of Chinese history from the early 19th century onwards (particularly the symbolic role of the Opium Wars). These nationalist voices meant that the EU and China could condemn the incident as much as they liked but the Chinese government would have been hard pressed to have backed down over this issue involving such an emotive subject. President Obama's meeting with the Dalai Lama in early 2010, and his final sanction for Taiwan to purchase over USD 16 billion of arms (an old deal, but one which had never been implemented) made things worse. A return state visit by Hu to the US planned for spring 2010 was postponed, though he did attend a counter proliferation summit in Washington in April.

When Hu finally did hold his valedictory visit to the US in January 2011, relations between the two countries had been in a downward spiral for over a year. The White House's treatment of Hu showed it clearly understood that any disunity amongst departments dealing with the visit was only going to be exploited by the Chinese side. For that reason, a remarkably consistent message was given to Hu on North Korea (see the next section), the value of the RMB and human rights. And this time, Hu was made to take part in a proper press conference in Washington, as opposed to the highly nervous and managed affair which had famously taken place when Obama was in Beijing just over a year before, where only statements were given and no questions from the press allowed. While Hu dealt relatively easily with questions from journalists about the importance of human rights with a powerful rhetorical flourish, declaring that China respected their universality even though it had a lot more work to do, his fumble beforehand, when it was clear he had misunderstood or misheard what had been asked about human rights and needed help from the translator to continue, showed a slightly flummoxed leader. At the black tie dinner at the White House in his honour the night after, he turned up in a western style grey suit, proving that for all their modernisation, modern Chinese leaders at least stopped at dinner jackets and black ties.

## 'A Spoilt Little Brother: The Issue of the DPRK'

One of the most widely reported batch of restricted US government cables leaked in 2010 by Wikileaks was that recording of Chinese perceptions of North Korea. According to He Yafei, the then Vice

Minister for Foreign Affairs (he was subsequently to be posted to Geneva as China's representative there), North Korea was like a "spoiled child". He stated in 2009 to a visiting US official that "We may not like them... [but] they are our neighbour".[18] Such voicing of frustration raised as many questions as it answered. If there was one area where China could claim to have real influence, it was over its impoverished, difficult neighbour. The Chinese army had lost hundreds of thousands of lives in the Korean War from 1950 to 1953 in order to protect the newly founded Democratic People's Republic of Korea (DPRK) from a UN led onslaught. One of the casualties was Mao Zedong's own son. Here was a country with a direct impact on China's interests, even if they were defined very narrowly. And yet, with its nuclear test bomb in 2007, the North Koreans had crossed a line, provoking the senior foreign affairs policy head under Hu, State Councillor Dai Bingguo to be despatched to Pyongyang to calm Kim Jong Il's government down.

China's diplomatic effort over the DPRK was one of the areas where it was expected to take an international lead, but it did so with what often seemed like great reluctance. At the same time as the DPRK was shelling a disputed island off the coast of South Korea in late November 2010, around the time the Wikileaks quotes above was published, the conservative number two in the Politburo Wu Bangguo met with a parliamentarian from Pyongyang and declared the eternal brotherhood and unbreakable bonds between the two countries. This concealed intense diplomatic effort, with the North Korean government somehow 'persuaded' to declare its interest in restarting the Six Party Talks which had been set up between Russia, South Korea, the US, China, Japan and the DPRK in the early 2000s. In November 2010, the PRC called for an emergency meeting of delegates to the Six Party Talks, though as at the

---

[18] BBC News, 'Wikileaks cables: China "Frustrated" by North Korea', November 30, 2010, at http://www.bbc.co.uk/news/mobile/world-us-canada-11871641 [22 December 2011].

time of writing (December 2011) the grouping has not formally reformed and possibly postponed indefinitely by the death of Kim Jong Il in December 2011. China's concerted efforts to restart the Six Party Talks have been motivated by its interests and desire to ease tension on the Korean Peninsula through diplomatic means, maintain its central role in the international response to the DPRK, and decrease international pressure on Beijing to take additional action.

Hu's government declared that it had limited leverage over the reclusive regime run by Kim Jong Il, one which had seen the country veer from starvation in the 1990s after the death of the founder Kim Il Sung to truculent defiance and an increasingly provocative nuclearisation from 2007 onwards. But whatever Hu may have thought of Kim personally, Beijing certainly pulled out all the stops when the Secretary General of the Korean Workers Party (the deceased Kim Il Sung remained as head of state) visited Beijing. Indeed, in 2010, Kim, one of the few leaders of a modern nation state who never flew, came by his armour plated train to China twice in the space of a few months, once closing down the centre of Beijing in early May because of his 100 strong car cavalcade, and once in August, when he was rumoured to be presenting his third son to the Chinese leadership for accreditation and legitimisation before making this succession implicit in public appearances with Kim Yong-un in October at the Congress to be held in Pyongyang. Kim Jong-Il revisited China in May 2011, reportedly with his third son. His death in December 2011 was marked by fulsome eulogies in Beijing.

Hu's own hands were certainly tied in his approach to the DPRK, even if he had wished to supply some fresh thinking. The historic links between the two regimes were deep and highly meaningful. Plenty of people pointed out that strategically there was little benefit for China in allowing the regime to collapse. Practically, it would cause a flood of refugees across the border, but far more significantly, it might also allow a potential US-influenced unified Korea to come into existence right on China's border. An ailing, weak, and preferably non-nuclear DPRK was the best outcome in all of this. In this relationship, at least on the surface, China held all the main cards. It supplied over half of the DPRK's aid on which it was dependent to feed its people and maintain its military, and over 90 percent of its energy. Hu's government was more than able to show it had the whip hand as and when it wanted. Rumours of it switching off the DPRK's energy supply for three days in 2007 during the first nuclear crisis were never definitely proved, but it seemed strange that North Korea had backed down so quickly after its test. To the more cynical, it seemed that with the DPRK, China was creating a vassal state. Indeed, in the words of one Russian analyst speaking in Moscow in late 2010, it "had already succeeded very nicely in doing that".

Attempts to encourage the DPRK regime to undertake some economic reforms along the lines of those used in China after 1978 were unsuccessful. During Kim's visit to the PRC, he was taken to look at the Shanghai skyline in the early 2000s, and then to Shenzhen and the special economic zone, and to Dalian, and Beijing. But he seemed largely unmoved by the prosperity he saw being created by 'socialism with Chinese characteristics'. This in part is a reflection of mistrust in the bilateral relationship stemming from disagreement over economic reform. Beijing has long encouraged the North Korean government to initiate economic reforms to boost its legitimacy and internal stability, but Pyongyang feels that reforms could undermine its long-insulated political and economic system.

Older officials of Hu's age, like Zhou Yongkang who attended the national day celebrations in Pyongyang in October 2010, and Wu Bangguo, maintained a public pose of unswerving faithfulness to the DPRK. In a message sent by Hu to Kim on the 65th anniversary of the foundation of the Korean Workers Party in October 2010, Hu was quoted by Xinhua as declaring that:

> For many years, the Workers Party of Korea (WPK) under the leadership of General Secretary Kim Jong Il has followed the will

of Chairman Kim Il Sung, and led the DPRK people in continuing to positively seek a development path suitable for the DPRK's own situation and has made delightful achievements in the DPRK-style socialist construction cause… As a friendly neighbour, close comrade and sincere friend, we sincerely wish the DPRK people, under the leadership of the WPK headed by General Secretary Kim Jong Il, continuously make new and bigger achievements in the historical process of building a strong and prosperous country.[19]

It would be nice to think that Hu was being ironic here, though it is unlikely. Whatever Hu said publicly, many Chinese shared the same disdain for the leaders of their impoverished neighbour as much as the rest of the world. There was a sense in which China might even argue that, with the Obama administration refusing to restart the Six Party Talks without specific conditions being met; the South Korean government hardening its position and burying the Sunshine Policy which had been tried under the former president the late Kim Dae Jung; and with a per capita GDP ranking, according to the CIA, last of the 192 countries in the world; the DPRK was looking dangerously like a problem that China had been saddled with. However, just as with the divisions on the economy and the role of the state between leftists and rightists in the CCP, the weight of shared revolutionary history meant China was incapable of ever finally pulling the plug on their 'spoilt little child' across the north east border. Here, whatever Hu may have wanted to do, he was the prisoner of history, and of divisions within the CCP.

## Frosty Neighbours: Japan

Hu was born during the peak of the Sino-Japanese War in 1942. It was a conflict which left deep marks on the Chinese psyche, ones which started to reopen with increasing intensity in the 2000s. Lobbying by Japan to have a permanent seat on the UN Security

---

[19] Xinhua, 'Hu Jintao sends congratulatory message to DPRK's Kim for 65th anniversary of ruling party', October 9, 2010, at http://news.xinhuanet.com/english2010/china/2010–10/09/c_13548536.htm [22 December 2011].

Council in 2004 and 2005 coincided with a particularly nasty riot in Beijing after the Chinese national football team lost to Japan in a round of the Asia Cup. A rethink by the leadership and the Ministry of Foreign Affairs about bilateral relations at the end of Junichiro Koizumi's period as Prime Minister (his annual visits to the Yasukuni Shrine in Tokyo where Class A Japanese war criminals are buried was a particular bone of contention between the two countries, in effect freezing top-level contact for the five years in which he was in power) meant that by 2008, for the first time, Hu could undertake a visit to Tokyo, boasting of 'a warm spring' between the two countries. During his May visit he made a speech at the elite Waseda University in Tokyo, proclaiming that the future of the two countries depended on the relationship between their youth. "Both China and Japan should make contributions to Asia's revival," he stated, "and work together to cope with global challenges and build a harmonious Asia and world."[20]

There was a stark contrast between what elite leaders like Hu and Wen (who went to Japan in 2007) said when either visiting Japan, or receiving Japanese dignitaries in Beijing, and what elements of the online community and others were stating. Popular views of Japan from the 1980s were increasingly mired in the rejuvenation of historic grievances. Many members of the Chinese public were particularly upset by what they charged were Japanese textbooks' incomplete accounting of war atrocities and emphasis on Japanese suffering rather than what had happened in neighbouring countries. "The Sino-Japanese relationship is a paradox," writes William Callahan, contrasting "the two countries' healthy economic relationship" to the coolness of their political links. Referring to clashes in 2005 and 2006 within China "with mobs attacking Japanese embassies, restaurants and businesses", Callahan comments that "these various protests... were not

---

[20] Xinhua, 'President's "warm spring" visit to Japan a complete success', May 11, 2008, at http://news.xinhuanet.com/english/2008-05/11/content_8143525.htm [22 December 2011].

sparked by a military clash, a diplomatic dispute or an economic crisis. Rather they erupted because of the two countries' 'history war'. Chinese people were insulted, over and over again, by what they saw as Japan's failure to properly atone for its imperial past".[21]

A further incitement was offered in 2010 when a Chinese ship and a Japanese coast guard vessel clashed in September in disputed waters in the East China Sea. The skirmish between the two vessels during which the Chinese ship and its crew were captured, exploded into a full-scale diplomatic incident. It culminated in the final release of the Chinese captain, after escalating angry words between the two governments. Protests against alleged Japanese incitement spread across China with rumours that in one city a woman wearing a dress deemed to be Japanese in style had it ripped off. In another, a restaurant serving Japanese food was attacked. Images of these protests were placed online, with placards in Xi'an showing some of the strongest, most insulting language. The incident showed that the ability of issues related to Japan to spark popular nationalist sentiment remained strong, despite the deep trade and investment ties between the two countries. Efforts to conduct a joint examination of historical issues surrounding the Sino-Japanese War and their interpretations, in order to reach consensus at least on the facts, only reached a small audience. For Chinese nationalists, China's replacement of Japan in 2010 as the world's second largest economy was a moment laden with symbolic, retributive satisfaction.

Hu's voice was silent when the 2010 Sino-Japanese crisis intensified, leaving Wen Jiabao to do most of the strong talking. But for the US and other powers in the region, there was a new awareness of 'assertiveness' by China that did not look and feel like a 'peaceful rise'. Instead, China showed brittleness in the way it was treating other powers in the region. This provoked US

---

[21] William Callahan, *China: The Pessoptimist Nation*, Oxford University Press, Oxford, 2010, p 162.

Secretary of State Hilary Clinton to state in mid 2010 that resolving disputes in the South China Sea was pivotal to regional stability. Secretary Clinton's statements deepened Chinese perceptions of a strategic 'return to Asia', the fact that for many years the focus of US interest had been in the Middle East but now there was a shift back to the Pacific, reinforced by President Obama's visit to the region in late 2011.

## Hu's Big Gamble: A Deal with Taiwan

Ironically, before the award of the Nobel Peace Prize to Liu Xiaobo in 2010, there had been a rumour for a number of years that Hu Jintao wanted to gain the prize himself for doing something to significantly improve relations across the Taiwan Strait. While it is clear now that even if offered the prize, Hu would no longer accept it (Liu's award had scuppered that!), it is his direct interest here where we can find the main outlines of something that looks like a lasting historic legacy.

Taiwan was an issue on which both Mao and Deng were willing to take the long view. Mao's famous and caustic remark to Nixon was that China was willing to wait ten thousand years to resolve the issue of the 'renegade province' (as it was called in Beijing then). Deng was equally sanguine, admitting that this was a problem which would need to be solved by his successors. During the era of Jiang Zemin in the 1990s, the greatest challenge from Taiwan was the inexorable move towards democracy on the island, culminating in the first direct elections for president in 1996. This provoked military manoeuvres from the Mainland, forcing the US to send two aircraft carriers to the area to calm things down. With the election of the more pro-independence Democratic Progressive Party (DPP) under Chen Shui-Bian in 2000, relations across the Straits moved to a knife edge, with the Beijing government constantly on guard for statements from Taipei that sounded like a covert declaration of independence. Along with the DPRK, Taiwan continued to be potentially the most destabilising diplomatic issue in the region, an issue exacerbated by what Alain Guilloux called the island's highly abnormal status:

> What is Taiwan? As it behaves like a state... should we suggest it is a state? Or a quasi state? Is it a 'like unit' in the neorealist sense? Is Taiwan more likely than its neighbours or other states elsewhere to disappear into a self-governing entity?... It is difficult to think of any other state or aspiring state that presents similar characteristics.[22]

This issue of status had meant that one of the best performing economies in the world, one with one of the highest per capita GDPs, best health services, and a population of 24 million, was unable to be part of the UN, or any bodies which implied recognition of it as a sovereign entity. Only in 2008 after many years of lobbying was Taiwan allowed to take up observer status at the World Health Authority (WHO) under the name 'Chinese Taipei'.

In fact, 2008 was a significant date and one which Hu was able to exploit. After eight years of DPP rule (Chen had been controversially re-elected in 2004 with the narrowest of victory margins, and in the final leg of the campaign someone had attempted to shoot him), the KMT (Kuomintang) Nationalist Party, which had ruled the island from 1949 to 2000, was voted back in. The new President, Ma Ying-Jeou, had stood on a programme of improving the economy. At the heart of this was creating better links with the Mainland. During his campaign, Ma even talked of creating a 'greater China market', despite the fact that a term like this aroused suspicion amongst some in the electorate who were much more wary of the Mainland's influence and intent. With a political Party back in after May 2008 which the Beijing government could deal with much more comfortably, the opportunity came for some new movement.

---

[22] Alain Guilloux, *Taiwan, Humanitarianism and Global Governance*, Routledge, London, 2009, p 174.

Taiwan is perhaps the most sensitive issue for a Chinese leader to deal with — even more so than Tibet and Xinjiang, which are at least part of the PRC's uncontested sovereign territory and where its levers of control are much stronger. Jiang Zemin had discovered in 1995, during the build up to the elections in Taiwan the following year, that reining in strong nationalist feeling in the military in particular was tough. One of his most important achievements was that he had managed to steer a more moderate course at the time, doing enough to show that he was not going soft on the PRC's territorial integrity, but also preventing things from getting out of hand and spilling over into a disastrous conflict. The reforms of the military that he promoted in the years that followed depoliticised it sufficiently for the 2000 and 2004 elections in Taiwan to be events that the mainland could deal with without major loss of face. By 2008 it had learned its lesson, keeping silent on the presidential election and gaining at the end a government it was able to cooperate with better. One of the greatest challenges Hu had to face when he finally gained control of the Central Military Commission over 2004–2005 was how to stamp his authority on this critically important issue.

He had a very restricted space to work in. For Taiwan and the Mainland, the overarching framework for their relationship is contained in 'the 1992 Consensus'. This was an agreement reached following meetings between officials from the PRC and Taiwanese government in Hong Kong that year. It stated that there was only one China, "with each side reserving the right to express its viewpoint" concerning the nature of that 'one China'. In this way the negotiators found a formula to sidestep the thorny issue of sovereignty. For all its flaws and ambiguities — and the contention by many DPP supporters in Taiwan that it was an *ex post facto* invention of a KMT dominated Taiwan negotiating team — it at least afforded a basis for future discussions by parking the most difficult issue for discussion at an unspecified later date.

Jiang Zemin's own contribution had been a policy statement on how the issue needed to be handled in January 1995. This was subsequently called the 'Eight-Point Proposal'. The eight points were:

1. Adhering to the principle that one China is the basis and prerequisite for peaceful reunification. China's sovereignty and territorial integrity must never be allowed to suffer division.
2. Allowing for the development of non-governmental economic and cultural ties between Taiwan and other countries.
3. Holding negotiations with Taiwan authorities on the peaceful reunification of the motherland.
4. Aiming to achieve the peaceful reunification of China since Chinese should not fight Chinese, but being prepared to use force to resolve the issue, if necessary, against the foreign forces who intervene.
5. Developing economic exchange and cooperation between the two sides separated by the Taiwan Straits.
6. Promoting cultural ties.
7. Respecting the rights of Taiwanese.
8. Welcoming and encouraging leaders of Taiwan to visit the Mainland and Mainland officials to visit Taiwan.[23]

These eight proposals combined a series of what can be called 'hard' and 'soft' measures to bring the two sides together. Cultural contact and the so-called 'three links' (postal, air, shipping) belong to the latter. Developing political links is also important. However, the key issue in the official Chinese position was refusal to relinquish the right to use force and insistence that Taiwan's future status must be addressed as a domestic issue, not internationalised. Without recognition of that, nothing else was possible.

The PRC's refusal to renounce force on the issue of Taiwan's status remains a major block to pursuing deeper political dialogue. Paramount leader Deng Xiaoping's vision in the 1980s was that

---
[23] Full summary text at http://english.cri.cn/4426/2007/01/11/167@184028.htm [23 December 2011].

the 'one country, two systems' formula could be used to resolve the outstanding issue of the three contended territories 'left over from history': Hong Kong, Macao and Taiwan. The 'one country, two systems' rubric did make a critical contribution to solving the issue of Hong Kong's status after reversion to PRC sovereignty from Britain in 1997. But from the outset, Taiwan's leaders adamantly rejected the notion that a formula applied to two foreign colonies could have relevance to a *de facto* sovereign entity governed and ruled by Chinese. The attempts by Deng and his team to sweeten the pill by granting a significantly more generous offer to Taiwan that included the ability, post-(re)unification, to maintain its own military, police force, political system, flag and other privileges befitting its special status were rejected. This objective of reunification under even the most generous terms became even harder for people in Taiwan to envisage once it had become a fully functioning democracy by 1996. Taiwanese might look at the Hong Kong Special Administrative Region over a decade after reversion to Chinese Mainland rule and feel that their caution had been vindicated. To this day, the Special Administrative Region remains only a partially democratic system, with a proportion of its legislative council elected and the rest indirectly elected by 'functional constituencies' representing business and professional interests. Arguments continue over the introduction of universal suffrage for the position of Chief Executive, something which was promised in 2012, and which has now been pushed back to 2018.

Over a decade after Jiang had made his contribution to resolution of the Taiwan issue, Hu Jintao issued his own six point declaration on December 31st 2008. Going by the grand title 'Let Us Join Hands to Promote the Peaceful Development of Cross-Straits Relations and Strive with a United Resolve for the Great Rejuvenation of the Chinese Nation', and delivered at a forum with Taiwanese 'compatriots' (the Mainland lingo for Taiwanese, to stress their closeness to people in the PRC), Hu declared that "our thirty-year practice further amply attests to the fact that the tremendous progress continuously achieved in the reform, opening up and modernisation of the Mainland of our motherland is a strong foundation and reliable safeguard for promoting the development of Cross Straits relations". Hu had been speaking only a few days earlier to mark the 30th anniversary of the reform and opening up policy in December 1978, and so he made the immediate link between the changes in the economy and the ways in which these had an impact on almost all areas of China's political and diplomatic life, not just the development of its economy. While constantly stressing the need to oppose factionalism and achieve the 'reunification of the motherland', Hu set out his own six principles:

1. To firmly abide by the one-China principle and enhance political mutual trust.
2. To advance economic cooperation and promote common development.
3. To promote Chinese culture and strengthen spiritual bonds.
4. To strengthen two-way visits of people and expand exchanges in various circles.
5. To safeguard national sovereignty and hold consultations on external affairs.
6. To end the state of hostility and reach a peace agreement.[24]

---

[24] President Ma Ying-Jeou's own position on the status of cross-strait relations was presented most recently in his National Day Address in October 2009, 'President Ma Ying Jeou's National Day Address', October 10, 2009, at http://www.mac.gov.tw/ct.asp?xlItem=66641&ctNode=5909&mp=3 [22 December 2011]. There he identifies the principal elements of his policy as:

- Acceptance of the 1992 Consensus.
- Support for links through visits to Taiwan by mainland tourists, direct air, sea, and postal links, food safety inspections, and cross-strait legal assistance.
- An attempt to extend these into the economic realm with a free trade agreement.
- Defence of Taiwanese national sovereignty and interests, in particular protections of its democratic system.
- Development of friendly relations with both Taiwan and mainland China and the promotion of 'flexible diplomacy.'
- A national defence strategy of "effective deterrence and resolute defence" developing a professional military based to protect the security of Taiwan.

By far the most significant of these was the last. There had even been talk after the six point proposal was issued that Ma Ying-Jeou might be able to visit the Mainland, perhaps to attend the Shanghai Expo being held from May 2010, and meet with President Hu there. Despite high level contacts over 2009 and 2010, however, there was no immediate major breakthrough simply because the main issue of how to describe and treat Taiwan's sovereignty to the satisfaction of both sides remained impossible. Some of the feelings aroused by this whole issue were clearly illustrated soon after President Ma's election, when Zhang Mingqing, a senior Chinese official from the State Council's Taiwan Affairs Office, was thrown to the ground while visiting the southern Taiwan city of Tainan, a stronghold of DPP supporters and pro-independence sentiment, on October 21, 2008.[25] When Chen Yunlin, former State Council Director of the Taiwan Affairs Office and newly named head of the Mainland Chinese Association for Relations across the Taiwan Straits, visited Taiwan in November, the first such visit by someone in his position, he was also greeted by street demonstrations in Taipei and Hsinchu.[26] The one tangible outcome of the new phase of relations was that an agreement on direct air, sea and postal links were made. For the million Taiwanese reputed to be living in cities in the Mainland doing business and studying there, this was good news, as at least it meant they no longer had to make time-consuming transits via Hong Kong or other places.

The Economic Cooperation Framework Agreement (ECFA), signed between Taiwan and China in June 2010 came as a surprise. Contentious in Taiwan, with a major and sometimes acrimonious debate before the deal went through, it happened just as President Ma's opinion ratings were falling. China under Hu however had shown a liking for signing Free Trade Agreements and had completed one with the Association of South East Asian Nations

---

[25] BBC News, 'Taiwanese attack Chinese envoy', October 21, 2008, at http://news.bbc.co.uk/1/hi/world/asia-pacific/7681711.stm [22 December 2011].
[26] See BBC News, 'Top Chinese envoy in Taiwan talks', November 4, 2008, at http://news.bbc.co.uk/1/hi/7705468.stm [22 December 2011].

(ASEAN) earlier in the year. That set the context in which the ECFA, which may well go down as one of the major achievements of the Hu years, was finalised. It has great political as well as economic significance, which Taiwan's President Ma himself, said showed "a correct decision at a decisive time" which would "break Taiwan's isolation and ... allow Taiwan to become a springboard for investors into the Mainland China market".[27] According to analysts Rosen and Wang of the Peterson Institute for International Economics, the ECFA "will be an ambitious accord that fundamentally changes the game between Taiwan and China".[28]

After months of debate within Taiwan and following long, intricate negotiations with the PRC side, a Basic Agreement was reached on June 13th at the Third Meeting of Experts in Beijing. The ECFA was formally signed by officials in Chongqing on June 29th, 2010. The signatories were Chen Yunlin of the Association for Relations Across the Strait on the PRC side, and P. K. Chiang of the Taiwan Strait Exchange Foundation form the Taiwanese side.[29] The text deftly avoids mention of the 'two states' issue, referring instead to "shore-to-shore relations". Its most immediate impact was to offer the potential for greater economic ties between the PRC and Taiwan by easing trade blockages, and to integrate the island's economy more deeply with the rest of the world.

ECFA was not an easy political sell for either side. President Ma was criticised for working at the limits of his political mandate. Dissonant voices in China argued that Hu had given up on Taiwan, and that far from being a bold move forward, ECFA was a sign of defeat. One of these, the academic Yan Xuetong, had stated on an internet article in 2008 that "[t]here is no more reunification... no

---

[27] 'Taiwan Vision Missing in Ma's ECFA Strategy', *Taiwan News*, at http://www.taiwannews.com.tw/etn/news_content.php?id=1310964 [23 December 2011].
[28] Daniel H Rosen and Zhi Wang, 'Deepening China-Taiwan Relations Through the ECFA', Peterson Institute Policy Brief PB10-16, June 2010, p 1.
[29] Alan D Romberg, 'Ma at Midterm: Challenges for Cross Straits Relations,' *China Leadership Monitor*, Issue No 33, has a full analysis of the political implications for Ma of the ECFA agreement.

more one-China principle. No more effort to get this island back". Speaking soon after the signing of ECFA, Yan told journalist Richard McGregor that "Chinese people are not that nationalistic... They are very money orientated. The dominating ideology is money worship. As long as the situation in Taiwan is favourable to making money, we don't care if [the island] becomes independent".[30] But Hu's support for ECFA was entirely consistent with his decisions on other major strategic issues like Tibet and Xinjiang (covered in Chapter Three). No matter what the context, whether it was an internal or external issue, economic development was placed at the heart of the resolution of everything — even a matter as complex as the relationship with Taiwan. Critics of the deal detected evidence of a clear strategy from Beijing, which was that the economic traction that ECFA would eventually lead to would give the PRC greater political influence. Free trade deals for Beijing were merely the sugar coating on a bullet which consisted of over a thousand missiles ranged along the Fujian coast and trained on the island.

Whether this strategy would work was another matter. The limitations of the Hu-ist view of human development (regardless of Ramo's argument in the 'Beijing Consensus' about China promoting a growth model that put quality of life indicators above simple production of GDP) will be dealt with in the final chapter. But even amongst the political elite in Beijing, there were plenty of arguments about what the ultimate direction of society needed to be. After China got rich, how was it going to become happy? The Olympics had shown that money could not, in the end, buy love. The brute fact remained that Taiwan's soft power influence over the Mainland in terms of pop stars and lifestyle trends had been disproportionate in the last three decades. And even the most PRC-friendly voice in Taiwan stressed that reunification could only happen after Beijing changed its political model. The idea of a democracy linking up with a non-democracy was not a tenable

---

[30] Richard McGregor, *The Party: The Secret World of China's Communist Rulers*, Harper Collins, New York, 2010, p 131–132.

one. The ECFA is therefore best seen as a first step towards thinking about what a long-term solution to the contradictory demands of both sides might look like. It is clear their economies are increasingly integrated. What political impact this might have is not so certain. If economic relations one day do lead to a final settlement that both sides can live with, then Hu's contribution in supporting the ECFA will have lasting historic implications. But that might be a long way down the line.

## Hard Power: When All Else Fails

The paradox that many grappled with during the Hu era was the lofty talk of harmony, peaceful rise and China offering win-win to the world by Hu and other elite politicians around him, contrasted with significant increases in China's military budget year on year, and the rumblings of a powerful military being built up. Suspicions that there was something ominous in the 24-character phrase attributed to Deng in the 1980s of "observe calmly; secure our position; cope with affairs calmly; hide our capacities; and bide our time" were never quite dispelled, and after the PLA was forbidden to involve itself in major business interests under Jiang in 1998, the resultant professionalisation of the military only intensified these worries.

Hu came to power with no military experience. This he shared with most of the figures in his generation around him on the Politburo. But the political role of the PLA was clear. It served the Party, not the state, faithful to its foundation in the 1920s as the Red Army. This gave it a slightly odd basis, almost outside of most other state actors, sometimes intervening as in the late 1960s during the most turbulent period of the Cultural Revolution where it was called to restore power, and then in 1989 when it was the defender of last resort when student protests looked to be getting out of hand.

What is not in doubt is the immense significance in contemporary China of the military. This was aptly symbolised by the fact that when Hu Jintao appeared on the 60th anniversary of the coming of the Communist Party to power in October 2009, he did so wearing the distinctive PLA green uniform, not his customary western style business suit. And the whole event itself turned out to be a showcase of the military hardware enabled by the budget increases that the PLA had been getting over the last decade. Military power obviously matters to Hu and his fellow leaders.

This was something that the world looked at nervously. The US Pentagon in particular had issued its reports each year highlighting significant rises in China's expenditure, usually around 15–20 percent increases year on year. In 2010, the report stated that China's economic

> achievements, combined with progress in science and technology, have also enabled [it] to embark on a comprehensive transformation of its military. The pace and scope of China's military modernization have increased over the past decade, enabling China's armed forces to develop capabilities to contribute to the delivery of international public goods, as well as increase China's options for using military force to gain diplomatic advantage or resolve disputes in its favor.[31]

In its assessment issued in 2011, the Stockholm International Peace Research Institute (SIPRI) showed that China had become the world's second largest spender on military equipment, with USD 119 billion compared to the US's 698 billion, a 189 percent increase over a decade before.[32] Such figures however were widely criticised for being underestimates, with the US in particular arguing that many costs that should have appeared in the Chinese figures had been put elsewhere, or were not calculated. That

---

[31] Office of the Secretary of Defense, 'Annual Report to Congress: Military and Security Developments Involving the People's Republic of China 2010,' p 4, at http://www.defense.gov/pubs/pdfs/2010_CMPR_Final.pdf [22 December 2011].
[32] SIPRI, 'Background Paper on SIPRI Military Expenditure Data, 2010,' issued April 11, 2011, at http://www.sipri.org/media/pressreleases/translations11/milexbackground.pdf [22 December 2011].

meant that a total sum that was at least double and perhaps more was likely.

China lay a long way behind the US, but then its strategic stretch was much more limited. It focused on Taiwan, and on the South China Sea. It did not get involved with the costly disputes in Afghanistan, the Middle East or North Africa. Hu's military was very aware of its limitations, even in this context. It had no aircraft carrier, despite discussions of this each year from the mid 2000s onward at the National People's Congress, and it had limited fire power. It was only in short bursts that it revealed something of its capability, surprising the world by shooting down a satellite in January 2007, putting a man into space for the first time in October 2003 (something Hu marked with an uncharacteristically enthusiastic comment that this marked "the glory of our great motherland and a mark for the initial victory of the country's first manned space flight"[33]). Chinese technical capability was little understood, but what evidence there was showed that it was coming on in leaps and bounds.

The government itself maintained the parameters of the rhetoric established under the 'peaceful rise' era, of its being a force for good in the region and the wider world, and its military expenditure being legitimate and not a cause for concern. The White Paper issued by the State Council in March 2011, one of a series of official policy pronouncements similar to white papers set out by other governments around the world, focusing on defence, contained the reassurance that in

> the second decade of the 21st century, China will continue to take advantage of this important period of strategic opportunities for national development, apply the Scientific Outlook on Development in depth, persevere on the path of peaceful development, pursue an independent foreign policy of peace and a national defence policy that is defensive in nature, map out both

---
[33] BBC News, 'China puts its first man in space', October 15, 2003, at http://news.bbc.co.uk/1/hi/world/asia-pacific/3192330.stm [22 December 2011].

economic development and national defence in a unified manner and, in the process of building a society that is moderately affluent on a general basis, realise the unified goal of building a prosperous country and a strong military.'[34]

Hu himself talked of creating a 'strong rich country' in ways which were similar to Mao Zedong who in 1957, two generations before, had stated that the Party's aim was to see China become a 'rich, strong, socialist country'. In this project, the need for a powerful military was clear. It was fundamentally important for the Party-station's ambitions of building a strong nation in the 21$^{st}$ century.

But China's military leaders looked as anxiously at the world as the world looked at them. They had had no proper combat experience since the disappointing attack on Vietnam in 1979. They were mindful most of all of a US which still maintained a powerful presence around the world, and which, according to American academic Bruce Cummings,

> runs a territorial empire... of somewhere between 737 and 860 overseas military installations operating in 153 countries, which most Americans know little if anything about. [This is] an American realm with no name, a territorial presence with little if any standing in the literature of international affairs.[35]

Chinese intellectual and writer Wang Hui was to ask

> [whether] America is an empire or a nation state? Does America have boundaries or not? It certainly has boundaries, since one has to go through customs when one arrives, yet its frontiers may also be Turkey, Iraq, Afghanistan and all along China's periphery. It has frontiers everywhere.[36]

---

[34] 'White Paper on National Defense in 2010', Information Office of the State Council, March 31, 2011, at http://www.china.org.cn/government/whitepaper/2011–03/31/content_22263357.htm [22 December 2011].
[35] Bruce Cummings, *Dominion from Sea to Sea: Pacific Ascendancy and American Power*, Yale University Press, New Haven, CT, 2009, p 393.
[36] Hui Wang, *The End of the Revolution: China and the Limits of Modernity*, Verso, New York, 2009, p 132.

Faced with this inescapable imperium, which China had the simple choice either to resist or accept, what was a consistent defence posture? If there was one area in which the PLA and the Chinese military establishment, with Hu's backing, had put major efforts into in the decade since he came to power, it was in what had become called 'informationalised conflict' — in other words, war in cyberspace. Here the enormous number of talented amateur and professional hackers spread across China supplied an almost endless pool from which the agents of the state could recruit. Some of their attacks managed to penetrate deep into other government systems. The Chinese Ministry of Foreign Affairs spokespeople were right to say that everyone was up to the same thing with varying degrees of success. But the Chinese managed to land some blows, disrupting systems in Germany, the US, the UK, and even the Prime Minister's office in Australia and India. China's cyber attacks fitted well with the counter-narrative of a Hu-led China which was slightly sinister and covert, and where many tens of thousands were silently working away snooping on the activities of web surfers elsewhere. The internet occupies a unique place between China as it looks out to the world and China as it control's its own internal issues. This will be dealt with more in the next chapter. But with cyber war and cyber attacks, the PLA and its agents could identify an area where they stood a chance of acquiring some competitive advantage against the immense US hegemony in the world around them. According to one news report in 2011,

> Though it is difficult to ascertain the true extent of America's own capabilities and activities in this arena, a series of secret diplomatic cables as well as interviews with experts suggest that when it comes to cyber-espionage, China has leaped ahead of the United States.'[37]

In this area at least, China could realistically be number one.

---

[37] Brian Grow and Mark HosenBall, 'In cyberspy versus cyberspy, China has the edge', *Reuters*, April 14, 2011, at http://www.theglobeandmail.com/news/technology/tech-news/in-cyberspy-vs-cyberspy-china-has-the-edge/article1985224/singlepage/#articlecontent [22 December 2011].

## Hu and Foreign Policy

Hu may have come to power as a relative novice on international affairs, but inevitably he had to pick up diplomatic skills quickly. His chairing of the Leading Small Group on Foreign Affairs shows that, whatever the complexities of foreign policy making in China,[38] the final say on China's international relations fell to him.

What conclusions can one draw over China's international role under Hu? For the first five years, until 2007, one can still discern the heavy influence of Jiang-era leaders — Zeng Qinghong, Tang Jiaxuan, and Liu Zhaoxing, the latter two both former Chinese Foreign Ministers in particular playing a role on maintaining lines that had been established under the previous President and Party Secretary. But from 2007, a more distinctive strategy has emerged, one which shows how important and powerful China has become, but in which it has veered between using its new powers with a mixture of assertiveness and reluctance which has often created confusion in the outside world. The eruption of protests in the Middle East and North Africa in late 2010 and early 2011, and the diplomacy around the intervention into Libya show this ambiguity well, with China responding to calls to repatriate 37 thousand of its citizens from the stricken country while abstaining from the UN vote on imposing no fly air zones, and expressing increasing unease over greater military involvement.

Surprisingly, the Chinese government throughout this period was coy about declaring anything that looked like 'core interests'. Hu's most senior foreign policy advisor, State Councillor Dai Bingguo, came closest to articulating this during the China US Strategic and Economic Dialogue in July 2009, when he stated that

> the core national interests of China [are] composed of defending its fundamental systems and national security, preserving national

---

[38] For an outline of this, see Linda Jakobsen and David Knox, 'New Foreign Policy Actors in China', SIPRI Policy Paper 26, September, 2010.

sovereignty and unification, and maintaining the steady and sustainable development of its economy and society.[39]

Dai restated this in May 2010 at the follow up dialogue in China:

> The Chinese side believes that [the] China-US relationship should be one between partners, not rivals, still less enemies; one of peaceful coexistence, not mutual suspicion and containment; one of mutual benefit, not pursuing one's own interests at the cost of the other; one of equality, not submission, or even subordinating of one side to the other. It should be a relationship in which we can have candid discussions, understand and trust each other, view each other's strategic intention in a rational and objective manner, respect and accommodate each other's core interests and major concerns, and skilfully handle disagreements and differences.[40]

Even so, this did not stop departing US Ambassador to China Jon Huntsman from complaining when speaking in Shanghai in April 2011, that leaders who "struggle with the legacy of outdated ideologies or past differences" and peddle "corrosive" misperceptions fed into the "lack of mutual trust" that bedeviled the US-China relationship. "Global challenges will not pause to wait for upturns in our bilateral relationship," he said. "Just the opposite — they will only worsen while we remain disengaged." Listing the human rights activists who had been taken in over the period from 2009, and the various blips that had occurred since President Obama had come to office, Huntsman sounded like a disappointed man. Many felt similar disappointment in the closing period of Hu's stewardship over foreign policy.[41]

---

[39] Quoted by Da Wei in 'A clear signal of "core interests" to the world', *China Daily*, August 2, 2010, at http://www.chinadaily.com.cn/usa/2010-08/02/content_11083124.htm [22 December 2011].
[40] Bingguo Dai, 'Remarks by State Councilor Dai Bingguo at Joint Press Conference of the Second Round of the China-US Strategic and Economic Dialogues', May 27, 2010, at http://www.fmprc.gov.cn/eng/wjdt/zyjh/t705280.htm [22 December 2011].
[41] James McGregor, 'Huntsman: Disillusioned and Disappointed by China', at http://onebillionambitions.wordpress.com/2011/04/14/huntsman-disillusioned-and-disappointed-by-china/ [22 December 2011].

In the Hu era, the country shifted from being viewed as a status quo power, to a power with a new positive model for the world to follow, to one which was disruptive. In this confusing context, the presiding impression of Hu diplomacy is of extreme cautiousness. There was one major accomplishment (the ECFA with Taiwan) and mixed results in other areas. Hu's greatest weakness was not speaking for China or being a mouthpiece for China at times when it was either being put under pressure or accused of assertiveness and pushy behaviour. His silence and invisibility may well have been linked with his desire to avoid blame should things go wrong, or because there was simply no consensus amongst the senior leadership on what position to take. Even so, as supreme leader, of the Party, state and military, Hu's importance as the ultimate spokesperson for a China that was emerging and becoming more and more prominent in the world was crystal clear. That he remained so silent was one of his greatest faults, and meant that at times when the newly prominent China needed an authoritative voice to explain its actions to the world and clarify its position, all it got was the subtle, enigmatic and silent smiles of the Party Secretary. This was not just a matter of the complex actors who had a voice or a role in the formulation of foreign affairs. In the end, Hu was the leader, and it fell to him to somehow chorale a uniform public response to these issues.

## Chapter Five

# WHAT DOES HU THINK?
# IDEOLOGY IN THE HU ERA

In the post-socialist, post-Marxist, post-Communist PRC, the proposition that ideology is still important might seem to be a strange one. And yet, from the vast and impressive infrastructure of cadre training at Party schools dotted across the country, to the ways in which leaders like Hu spoke publicly, to the resources put into campaigns, ideology still seemed thick in the air of political life in Beijing, and its effect could be seen even in the work of business people, journalists, and those who superficially looked to be very remote from the world of thought organisation and intellectual political arrangement that ideology was meant to fill.

Associating Hu Jintao with a particular ideology seems odd. There was no 'Huism', a unifying body of thought with which his name was associated. The Xinhua bookshops from one end of China to the other were not piled high with the distinctive light yellow 'collected works' of his, the way they were of those of Mao, Deng, and Jiang. Nor was Hu's 'thought' enshrined in the Constitution the way that those of his predecessors' had been. The lack of ego and self-promotion that characterised Hu's political life also reached into his ideological way of operating.

Some grappled with whether there were new dominant strands of thought in Hu's China. One of the most concise accounts of this was by the British writer Mark Leonard whose *What Does China Think* had been produced after a stay in Beijing, looking at some of the think tanks there and elsewhere in China. Leonard talked to some of the more vocal leftist voices — people like Pan Wei, a professor at Beijing University, whose shrill declarations of the need for China to find its own distinctive path away from western-dominated political models had resonance in a country where the historic grievances mentioned in previous chapters against the west and modernity in particular never seemed to go away. On a visit to Chongqing, the vast south western city which had attracted notice in the mid 2000s after it had been made a municipality directly under the central government by having ostensibly the largest urban population in the world, Leonard declared that he had seen a place grappling with new modes of governance and public participation in decision making. But the one group whose voices were most conspicuously absent in his book were those right at the top — Hu, his advisors like Wang Huning, and the key people at the Party School, who were mandated to try at least to think the unthinkable — but with Chinese characteristics.[1]

If ideology was no longer important in China, then why was there a network of over 2000 Party schools, stretching across every province and into most cities and prefectures? Cadre training was, according to Frank Pieke, "a crucial but almost completely overlooked aspect of the Chinese Party-state". It was, he went on, "Mao Zedong's worst nightmare become real. Gone forever are first hand revolutionary experience and direct involvement in the life and work of China's toiling masses. Instead, cadres have become a ruling elite who worship book learning and formal educational qualifications". Party schools with their highly intensive training "provide... a key transformational experience in the construction of cadres' unique personhood, a sense of the self that straddles the boundaries between strong individuality, total submission to the Party's will, elitist exclusivity and faceless anonymity".[2] The amount of resources, time and effort put into this training was formidable. And the Chinese system remained one of the few in the world where officials and politicians at the most senior level were taken out of their daily jobs running ministries and departments, sometimes for

---

[1] Mark Leonard, *What Does China Think*, Fourth Estate, London, 2008.
[2] Frank Pieke, *The Good Communist: Elite Training and State Building in Today's China*, Cambridge University Press, Cambridge, New York, 2009, p 1.

up to half a year, in order to attend intensive courses, from those on new adaptations of Marxist ideology, to introductions to new strands of thought and research from the west which were presented either as things to be adapted and used in China, or models of what the Communist system was up against in the impurity of the world around them. Ideology remains important even in the pragmatic world of Hu Jintao's PRC because it gives "understandings of the political environments in which we all are part".[3] Talk of a post ideological China therefore falls far wide of the mark.

This chapter will look first at the context in which the various parts of the CCP in Hu Jintao's China created ideology. It will then focus specifically on the statements that Hu made, particularly around scientific development and harmonious society, which were most strongly associated with him, particularly through three key speeches. It will analyse the ways in which these ideological points were partly the result of evolution from previous positions, partly the attempt to build consensus, and partly a legitimising mechanism. It will finally draw some conclusions about the likely historic impact of Hu's ideological imprint.

## Worrying About China — The Historic Path to 21st Century PRC Ideology

The great divide in the PRC's ideological history corresponds, unsurprisingly, with the same transformation visited on its economic policies. From 1980, the Party's commitment to Maoist class struggle and social activism, with its devastatingly destructive outcomes, was abandoned. And while Maoism remained a disruptive and surprisingly persistent element of the intellectual and political world in the PRC, it has, at least till 2011, never again infected the political elite, many of whom know all too well its highly undesirable effects, through their suffering in the Cultural Revolution.

---

[3] Michael Freeden, *Ideology: A Very Short Introduction*, Oxford University Press, New York, 2003, p 1–2.

There were many debates in the 1980s and 1990s about the ways in which opening up and reforming China's system might carry destabilising risks, and how the modes of economic and structural engagement with the developed world might persist while seeing off some of its less welcome impacts. The collapse of the Soviet Union in 1991, so soon after the CCP's own nasty experiences with popular unrest in 1989, provoked deep soul searching about how the project of modernism, albeit on the CCP's terms, might continue. Deng's final political intervention in 1992 during his Southern Tour partially resolved this. Reform was irreversible. Going back to the past (if that is what Deng's opponents were arguing, which wasn't clear) was impossible. The Party lived or died on its link with modernity. The problem was what 'modernity' in this context meant.

'Socialism with Chinese characteristics' and 'market socialism' were the two great ideological mantras in the 1980s and 1990s. Embracing the market, within strict Party-state parameters, was the objective. What was finally created was a cause of some controversy — an authoritarian centralised model, a Party-state with unique characteristics, one where rhetorical commitment to Marxism-Leninism was maintained, while pragmatism (after all another ideological standpoint) was dominant; all of these external descriptions were used to try to pin down what China post-Mao had become.

At the heart of this talk about it being different, unique, and offering an alternative, was the discourse created in China about modernity being a specifically western influence, something which had come from outside and which had no roots in the country. Where was the unique Chinese form of modernity? How could it be expressed, described, promoted and followed? Once this issue became clear, then observers and those engaged in the process of self-articulation and analysis could connect to a long process, since the Qing Dynasty over a century before, of Chinese wrestling with the ideas, and the social and economic and political impact, of modernity, and in particular of modern industrialised, urbanised social formations. There was a clear link to the students agitating for greater national self-determination and engagement with science and democracy during the May 4th Movement at the end of World War One in 1919, and those who, within the Party school structures or the dissident communities in the PRC, were trying to spell out what was the Chinese vision of modern life. The Party had to find itself at the heart of this debate. Hu's speeches contain plenty of statements about this (see section 'Ideology in the 1990s and the Early 2000s' below).

In *Worrying about China*, Gloria Davies maps out the entangled, often antagonistic responses of key modern Chinese intellectuals to the question posed about how much modernity with Chinese characteristics made sense. "Modern Chinese intellectual discourse then, unlike its EuroAmerican counterpart, has always been forced into the position of having to either acknowledge or deny the pre-eminence of Western thought", she argues, "and this necessity of having to cope with both the unknown and foreign invests Western thought, as it appears in the language of Chinese critical enquiry, with an ambience of at least potential inimicality or incommensurability".[4] But this search for an indigenous intellectual foundation for a Chinese voice and place on modernity has been fraught with problems.

> When Chinese intellectuals imply that authentic presentations of the Chinese past and present can be produced only by people who have an innate empathy for their object of enquiry… In this view, they are the true spokespersons for China and bear the responsibility for voicing concerns on their nation's behalf, and for 'appropriating' Western ideas in ways which suit China's national cultural development *specifically*. A particular version of Chinese culture is proffered by authorial fiat, as the true account, regardless of the infinite heterogeneity of lived experience in Mainland China. Cultural and linguistic hybridity are gathered up, distilled and essentialised to conform to the bifurcated vista of China and the West.[5]

---

[4] Gloria Davies, *Worrying About China: The Language of Chinese Critical Inquiry*, Harvard University Press, Cambridge, MA, London, 2007, p 47.
[5] *Ibid.*, p 40–41.

This argument may seem to be about remote areas of intellectual contention and debate, but in fact, the political elite were deeply involved in the constant need to reassert a 'Chinese way' to do things, a Chinese path, something which was even enshrined in the language which talked of *guo qing* — the specific national characteristics and situation which needed to be known and understood for any policy to have a chance of working. The elite, like intellectuals, had one other major problem. Davies quotes the Beijing-based literary historian Qian Liqun's remark in the late 1990s that "Chinese national characteristics are actually altered by Mao. To this day, observers of Mainland ways of thinking and behaving, even of orating, notice traces of this legacy". Another, Li Jie, commented that "by 1966 the Chinese could only think Mao Zedong thought, they had suffered a complete stupefaction of their own thought processes".[6] This legacy had cast a long shadow, however actively it had been rejected, and for those working in elitist political structures, from Hu downwards, they were living, breathing and surviving in a landscape where any moves against the fundamental tenets at least of Marxism were catastrophically perilous. The one sure and safe territory for change was to appeal to the vast, unexplored areas of 'Chinese reinterpretations of Marxism for the reality in China'. There was ample room for manoeuvre, although the side effect of this was to create the exaggerated disjuncture between a strongly posited oppositional 'West' and the PRC.

British Prime Minister Clement Attlee had famously remarked that "when you scratched a communist, you found a nationalist underneath". In many ways, the strength, and the danger, of a discourse where the specificity and uniqueness of Chinese modernity was stressed was that it fell into some of these nationalist traps. 'China is Unhappy' has skirted round some of these, arguing for the existence of two great enemies — foreign exploitative trade practices on the one hand, creating a China that was becoming

---

[6] *Ibid.*, p 146.

a 'sweat shop for the world', and elites in China itself who were creating more inequality, controlling more of the material benefits that development was bringing, and fobbing off a partially enslaved population with aspirations and hopes of a never-arriving tomorrow, while they enjoyed everything today. The harsh polemic of the co-authors of this book was more elegantly presented by academic Wang Hui, who wrote of the ways in which the PRC broke away from the socialist camp very early after the revolution in 1949, stressing self-reliance. "Absent this condition of self-reliance, and it would be very difficult to picture how China's path to reform and opening up would have looked".[7] Acknowledging the profound impact the Cultural Revolution had on the development of political life in China, he states that "every great political battle was inextricably linked to serious theoretical considerations and policy debate".[8] The instability and violence of the 1966–1976 era had prompted one major change in the Party's evolution, which was that it had metamorphosed into a "bureaucratic machine", without "a distinctive evaluative role", but more a "structuralist functionalist relationship to society".[9] In the official language, the Party existed almost above everything else, in a zone where it neutrally balanced interests and potential conflicts, creating consensus so that the vast complex nexus of Chinese modern society during the transitional impact of intense industrialisation might still have some functionality. This 'bureaucratic machine' was serviced by precisely the highly technically trained cadres who had been through intense specialist training as administrators in the national Party school system mentioned above. The CCP after 30 years of modernisation, therefore, had made itself into something that almost transcended political division, that represented, preserved and embodied unity. The great challenge was how to square this function with its strong historic legacy of ideological commitment to revolution and to the goals of Marxism.

---

[7] Hui Wang, *The End of the Revolution: China and the Limits of Modernity*, Verso, New York, 2009, p xix.
[8] *Ibid.*, p 6.
[9] *Ibid.*, p 9.

## Ideology in the 1990s and Early 2000s

When the commitment to Leninist class struggle had been lifted at the Congress in 1992, the Party ideologues had created enough space to re-engage with marketisation and push forward with justifications for deeper opening up to the outside world, which had been set back by the shock of Tiananmen Square in 1989. The kind of challenges to this position have been mentioned in the first and second chapters. There were plenty who had influence in the Party who believed that it was losing sight of its roots, and undermining the fundamental creed on which the Party had built its legitimacy. The unavoidable fact remained, however, that the non-state sector was growing, and becoming increasingly important to China's economy. How could entrepreneurs, some of the most productive and important figures in society, live a kind of twilight life, where they were tolerated, but give no substantial footing on which to operate?

Entrepreneurs, after all, had been amongst the great enemies for much of the CCP's history. From the 1950s, they, intellectuals and those accused of supporting the KMT had been the main targets of campaigns ranging from the anti-Rightist onslaughts in 1957 after the period of false-liberalism during the Hundred Flowers Campaign to the Armageddon of the Cultural Revolution, when anyone with a remotely 'capitalist' background was a prime target for attack and imprisonment, sometimes even leading to death. The small capitalists that had been created during the 1980s reforms had been tolerated until 1989, but, in the words of Jie Chen and Bruce J Dickson in their book on entrepreneurs in modern China, after June 1989 "the starkest symbol of the backlash against reform was the decision in 1989 to ban the recruitment of capitalists into the CCP".[10] That remained the formal position throughout the 1990s.

The fall of the Soviet Union posed many existential problems for the Chinese CCP after 1991, ones which only accentuated

---

[10] Jie Chen and Bruce J Dickson, *Allies of the State: China's Private Entrepreneurs and Democratic Change*, Harvard University Press, Cambridge, MA, 2010, p 26.

the issue of how to enfranchise capitalists who were the result of further embrace of marketisation, without carrying political risk. Gorbachev was criticised in internal reports commissioned from Chinese think tanks for allowing too much political reform without proper economic reform, for being far too tolerant of dissent and not clamping down violently or promptly enough. For the CCP, entrepreneurs were half wanted, half feared. The challenge was how to create the framework and ideological rationale for their secure enfranchisement within the CCP system.

Jiang Zemin's contribution here was a significant one. On the 80th anniversary of the foundation of the CCP in July 2001, Jiang outlined a way in which specialists and other elites would be able to join the Party. According to one analysis, "Commentators [argued] that the decision to admit capitalists into the Party and institutionalise the Party's rule downplays the ideological role of the CCP". In fact, "[i]t is clear that the Party's ideological role has not been reduced at all".[11] The author continues,

> Since the CCP launched its economic reform movement in late 1978, ideology has become an important vehicle for communicating regime values to the Party rank and file and to the whole population. The logic is continued as the CCP adapts its traditional ideology by assimilating new elements of China's modernizing society through the Three Represents Campaign.

The *san ge daibiao* ('three represents'), while associated with Jiang, is also a bridge to Hu. The theory is a simple one and had its origins in talks Jiang had given in 1995 on the 'three stresses' (*sanjiang*) — to stress study, stress politics and stress healthy trends. With Deng Xiaoping Thought officially written into the Chinese Constitution at the Party Congress held a year after his death in 1997, Jiang was able to formulate his 'theoretical contribution' more completely. The key task was how to deal with the major upheavals caused

---

[11] Hepeng Jia, 'The Three Represents Campaign: Reform the Party or Indoctrinate the Capitalist', *Cato Journal*, 24(3), p 262.

by the reforms of the state owned enterprise system, which was seeing as many as 60 million workers for state companies lose their jobs. Three Represents Theory created the basis for this. In one pithy formulation it focused on what the Chinese Communist Party currently stands for. That is:

- It represents the development trends of advanced productive forces.
- It represents the orientations of an advanced culture.
- It represents the fundamental interests of the overwhelming majority of the people of China.[12]

The practical impact of this was that from the 2002 Congress, the private sector was recognised in the Constitution and entrepreneurs were finally allowed to join the CCP. The move was a timely one.

> The emergence and growth of the private sector in China has been one of the most profound socioeconomic changes in China since the onset of Post-Mao reforms. From the early 1990s, the number of private enterprises increased by 35 percent annually and now totals over 5 million. The private sector is the main source of growth in China; by 2007, it contributed 66 percent of gross domestic product, and 71 percent of tax revenues… As private enterprises have gained increased prominence in the national economy, private enterprises have begun to play an increasingly important role in China's political life. Their economic and political status has been further enhanced and institutionalised by the constitutional protection of private property promulgated in 2003… and the Chinese Communist Party's lifting of its ban on recruiting private entrepreneurs into the Party in 2001.[13]

This was not to say that there were no other competing ideological currents in the 1990s. When President of the Party School, Hu had

---

[12] 'What is the Three Represents' at china.org.cn, http://www.china.org.cn/english/zhuanti/3represents/68735.htm [22 December 2011].
[13] Jie Chen and Bruce J Dickson, *Allies of the State*, p 1.

allowed theorists and ideologues to experiment with ideas from neo-conservatism to a brief interest in the Third Way, with lectures by London School of Economics guru Anthony Giddens, Jurgen Habermas on civil society, Jacques Derrida on structuralism, and even forays in Foucault and Sartre, rumours had started to circulate that the man likely to next lead China was a closet liberal. But on hindsight it is now clear that the presiding ambition had been to identify useful ideas by which to give the CCP greater flexibility and traction on a society going through immense, rapid and potentially destabilising change. The old mantra of 'using foreigners to serve China' never completely disappeared.

Some of the continuity between the era of Jiang and that of Hu in terms of ideology can be seen in the figure of Wang Huning, an academic from Shanghai's elite Fudan University, who had worked in the Department of International Politics before being brought to Beijing by Jiang in 1995 to head the Political Section of the Party's Policy Research Office. Wang had written widely in the 1980s about the need for deeper democratisation in the Party, saying that China's culture was changing from "conservative, closed, subjective and arbitrary" to one that is "renewed, open, objective and democratic".[14] Wang's interest in stability, efficiency and cautiousness however meant that he appealed as much to Hu as to Jiang, and was able to maintain strong influence from 2002 onwards. Wang Huning was promoted to the Secretariat of the 17th Party Congress in 2007 as a sign of this, a critical position in charge of Politburo Leaders' speeches, documents, and travel.

## Huism from the Start

On December 5th, days after his election as General Secretary of the CCP, Hu visited Xibaipo in Hebei, an isolated town which had served as the last revolutionary capital before Mao Zedong had arrived in

---

[14] Quoted in Joseph Fewsmith, *China After Tiananmen*, Second Edition, Cambridge University Press, Cambridge, 2008, p 96–97.

Beijing in 1949. The symbolism of revolutionary geography and of linking with the leader who had founded the regime and was the core of its first generation was clear. In a speech given here, Hu talked of the 'two musts', upholding the spirit of plain living and hard struggle and enjoining the Party members listening, and the wider community to which he was speaking beyond, to "remain modest, prudent and without arrogance and rashness".[15] In this way, Hu "linked the Three Represents to the hardworking attitude and the so-called fish-water connection between the Party cadres and the masses".[16]

This desire to speak to the grassroots after years in which inequality had grown and in which the impact of rapid growth on society had at times been highly destabilising was a theme that was to continue throughout Hu's early months. Wen Jiabao had stated in 2003 that "the level of relative affluence that China has now attained is not comprehensive or balanced and the main discrepancy is in the rural areas".[17] Hu's own belief in reaching out to as broad a social constituency as possible became clear in his speech on July 1st, 2003 when he talked of "the need to build a Party that serves the interests of the public and governs for the people".[18] The phrase 'taking people as the centre/core' (*wei ren you ben*) became a critical one, with the 3rd Plenum of the 16th Congress in October 2003 being a key moment to shift from talking not just about 'economic development' but also to include social ones. The aim was to build a "Party that serves the interests of the public and governs for the people", to be "people centred", and to use "scientific development"; in order to create "comprehensive, co-ordinated, sustainable development".[19]

---

[15] *Ibid.*, p 243.
[16] Hepeng Jia, 'The Three Represents Campaign', p 262. The reference to fish-water connection is to a former Mao dictum about the essential relationship that links the CCP to people like a fish needs water.
[17] Quoted in Fewsmith, p 244.
[18] *Ibid.*, p 251.
[19] Fewsmith, p 252.

If these were the objectives, what were the means of delivering this within the historic ideological parameters which had been bequeathed Hu and his fellow elite leaders? The key buzzwords of the Hu era were 'scientific development' and 'harmonious society'. These in fact were written into the Chinese Constitution in 2007, though not as parts of what was signed as a Hu Jintao-sponsored ideological contribution to Party development. They were simply marked as contributions to the development of 'socialism with Chinese characteristics', a project consistently followed from 1949 onwards.

Hu made three important ideological statements in a speech made to celebrate the 85th Foundation of the CCP on June 30th, 2006, the speech at the Party Congress in October 2007, and a talk to celebrate the 30th anniversary of reform and opening up. Important additional material is also contained in a talk at the 6th Plenum of the 17th Congress Discipline and Inspection Committee on January 10th, 2011. Each of them contains statements which Hu made about key parts of the elite, establishment ideology under him. And each were the result of the strong impulses for consensus and working to create a collective voice which was the workstyle he personified and supported. As such, it is hard to say that these are statements of personal belief, but nor can Hu's important agency in their content and construction be ignored.

Hu's speech on June 30th, 2006 contains the central elements that dominate elite discourse in the PRC in the first decade of the 21st century. Firstly, there is a strong attempt to appeal to the narrative of revolutionary history for legitimacy. Secondly, there is the continuous effort to present the CCP and its ideology as the key embodiment of modernity and its most important driver in the PRC. Thirdly, there is the tension created in trying to handle post-socialist belief systems while embracing issues which might seem contradictory to them or antithetical. Fourthly, there is a focus on the political objective of making a message, or a declaration, for 'all the people' and for the whole of society, showing that the Party delivers and represents the best hope for all, not just a self-defined and protected elite.

Hu's lack of any personal voice in his statements has already been noted. His public utterances are those embodying consensus, emanating from a collective, created by committees and speechwriters with not a shade of personal colour. Mao was famously demotic and vulgar in his utterances, so that the finest writers needed to be recruited to polish up his somewhat rough statements (amongst them the great novelist and scholar Qian Zhongshu, who served on the committee that saw through some of Mao's posthumously published works). Jiang and Deng allowed themselves the odd moment of subjectivity, and Zhu Rongji's sometimes emotional mode of address represents possibly the acme of the post-1949 leadership getting personal in their public utterances. But Hu's are the most impersonal, delivering their version of the post-Maoist Marxist truth with lapidary grandness.

The speech commemorating the 85th anniversary of the Party's founding in June 2006 was one of the most developed expressions of 'harmonious society' and 'scientific development'. Nodding to the narrative of Party history which was now accepted as the 'historic truth', Hu stated, 'During the construction period of reform and opening up and socialist modernisation, we have opened up the path of socialism with Chinese characteristics, persisting in taking economic development as the central task, persisting in the four basic founding principles, persisting in reform and opening up, making advances in the setting up of a socialist market economy, improving the comprehensive power of our country and the living standards of the people, in order to fully create a middle income society, basically realising social modernising to open up a vast future'.[20] The sense of the Party being the vanguard leading to the future and the main engine of modernity is returned to again soon after: 'Only our Party can become the nucleus of power to lead the Chinese revolution, construction, and reform, only it is able to bear

---

[20] Author's translation.

the great trust of the Chinese people and the Chinese nationality... In the last 85 years, our Party has preserved and developed the progressive creative line'.[21]

People 'are the force for creating history'. In the 1970s when 'the international environment was dominated by peace and development', the Party 'faced the contradiction between the daily increase in the material and cultural needs in society and the backwardness in the productive capacity of China'. Reform and opening up were implemented in order to address this contradiction. The CCP is the guarantee of historic scientific-based progress — where science is posited as a concrete expression of empirical truth and social development. But in order to have stable development and to take China towards 'a harmonious (*hexie*) society and scientific development', and to construct 'the new socialist countryside' (*shehui shuyi xin nongcun*) it is necessary to take the CCP as representing the best interests of the people, the repository of their collective modernist hopes and aspirations. 'History proves, only with the deep recognition of the mighty force of people creating history, sincerely representing the basic interests of the vast numbers of Chinese people, together with the people, relying on the people, can our Party get the complete trust of the people, and gain victory'.[22]

And to do this, to be a modernising force, linked to the productive vanguard of the people, the Party relies on the fundamental tools of theory and strategic policies. These are the 'life' (*shengming*) of the Party. Having a correct theoretical understanding, based on the development in China of Marxism, is crucial. 'Our Party persists in liberating thought, seeking truth from facts... combing the fundamental tenets of Marxism with the actual situation in China'. Only with the 'non-stop progress of the realisation of theory and

---

[21] Jintao Hu, 'Zai Qingzhu Zhongguo Gongchandang Chengli 85 Zhounian Ji Zongjie Baoche Dangyuan Xianjinxing Jiaoyu Huodang Da Huishang De Jianghua' (Speech made at an Advanced Educational Meeting of Cadres Celebrating and Summarising the 85th Anniversary of the Founding of the CCP), Xinhua, July 1, 2006.
[22] *Ibid*.

policy can our Party... find the right path, the scientific manner, in which to push forward the Party and the people's enterprise from victory to victory'.[23]

The impact of modernity, through the reform and opening up process since 1978, has created problems, contradictions, threats and imbalances. Hu admits this. 'From first to last the Party knows that its central task during different historic periods' is to deal with these contradictions. But the Party is at the heart of all attempts towards progressiveness in society, pushing forward the advancement of Chinese productivity, advancing its culture, being 'the embodiment of the basic benefits of the great mass of the Chinese people'.[24]

Progressiveness (*xianjinxing*) after all 'is the essence of Marxist Party building', the 'basic service and the eternal theme' of Marxism. Despite daily changes in the international system, therefore, the Party's consistent commitment to this on behalf of the people acts as a foundation for stability. In essence, the Party is progress, giving a framework in which the forces of productivity can be unleashed, continuing the historic project started in 1949 of building a 'new, strong country'. There is space in this to talk about developing democracy, but one within the framework supplied by the Party, which represents the interests of all people, and which remains the sole guardian of modernity in the PRC.[25]

The speech made a little over a year later, at the 17th Congress of the CCP on October 15th, 2007, carried the cumbersome title 'Hold High the Great Banner of Socialism with Chinese Characteristics and Strive for New Victories in Building a Moderately Prosperous Society in All Respects'. Making his report reviewing progress in the last five years, Hu declared that this was 'an extraordinary period'. 'At its Sixteenth Congress', he went on, 'the Party established the

---

[23] *Ibid.*
[24] *Ibid.*
[25] *Ibid.*

important thought of the Three Represents as its guide and made the strategic decision to build a moderately prosperous society in all respects'. Hu listed a long menu of great successes: economic strength grew, reform and opening up continued, 'living standards improved significantly'. Fresh progress was 'registered in improving democracy and the legal system', and 'social development proceeding in an all round way'. However, 'while recognising our achievements we must be well aware that they still fall far short of the expectations of the people'.

One threat that faced Hu during this Congress was continued leftist anxiety about the propriety of importing so many ideas from the West and adopting too much marketisation. To head this off, Hu spent a whole section speaking of the correctness of the decision made at the 1978 'historic Third Plenary Session of the 11th Central Committee which ushered in the new historical period of reform and opening up'. Reform and opening up 'represent a great new resolution carried on by the people under the Party's leadership in a new era to release and develop the productive forces, modernize the country, bring prosperity to the Chinese people and achieve the great rejuvenation of the Chinese nation'. It also had historic legitimacy: 'the great cause of reform and opening up was conducted on a foundation laid by the Party's first generation of collective leadership', and continued by its second and third generation leaders. On this reading of the Party's history, there had been only consistency since 1949 in terms of overall direction and strategy. There had been no hiatuses in terms of policy or elite leadership decisions. The new research being undertaken by scholars like Yang Jisheng on the tragedy of the great starvations in the 1960s, and the work others were doing on the most violent aspects of the Cultural Revolution and even the murder and torture that it was claimed took place after 1989, was sidelined. The Party has only ever had one direction, and that is to pursue modernity, progress and development. 'Rapid development represents the most remarkable achievement of this new period [since 2002]'. Hu's final statement on reform is emphatic: 'Facts have incontrovertibly proved that the decision to begin reform and opening up is vital to the destiny of contemporary China'. There was no other alternative.

The key task of the new leadership is therefore to offer refinements and improvements, to build, as it were, on the shoulders of the founding giants Mao, Deng and Jiang. The 'scientific outlook on development' is a key tool in this, acknowledging the economic achievements but also recognising that 'overall productivity remains low, the capacity for independent innovation is weak and longstanding structural problems and the extensive mode of growth are yet to be fundamentally addressed'. Lurking behind this is the intense debates about sustainability, whether of the growth model, the economy or the infrastructure of society, which had been ongoing since the very start of the reform era in 1978. Imbalances abounded, between the cities and the countryside, between the rich and the poor, and between the different, newly created and defined social groups which will be considered in the next chapter. People are becoming more demanding, 'our society is becoming more dynamic, but profound changes have taken place in the structure of society, in the way society is organised, and in the pattern of social interests, and many new issues have emerged'. The scientific outlook on development 'takes development as its essence, putting people first as its core, comprehensive, balanced and sustainable development at its basic requirement, and overall consideration as its fundamental approach'. Governance, putting the people first, pursuing sustainability, and striving to find balance while remaining a dynamic, ever changing society were critical in order to build a harmonious society. 'Scientific development and social harmony are integral to each other'. In order to do that, somewhat circuitously, Hu states that 'we must continue to deepen reform and opening up'. The Party needs to be strengthened (see the next chapter for the implications of this). The whole of society needs to be recruited to strive towards this common goal.

The policy goals set out by Hu in this speech for achieving a 'harmonious society' and pursuing 'scientific development' were to 'promote balanced development to ensure sound and rapid economic growth', to increase citizen's participation in political affairs, and to promote socialist core values so that 'fine ideological and ethical trends will be encouraged'. By 2020, therefore, after the implementation of these measures, 'China, a large developing socialist country with an ancient civilisation will have basically accomplished industrialisation, with its overall strength significantly increased and its domestic market ranking as one of the largest in the world'. It will be a country 'whose people are better off and enjoy markedly improved quality of life and a good environment'. Its citizens 'will have better institutions in all areas and Chinese society will have greater vitality coupled with stability and unity'.

Discrete areas of policy focus consisted of enhancing Chinese innovation, upgrading the industrial infrastructure, building a new socialist countryside (one where the stark imbalances in terms of wealth, provision of education and medical care, and infrastructure which still existed would be ameliorated) and addressing some of the country's immense energy efficiency and environmental problems. Beyond these practical policy objectives, there was also the equally critical ones connected to 'promoting... socialist culture'. Whatever happened, it was important to 'build up a system of socialist core values and make socialist ideology more attractive and cohesive'. Despite Hu's talk of the need to 'educate the people in the latest achievements in adapting Marxism to Chinese characteristics', and 'make every effort to carry out theoretical innovation and give Marxism in China distinct characters of practice', little of the content of this new innovative Marxism was alluded to. There seemed to be, in much that Hu went on to say, an encoded bias towards conservatism, the preservation culturally at least of the status quo, with constant reference to 'harmony' and the need to control 'the press, publishing, film, radio', etc. with 'correct guidance'. The foundation was still located in 'Chinese culture', with absolute certainty posited about what Chinese culture was, and how it was linked to the economic modernisation drive of the CCP by supplying a kind of spiritual ballast. 'Chinese culture has been an unfailing driving force for the the nation to keep its unity and make progress from generation to generation'. Despite the exhortation to 'innovate and move forward' therefore, there was a still point at the centre, a constant focus for reference. The question of what the core values derived from this national culture were, however, remained illusive in both Hu's talk, and that of his fellow leaders around him.

In a final flourish, at the end of this two hour tour de force, Hu struck a note of caution. 'We are bound to meet difficulties and risks in our endeavour. We must therefore stay prepared for adversities in times of peace, be mindful of potential dangers, and always maintain our firm faith in Marxism, socialism with Chinese characteristics and the great rejuvenation of the Chinese nation'.

'Faith' in Marxism might strike a slightly discordant note here, with the dense talk of scientific development. One thing that was lacking in Hu's long declaration was any specifics on what the core beliefs of this faith was. His interpretations of Marxism were surprising vacuous, especially in view of the fact that the kind of ubiquitous marketisation that Marx so profoundly criticised was something that, at the policy level at least, the PRC had embraced with abandon. The vestiges of the old Maoist system still lived in the utopianism that lingered in some of what Hu said, implying that history was an onward march to better and better things, and greater and vaster progress. Some of the grandiloquence of his language too contained memory traces of the linguistic stable from which it had come, with the long years of political manipulation and deformation of language, particularly during the Maoist period. 'Faith' was the word Hu used, however, and faith was what he meant, in as much as one talks of an American president always speaking in a faith context supplied by Judaic-Christianity. Faith in Marxism was postulated as a given, an uncontested part of the intellectual universe from which this speech came. Issues about the profound choices to be made between some interpretations of Marx and others were left aside.

Much of the 2007 speech, in any case, dealt not so much with the ideology of the Party and the policy outcomes that derived from this, but with the thorny issue of what the Party was to itself — this will be dealt with in the next chapter. But the business of establishing its own governance, within this ideological framework where 'people were taken as the core', and the stress was on delivery of sustainability and development, was more pressing than coming up with some grand uniform theory on which everything else could be predicated. While entreating citizens to be creative and innovative, therefore, the great contradiction of Hu's speech was the constant veering towards conservatism, maintenance of the status quo, adherence to Party orthodoxy, and a final, emotional and somewhat romantic view of the unifying, uplifting force of Chinese traditional culture.

Mao had embraced contradictions, and sometimes delighted in them, with his essay 'On Contradictions' being one of his significant contributions to Marxist thinking. For Hu the opposite was the case. The challenge was to find balance, stability, and ways to address contradictions. While he avoided the words 'Confucius', there were plenty around him who started to appeal to some sense of ancient Chinese values which reached back two and a half millennia to the time of the great philosophers. 'Taking people as the base' was ascribed to Mencius, a near contemporary of Confucius (and someone who offered almost the exact opposite of the Sage's highly pessimistic views on human nature). That harmonious society was placed at the door of Confucius, a figure who had been virulently attacked in the early 1970s but who made a spectacular comeback in the late 2000s, was ironic. Professor Jiang Qing, a commentator based at Beijing University, and others within China developed new ways of writing about the relevance of Confucian thinking in the new, reforming China. A lively debate about the ways in which this finally presented a new alternative to the Christian dominated West and its ideology started, linked to the vague concept of Asian values. All that one could say safely is that Hu was striving for the same expression of a uniquely Chinese mode of doing things, and of modernising that was referred to in the opening of this chapter. But the more cynical might see in his words only the Party's self interest writ large, and a continuation of the Party's long history of delivering solemn promises, and then evading or ignoring these no sooner than they were said. Hu's speech was criticised by some as airy rhetoric, and its key words of harmony and scientific development received either with indifference, or suppressed cynicism.

## Reform or Die — 30 Years of Opening Up

Indeed, the consistency of the Hu-as-core (though this formulation was never used in Chinese) world view can be seen in a speech he made a year later, on December 18th, 2008, to mark the 30th anniversary of the reform and opening up process. His main objective then was to demonstrate legitimacy by being linked seamlessly with the reform process instigated in December 1978. And he specifically mentions, right at the head of the speech, the leftist enemies who had dogged the progress of Party modernity in the last decades — 'Under the leadership of Comrade Deng and other lifelong revolutionaries, the Third Plenum of the Central Committee of the Tenth Party Congress [in December 1978] conscientiously corrected the leftist aberration of the Cultural Revolution, criticising the 'whateverists' [those that claimed that whatever Mao said or did was correct]', ending the conflict caused by class struggle, and taking economic development as the key task. The emphasis now, after 'following the correct line of Marxist Thought, the political line and the organisation line' was to 'liberate and develop social productive capacity', modernising the country, allowing the people to get prosperous'.[26] The great transition in the last three decades

---

[26] Translated from Jintao Hu, 'Zai Jinian Dang de Shiyi Xu San Zhong Quanhui Zhaokai 30 Zhounian Dahuishang De Jianghua', (Speech Remembering the Thirtieth Anniversary of the Third Plenum of the 11th Party Congress), reprinted in *Liu Ge Weisheme*' ('The Six Why's'), People's Daily Publishing House, Beijing, 2009, p 1–2.

had been to go from being a planned economy (99 percent of economic activity in the late Mao period was under central state control) to the market economy, 'a great historic shift'.[27]

In rising to be what was then the world's fourth largest economy, the PRC, according to Hu, had increased its annual GDP from 1978 by 9.8 percent per year. This prosperity had proved that 'in striving to develop socialist democratic politics, the people, in becoming the masters in their own houses, have received an even better safeguard'.[28] Over this, relations between all nationalities in China, all religious groups, all classes of society, and between China and the Chinese compatriots (*tongbao* — a code for the Chinese in Taiwan) in the outside world should become 'more harmonious'. As in the speech at the 17th Party Congress, Hu states that the 'meaning and deep impression of the 11th Party Congress Third Plenum' was absolutely correct: 'The great achievements of reform and opening up are the result of the unity between the Party and the people of all ethnic groups in the PRC'.[29] And just as in 2007, this all had an ideological basis, creating consistency in the social beliefs across the new groups emerging in Hu's PRC (see section 'Taking Class as the Key Link — Again' below). 'The theory of socialism with Chinese characteristics', he declares, 'is the latest success of the Sinification (*zhongguohua*) of Marxism, the most precious riches of the Party's politics and spirit, and the foundation of the common thought of the whole people's struggle for unity'.[30] In order to continue the critical reform process, China had to deepen its own development, making productivity the key, under the joint leadership of the Party and the people, with Marxism seen as the expression of the people's will: 'The mass of the people are the fundamental source of the Party's strength and victory'.[31] Uniting socialism with market economy had been one

---

[27] *Ibid.*, p 3.
[28] *Ibid.*, p 5.
[29] *Ibid.*, p 7.
[30] *Ibid.*, p 9.
[31] *Ibid.*, p 11.

of the great ideological and political successes of 'Marxism with Chinese characteristics'. The new stage was to push forward with political reform, still led by unity between the working class and the farmers: 'People's democracy is the lifeblood of socialism... without democracy there is no socialism, and there can be no socialist modernisation'.[32] This did not mean 'using the western models' (more of that later). It did mean creating a more balanced, equal and stable society, with socialism bringing about justice, China's sovereignty being preserved, and the country's interests being tightly defined and defended. 'Without stability, then nothing is possible'.[33] Therefore the Party needed to have 'unified thought'.[34] The objective of the Party now after six decades in power, and three decades of reform, was 'building a rich, democratic, civilised, harmonious, modern socialist country'.[35]

In a modernising state where 'the Party and the people are one', as Hu declared when speaking to the discipline committee in January 2011, the Party had to act for the whole good of the people. But beyond generalities, when coming close to the specifics of political decision making and the basis that these were made on (after all, politics is almost always about choices and the contestation of groups advocating benefits between these alternatives), what was Hu's belief system? His aim in his speeches was clearly to speak only in a way that ensured agreement across almost all the complex interests groups and factions and other shades of opinion that constituted the CCP in the 21st century. It was easy to speak about the need to reform, modernise, and create greater prosperity. But at heart, what was the specific Hu line? Curiously, Hu was happy to use big words and terms that fitted somewhat strangely in the discourse of a supporter of dialectic materialism — spirit, justice, democracy all tripped off his tongue easily. But it was more the fears that appeared in his public utterances that

---

[32] Ibid., p 13.
[33] Ibid., p 18.
[34] Jintao Hu, Ibid., p 19.
[35] Jintao Hu, Ibid., p 21.

staked out his real interests — the 'complicated internal issues' that he spoke of when addressing the Party discipline commission in January 2011, and the need to maintain stability, along with the need to build law in order to maintain stability and sort out possible contention between people in society. What Hu and his co-leaders were really wrestling with was the explosive social impact derived from rapid economic development. And the challenge this created had been to make new links in society, reassemble certain key lines of connection, break up others, and create new social classes with distinct differences between each other. Class, far from going away in the new modernising China under Hu, was as much a problem as it had been when Mao was in charge. The issue was to find a new way of talking about it, a new framework, which dealt with some if not most of the immense fractiousness that could grow from new imbalances and inequalities.

## Taking Class as the Key Link — Again

Fundamentally, ideology had given elite Communist leaders in China in the past a way of identifying and then finding a political programme to deal with the profound fragmentation of Chinese society and its immense power imbalances. Communism had, in the early decades of the PRC, cut largely across tribal alliances, and created a national common purpose. It had also addressed the age-old divisions between the haves and have-nots, the rural and the urban, and it also had something to say about the political impact of the very modest industrialisation that had occurred in China up to 1950. For Mao, a precise taxonomy of class structure had supplied him with the basis on which to wage a form of permanent war against those classes who were antipathetic to the new revolutionary, utopian programme. His 1957 speech, 'On the Correct Handling of Contradictions Amongst the People', had been the classic statement of this.

> In the conditions prevailing in China today, the contradictions among the people comprise the contradictions within the working class,

the contradictions within the peasantry, the contradictions within the intelligentsia, the contradictions between the working class and the peasantry, the contradictions between the workers and peasants on the one hand and the intellectuals on the other, the contradictions between the working class and other sections of the working people on the one hand and the national bourgeoisie on the other, the contradictions within the national bourgeoisie, and so on.[36]

On how to handle these social conflicts, Mao had initially sounded reasonable:

The only way to settle questions of an ideological nature or controversial issues among the people is by the democratic method, the method of discussion, of criticism, of persuasion and education, and not by the method of coercion or repression.

But a more prescriptive tone then appeared:

To be able to carry on their production and studies effectively and to arrange their lives properly, the people want their government and those in charge of production and of cultural and educational organisations to issue appropriate orders of an obligatory nature. It is common sense that the maintenance of public order would be impossible without such administrative regulations. Administrative orders and the method of persuasion and education complement each other in resolving contradictions among the people. Even administrative regulations for the maintenance of public order must be accompanied by persuasion and education, for in many cases regulations alone will not work'.[37]

The persuasive method reached its apogee in the Cultural Revolution, an era when all-out war prevailed for a period between different groups that defined themselves separately and linked themselves to what were presented as legitimate strands of

---

[36] Zedong Mao, *On the Correct Handling of Contradictions Among the People*, Foreign Language Press, Peking, 1957, p 3–4.
[37] *Ibid.*, p 11–12.

revolutionary activity. This, as was stated in the first chapter, was a period that had a profound impression on Hu and those in his generation.

Since 1978, the relationship between the individual and the state has been redrawn. But the need to create a new taxonomy of social classification has not gone away. Of course, the impact of rapid growth on social development had been disruptive, and allowed a reconfiguration of social groups, creating a swath of winners and losers, and redrawing the boundaries of different kinds of elites with their access to sources of power. Slavoj Zizek, in a review of a study of the CCP, had caustically pointed out some of the contradictions in the rhetoric of leadership and what his perception of reality on the ground in contemporary CCP was: 'One should bear in mind', he argues, 'the basic rule of Stalinist hermeneutics: since the official media do not openly report trouble, the most reliable way to detect it is to look out for compensatory excesses in state propaganda: the more 'harmony' is celebrated, the more chaos and antagonism there is in reality. China is barely under control. It threatens to explode'.[38]

This is an overstatement. Social conflict had increased, but many parts of the Chinese political, economic and social state functioned better than ever before. The main issue was the creation of new identities for social groups. Political scientist Teresa Wright looks at some of these new categories in her book, *Accepting Authoritarianism*. In what she calls the 'Late Reform Era' (from the early 1990s onwards), with "a dramatic acceleration and expansion of state-led economic privatisation and marketisation", where the CCP has "moved from tolerating the private sector to embracing it", entrepreneurs have become increasingly wealthy, but there has been "an even more highly polarised socioeconomic structure" resembling an onion dome, where "the wealthiest 20 percent of Chinese citizens earned more than 59 percent of China's income" with the bottom 20 percent getting only 3 percent of the country's

---

[38] Slavoj Zizek, 'Can you Give My Son a Job', London Review of Books, 32(20), October 2010, p 9.

wealth, a difference of 18 to 1 compared to the US, where the difference is 15 to 1.[39] In this society, the CCP has expended huge effort and time in order to broker deals and accommodations with new social classes, from private entrepreneurs, to professional urban dwellers, rank and file private sector workers, migrant labourers and farmers. It has achieved its greatest success with entrepreneurs, of whom a staggering third are now Party members. But the different kinds of deals that the Party has been able to strike have also been supplemented by the ways in which these separate social classes see their best interests served by the ruling elite. "For private entrepreneurs" for instance, "who have garnered their wealth through their connections with the ruling Party-state, political change would similarly threaten their economic advantage".[40] Almost all the social groups see elements of the CCP's message as protecting their best interests, with the possible exception, worryingly for the Party, of farmers, who "sit at the bottom of the lower tier of China's onion dome-shaped economic structure",[41] and whose experience of the sometimes highly unequal benefits of the central government's development strategies have led them to "be restless and only tenuously tolerant of the political status quo". The Maoist legacy of collectivisation had left a nasty memory stain, but even policies like the introduction of the Household Responsibility System in the early 1980s had created new power blocks and elites, with farmers able to sell back surpluses to the state and invest this money in other economic activities. Land ownership problems, the inherent prejudice in the maintenance of a dual citizenship system, and a range of other issues meant that "many peasants felt that their ability to rise economically was limited by socialist legacies and state controls". The impact of the late reform policies had mixed effects, "in some respects improving their quality of life and diminishing their political

---

[39] Teresa Wright, *Accepting Authoritarianism: State-Society Relations in China's Reform Era*, Stanford University Press, California, 2010, p 6–7.
[40] *Ibid.*, p 8.
[41] *Ibid.*, p 137.

dissatisfaction, yet in other ways creating new types of hardship and political complaints".[42] The impact of market forces, exposing the agricultural sector to fierce competition, and the increase in the requisition of farming land for non-agricultural development had all taken a toll on the popular rural attitudes towards Party elites, and the CCP's message of "taking people as the base". "Peasants who have continued to depend on agriculture 'have experienced absolute, not just relative, declines in their standards of living'".[43] Peasant-based challenges to the ruling elite, Wright concludes, are "likely to increase".[44]

Hu's constituency includes all of these groups, from the highly internationalised returned-students, of which there were about one million, to the private business people with their deepening links into the global investment system, and the urban professionals with their interest in protecting their property, their lifestyles and their rights, to the farmers and migrant labourers, who clearly wanted more of the pie created by the policies of the previous three decades. How could an elite leader frame, from a Marxist discourse first used in China in a period of huge unrest and poverty and state breakdown, a message for a country careering towards modernity? Hu's problems were compounded by the fact that at least for the elite, the ideology did matter — it was a basis for legitimacy, and for a cohesive world view which had brought the CCP to power. The force of conservatism in this elite could not be underestimated. Even if we credit Hu with latent liberal tendencies (and as I argue in the conclusion, that is unlikely, with the best description likely to be a chameleon-like ambiguity on most ideological and political issues) he was surrounded largely by those who were publicly known as supporters of a more cautious, conservative line. The second (Wu Bangguo), fourth (Jia Qinglin) and fifth (Li Changchun), eighth (He Guoqiang) and ninth (Zhou Yongkang) in command in

---

[42] *Ibid.*, p 148.
[43] *Ibid.*, p 153.
[44] *Ibid.*, p 160.

his second Politburo Standing Committee were all described as hardliners. The remainder were hardly free thinking liberals. At best, Hu's ideological position was to create a transient space within which the painful social contradictions could be controlled until wealth creation had enlisted most of the people into the project of keeping the CCP in power.

And whatever the Hu-ist CCP's ideological position was, in the end the key issue was the organisational powers of the CCP itself, and its ability to demonstrate efficiency, relevance, and legitimacy to the whole of society. That remained the fundamental challenge of the CCP in late Chinese post-reform modernity. It is to this issue that we now turn.

## Chapter Six

# ALWAYS THE PARTY MAN: HU AND THE CCP

During his Work Report to the Party Congress in 2007, the final sections had been not about ideology, or the need for deeper economic reforms, but the task of 'carrying forward the great new undertaking to build the Party in a spirit of reform and innovation'. Hu declared that 'the Party's task to build itself has become more arduous than ever before'. The CCP was beset by the challenges of governing a vast, complex society undergoing dramatic change, but also struggling within itself against corruption and factionalism. To some, it often seemed like a country within a country, a shadow of its historic strategy in the first years of Mao control in the late 1920s of being akin to a 'state within a state'.

There had never been a political force quite like the CCP. With 80 million members, and a youth wing of a similar size, the CCP stretched into every area of political life in contemporary China. It was present in Party Branch Secretaries in the 800 thousand villages of China, in the townships, prefectures, and provinces, in the state owned enterprises, and even in the non-state enterprises where rules enjoined the need to have Party Secretaries and a Party branch if there were more than eight workers. It was in control of the media, and had full control of the army, and of the security forces, an immense capacity which meant that it could keep an eye not just on the enemies without, but more critically the enemies within.

The CCP is shy of its power. As the Financial Times journalist Richard McGregor wrote, "The Party has made strenuous efforts to keep the sinews of its enduring power off the front page of public life in China and out of sight of the rest of the world." However, "Peek under the hood of the Chinese model... and China looks much more communist than it does on the open road."[1] Organisationally, it has been able to operate a shadow structure, working around, above and within the government. Party Secretaries famously hold the upper hand from top to bottom of the PRC system, creating its unique form. The Party's opaqueness is legendry, with its finances shrouded in mystery, Politburo meetings being famously out of sight (even despite the Hu era innovation of sometimes publicising their study days) and its control over news management and personnel as rigid as at any time in the past.

Hu's CCP was a force to behold. Its highly organised conventions and congresses closed down Beijing for the periods when they were held. It maintained an extraordinary discipline on its members, with hardly any signs of open elite dissent, giving a field day to speculation, but none of the concrete evidence of dissatisfaction that had existed in previous Politburos. Unity seemed to prevail over the key challenges of clamping down on unrest in Tibet and Xinjiang, responding to the problems created by dissident Liu Xiaobo, rising to the challenge of the 2008 global economic downturn, and dealing with international affairs. The Party continued its strategy of professionalising and expanding, seeming to inexorably go from strength to strength under the stewardship of a man who was, whatever else that might be said of him, the ultimate Party man.

Part of the CCP's experience since 1991 has been in thinking long and hard about the collapse of the Soviet Union, and then the colour revolutions that swept states that had broken away from the USSR in the mid 2000s. The long process to 'reinvent itself,' involved assessments of the events of 1989 in China, the fall of the Soviet Union, the colour revolutions and the 'political systems of a variety of non-communist states in Asia and the Middle East, Europe and

---

[1] Richard McGregor, *The Party: The Secret World of China's Communist Leaders*, Harper Collins, New York, 2010, p xiii.

Latin America',[2] particularly after the Jasmine revolutions of late 2010 and early 2011 in North Africa and the Middle East. The long soul-searching over the collapse of the USSR in particular continued over 13 years, and culminated in the decision issued at the fourth plenary of the 16th Congress in 2004, entitled 'Decision of the CCP Central Committee on Enhancing the Party's Ruling Capacity'. As Shambaugh comments

> It is most interesting, that the Chinese critiques of the failure of the CPSU and collapse of the Soviet Union were *systemic* in nature... They found that, instead of a "perfect storm" of events culminating together in August 1991, in fact the sources of Soviet collapse lay in long-term Soviet decline, mismanagement, wrong judgements and policy mistakes, systematic distortions, an inability to react to failures and innovate, excessive dogmatism, bureaucratic inefficiency, an inappropriate foreign policy, and a variety of other maladies.[3]

The failure of the CPSU had been like a looming shadow behind much of the CCP's attempts to redirect itself over the late 1990s and into the 2000s, and is one of the most powerful influences on Hu's attempts, in his words as quoted earlier, to professionalise the Party, to develop it and make it more efficient in its internal governance. In his 2007 speech, he presents six key tasks which are relevant to the CCP:

1. To thoroughly study and apply the systems of theories of socialism with Chinese characteristics and focus on arming the whole Party with the latest achievements of adapting Marxism to Chinese characteristics.
2. To continue to strengthen the Party's governance capability and focus on building high-quality leading bodies.

---

[2] David Shambaugh, *China's Communist Party: Atrophy and Adaptation*, Woodrow Wilson Centre Press, New York, 2008, p 41.
[3] *Ibid.*, p 60.

3. To expand Inner Party democracy and focus on enhancing the Party's solidarity and unity.
4. To continue to deepen reform of the cadre and personnel system and focus on training high-calibre cadres and personnel.
5. To consolidate and develop all the achievements and campaigns to educate Party members to preserve their vanguard nature and focus on strengthening primary Party organizations.
6. To effectively improve the Party's style of work and focus on combating corruption and upholding integrity.

The last point in particular got Hu's stern endorsement: 'The CCP never tolerates corruption or any other negative phenomena. This is determined by its nature and purpose. Resolutely punishing and preventing corruption bears on the popular support for the Party and its very survival.' If there could be a Hu manifesto for the CCP under this leadership, this is it. But the question it raised was a massive one: could the CCP be its own manager and source of discipline? Was it, in the end, possible to create a political entity which was able to be at the same time its own judge and jury, and would society trust this if it were the case, even if it were possible?

## Forms of Party Discipline

How could the CCP discipline itself? Since the 1980s, there had been a raft of village elections, to restore legitimacy to governance in the countryside, where the impact of state breakdown in the Cultural Revolution had been gravest. These had culminated in the passing of a national Organic Village Election Law in 1998, which mandated that all villages in China had elections every three years where there was a choice of candidate, secret ballots, and one person one vote. Assessments showed that half of these had been successful. This lay behind the claim by some inside and outside China that it was already democratising.[4] But the lack

---

[4] For an overview of village democracy, see Kerry Brown, *Ballot Box China: Grassroots Democracy and the Final Major One-Party State*, Zed Books, London, 2011.

of other political parties and the ways in which these elections had frequently been controlled by Party leaders in the districts where they occurred left a big question mark over them. In the early 2000s, some elections have been held at township level, with the first held in Suining City, Sichuan Province in 1998, and Shenzhen in January to April 1999. In October 2001, however, the Party Central Committee, in its 'Opinion of the NPC Core Group on Conducting Well the New Round of Town and Township Elections' forbade the implementation of elections at this level.[5] Since then, despite motions passed at NPC's to reenergise the election process, and talk of elections in other parts of China, the process has been stalled, with a number of separate options considered.

Hu's interest was more in rebuilding the Party's accountability to itself, and it was for this reason that 'Party building' and 'Inner Party democracy' became phrases that he used frequently from the mid 2000s onwards. In September 2009, in particular, at the fourth plenary session of the CCP 17th Party Congress, Inner Party democracy was called 'the lifeblood of the Party' (*dang de shengming*), helping it deal with the cancer of corruption and complacency.[6] Wu Banguo, as usual the standard bearer for the hardliners, simply stated at this meeting that "Western models of democracy, which emphasize multi-Party competition for power, the separation of three branches of government, and bicameralism, is not suitable for China".[7] Introducing a range of governance mechanisms into the CCP so that it could set up systems by which to decide amongst different competing power holders and to break apart any hold of a faction that might be emerging over key areas was becoming more important.

---

[5] See Lisheng Dong, 'Direct Township Elections in China: Latest Developments and Prospects', in Kevin O'Brien and Suisheng Zhao (Eds), *Grassroots Elections in China*, Routledge, London, 2011 p 195.
[6] See Cheng Li, 'Intra-Party Democracy: Should We Take It Seriously', *China Leadership Monitor*, Issue No 30, p 2.
[7] *Ibid.*, p 4.

Cheng Li sets out four examples of the CCP setting down rules for itself:

1. Setting up an ombudsperson mechanism to inspect and monitor ongoing anti-corruption work at lower levels of the Party.
2. Making high ranking leaders declare their property interests, business activities of the families around them, and other financial matters.
3. Establishing a public anti-corruption reporting mechanism with telephone hotlines and internet reporting websites to enable the public to report officials' wrongdoings.
4. Perhaps most importantly, implementing an institutional separation mechanism whereby the Party is divided into three divisions: decision making, policy implementation, and supervision.[8]

Just how credible these measures were was a subject of debate. But it was clear that Hu and the leadership around him regarded more transparency and greater internal governance as crucial to their moral standard and their right to rule. The lofty tone of the leadership needed to be protected from criticisms of hypocrisy and setting one standard for the rest of society, and another for themselves. Anger at elitist disconnect in China, however, as the discussion of 'China is Unhappy' mentioned in previous chapters, was not hard to come by.

Ideologues in the Party found it easier to spell out what it did not want rather than what it did. In 'The Six Why's', a series of talks presented on TV and then published in book form in the summer of 2009, the editorial team of the *People's Daily* presented a list of things, in question format, that China did not want:

— Why we must resolutely persist in placing Marxism in a leadership position on the ideological realm, and not introduce pluralism
— Why is it that only with socialism can we save China, only with socialism with Chinese characteristics can we develop China, and not with democratic socialism and capitalism

---

[8] *Ibid.*, p 10.

— Why we must resolutely persist with the structure of the People's Congresses, and not introduce 'the tripartite division of powers'
— Why we must persist with the united front under the CCP, and not have a western style multi-party system
— Why we must persist with public ownership as the base, with a mixed economy, and not have privatisation
— Why we must persist with opening up and reform, and not return to the past[9]

Lurking behind this was the fear of the colour revolutions that had occurred internationally in the mid 2000s. While Hu never used this iteration, it was clear from his emphasis on the Party, its need to build up its capacity and professionalise itself, and its central part in the political and cultural life of the country, that he would have accepted the drift of the Six Why's against allowing in the importation of what Deng Xiaoping had famously called 'flies from outside'. Hu's talk had consistently focused on the "need to build a Party that serves the interests of the public and governs for the people".[10] He had talked at the Fourth Plenum of the CCP 16th Congress in 2004 of "reforming and perfecting the Party's leadership structure and work mechanism", and of "adhering more closely to formal procedures and socialist democracy", with the introduction of rules into the CCP to control "the concentration of power into the hands of individual leaders".[11] The great fear was the rise of a leader like Mao, who had managed to run roughshod over Party procedure, nearly destroying it in the 1960s, and allowing 'rule of man' to win over 'rule of law'.

While the need to focus on internal development was important, it was connected to a range of other debates and issues which raged

---

[9] *Liuge Weisheme* ('The Six Why's'), People's Daily Publishing House, Beijing, 2009.
[10] Quoted in Joseph Fewsmith, *China Since Tiananmen*, Second Edition, Cambridge University Press, Cambridge, 2008, p 250.
[11] *Ibid.*, p 257.

around the Party, and which the Party seemed reluctant to make strong decisions about. These became visible from time to time and gained more traction in 2010 when Wen Jiabao in particular became more vocal, at least in the eyes of some observers, about the need for faster political reform. The Party elite, with Hu as the spokesperson, had talked of the need for 'economic and social' outcomes from their first year in power. But unpacking what this meant in terms of introducing reforms in society in the area of rule of law, civil society, the relationship between the state and the individual, and political reform itself proved difficult.

Wen's article in the *People's Daily* on April 15th, 2010 about his work with and fond recollections of the former Party Secretary Hu Yaobang who was forced to resign his office in 1987 after criticism of mishandling student demonstrations that year, and who died in April 1989, was of particular interest. Hu, after all, had been, along with Zhao Ziyang (his replacement) a semi-taboo figure for much of the last two decades. But Wen's memories of Hu being a man who 'wanted hard to try to understand the real truth at the grassroots level' fitted well with the concerns of the current administration.[12] Wen continued

> I worked by Yaobang's side for two years, I experienced personally his close connection with the people, his concern for the people's suffering, his excellent way [of being an official] and his unselfishness, his open and above-board-ness, and his moral character. I witnessed firsthand how completely he threw himself into his work, struggling day and night for the Party's cause and for the people's interests. What he taught me in those years is engraved on my heart, and his constant leading by example keeps me from [allowing myself to] be lazy. The way he handled things had a huge influence on my work, studies, and life.

Was this a sign of Wen's staking out a greater space for his supposedly more liberal, reformist ideas? Some thought so. But

---

[12] Wen Jiabao, 'Returning to Xingyi, Remembering Hu Yaobang,' translated at http://chinageeks.org/2010/04/wen-jiabao-returning-to-xingyi-to-remember-hu-yaobang/ [15 February 2011].

others reminded those jumping to conclusions that Hu Jintao as well as Wen had been a protégé of Hu Yaobang, and had sanctioned, and wanted to attend, the commemoration of Hu Yaobang's 90th anniversary of his birth in 2005 (but in the end been preventing from attending because of hardliner resistance in the CCP).[13] That Wen would have gone out on a limb and written the article without sanction at least from Hu and others in the Politburo seemed unlikely. A more likely interpretation was that Wen was working as a voice to at least speak to some disaffected elements in the Party as it attempted to be all things to all people, leaving Hu to occupy a space of privileged, remote aloofness.

Dealing with contentious figures from the CCP's very recent history was a real issue, something brought sharply to the forefront by the appearance of the smuggled out, recorded, and then transcribed memoirs of Zhao Ziyang in 2009. Zhao had died in January 2005 under house arrest in Beijing, 16 years after the events of June 3rd and 4th in Tiananmen Square 1989 which had caused him to be criticised by other leaders and removed from his position as Party Secretary at the behest of Deng. Zhao had been briefly glimpsed over the years, kept tightly under control, and silenced. But his taped recollections, when they were finally assembled in Hong Kong and published in book form, showed the direction that divisions could go in the Party, and how, over some issues, it remained vulnerable to deep schisms. That Zhao's death had been marked only a few days after it happened by the briefest of obituaries in the *People's Daily*, and that his funeral had been a cursory, secret affair at which none except the closest relatives had been able to attend, showed just how sensitive his name remained.

But to those on the liberal side of the Party, Zhao was the great lost hope, a man who had represented the real possibility for change not just to the economy, but to the governance of China itself. This high regard meant that his name cropped up covertly

---

[13] Wu Zhong, 'Hu, Wen and why,' *Asia Times Online*, April 21, 2011, at http://www.atimes.com/atimes/China/LD21Ad02.html [15 February 2011].

in many different kinds of blogs and discussions in China, and he remained a deeply respected, sometimes almost revered figure.

## Democracy and Wen: A Good Thing?

When Wen Jiabao appeared only a few days before Hu at the commemoration for the creation of the Shenzhen Special Economic Zone in August 2010, however, he made remarks which were much more nakedly political in nature. Shenzhen was one of the hallowed spaces in the geography of Post-Reform China, the place where the first economic zone had been created in 1980, which had literally risen from nothing in the space of a few years, embodying all the energy, confusion and ambition of the reform programme. Wen's talk while in the city of the need for the Party to innovate more, and accelerate its reform model were all easily compatible with statements Hu had made. His comments however, reported on the official Chinese government website, that "China should push forward not only economic restructuring but also political restructuring" were less conventional. "Without the safeguarding of political restructuring," the report went on, "China may lose what it has already achieved through economic restructuring and the targets of its modernization drive might not be reached." Wen said people's democratic rights and legitimate rights must be guaranteed. People should be mobilised and organised to deal with, in accordance with the law, state, economic, social and cultural affairs. He said the problem of over-concentration of power with ineffective supervision should be solved by improving institutions. He demanded the creation of conditions to allow the people to criticise and supervise the government. Wen pledged to build a fair and just Chinese society, and in particular, to ensure judicial justice.[14]

A few days later, on September 7th, Hu was also in Shenzhen, to mark the anniversary, along with the Hong Kong tycoon Li Ka-Shing.

---

[14] 'Chinese premier calls for further reform, ideological emancipation', at http://www.gov.cn/english/2010-08/21/content_1685351.htm [22 December 2011].

His reflections on the need for greater reform were less expansive: "The SEZs could experiment with reforms in economic, political, cultural and social systems," he was reported as saying by the state owned *China Daily*. "Hu called," the report continued, "for 'expanding socialist democracy' and speeding up the construction of 'a socialist country under the rule of law.' He said efforts should be made to carry out democratic elections, decision making, management and supervision in order to safeguard the people's right to know, to participate, to express and to supervise."[15] According to veteran observer of Chinese elite politics, Willy Lam,

> The stark contrast between the Wen and Hu speeches — and, in particular Wen's single-minded championship of political liberalisation — has raised a host of questions about key issues in elite Chinese politics. Is the progressive-minded premier engaged in a struggle with an "anti-reform" faction within the CCP? Is there an ideological split between the Premier and the President? Equally importantly, will Wen really go about picking up the threads of political reform, and if so, will he succeed?[16]

The plot thickened in early October 2010 when CNN broadcast an interview with Wen, in which he made strong statements about the need to promote freedom of speech, and of democratic reform. "I believe freedom of speech is indispensable, for any country, a country in the course of development and a country that has become strong," he stated. "Freedom of speech has been incorporated into the Chinese Constitution… I believe I and all the Chinese people have such a conviction that China will make continuous progress, and the people's wishes for and needs for democracy and freedom are irresistible." The fact that the interview was blacked out in China

---

[15] Chen Hong, 'President Hails Shenzhen SEZ a world "miracle"', *China Daily*, September 7, 2010, at http://www.chinadaily.com.cn/china/2010-09/07/content_11264644.htm [23 December 2011].
[16] Willy Lam, 'Wen, Hu speeches hint at ideological rift', Asia Times Online, September 30, 2010, at http://www.atimes.com/atimes/China/LI30Ad01.html [22 December 2011].

and went unreported in domestic media only served to create the impression that Wen was making some kind of personal bid for reform which his colleagues on the Politburo, and especially Hu, did not support. But a more hardened view came from Chinese writer Yu Jie, author of a book only allowed to be published in Hong Kong in 2010, who simply stated in an interview with the BBC that "The policies supported by the Premier are very different from his behaviour in front of the media and the public. Sometimes they contradict each other."[17] In fact, Wen was just producing rhetoric on this account. His words meant little.

Insincerity is not exactly in short supply in modern Chinese politics. Politicians in this culture, like any other, are fond of making promises which turn out to be empty. And Wen was hardly an outsider. He was central to a collective leadership throughout the last decade, and had worked with Hu since their time in Gansu in the 1970s. The idea of them having stark ideological differences was unlikely, and made all the more so by the fact that over key issues like the government response to Nobel Laureate Liu Xiaobo, and the Jasmine Revolutions, utter consistency and consensus reigned. Wen spoke within the parameters of what was acceptable, and in language which never strayed from its commitment to the primacy of the CCP in the PRC's development and in the nation's political life. Those who saw Wen as the promoter of a less strident, repressive system had to explain how it was that on the assault on lawyers, rights activists, and other dissidents, and on the main issues of independence for the courts, legal status for civil society, and greater role out of elections, there was hardly any light between Wen and his fellow elite leaders.

## Dealing with Dissent

Hu talked of innovation a lot. But in terms of political innovation, and trends of thought that veered towards areas the Party

---

[17] Michael Bristow, 'Is "Grandpa Wen" as nice as he seems?' BBC News, August 16, 2010, at http://www.bbc.co.uk/news/world-10964615 [22 December 2011].

regarded as threatening, the Hu era was a continuation of the pattern established almost the moment that opening up and reform started — brief periods of intellectual liberalism followed by heavy clampdowns. On the eve of the 1978 Party meeting that kicked off the reform process, Democracy Wall, a few streets away from the hotel where the meeting was being held, was thriving in the Xidan area in central Beijing. But by early January, many of the most active, vociferous activists, people like Xu Wenli and Wei Jingsheng, had been taken in, ultimately serving long sentences in jail before being exiled to the US or elsewhere. The 1980s proceeded with 'Strike Hard Campaigns' against what were regarded as socially undesirable elements (usually entrepreneurs who had gone too far in their money spinning schemes) or spiritual pollution clampdowns, where the more daring intellectuals were slapped down, and in the worst cases, jailed. The fallout from 1989 included a period of brittle and large scale clampdowns, a period still little understood and studied today, where many were horrifically treated by police and security agents because of being associated with the rebellious students.

The 1990s were the same. Under the smiling Jiang Zemin, first the spiritual sect Falungong and then the China Democracy Party suffered brutal campaigns to extinguish them. The attempts by a few dozen activists in 1998–1999 to register their independent political party according to what they claimed were their constitutional rights, met with immediate and comprehensive reactions. Most were rounded up, many sent to prison for sentences of up to a decade; the Falungong practitioners were of a different order, with a long-term campaign to exterminate their influence, carried out in some areas where the sect had been strong like the north east with particular viciousness.

Hu's response while being Party boss of Tibet in 1989 had shown that when it came to the crunch, the use of violence as a political tool of repression was not an issue. And despite some wishful thinking that he would revise the Party's strategy towards those who were its most worrying and challenging potential opponents, China under him saw a slowly escalating campaign against those labelled as subversive. Lawyers, some civil rights activists, dissidents, and even artists were targeted, in an expanding circle of people whom the Party regarded as a threat.

The first sign that Hu's leadership might not be the dawn of a new and more liberal era in this respect was the treatment of a series of activists like Hu Jia, who had migrated from AIDS work into more politically charged projects in the mid 2000s, and who was detained in 2007 and sentenced to three and a half years in 2008 for 'inciting subversion of state power'. Hu Jia was to join Chen Guangcheng, a blind lawyer from Shandong province who had helped first fellow villagers in their attempts to get redress for crimes they believed to have been committed against them, and then, much more contentiously, women who said they had suffered forced abortions. For this he was sentenced to five years in prison in 2006. Overshadowing these was the case of Gao Zhisheng, another self-trained lawyer, who had been detained for representing Falungong cases in 2007.

Gao's case represented much of what was worrying about the impact of the powers of unaccountable state agents in the PRC under Hu, and as such, became one of the most intensely covered abroad. Gao had a modest background and had become a Christian while representing clients. It was perhaps that that gave him his messianic qualities — according to someone who met him before his second 'disappearance', he looked 'like a man who wanted to sacrifice himself'.

Hu and Wen's leadership had seemed like sticklers for the rules, and had spoken frequently of the need to establish the rule by law more deeply in China. Judges had been trained, and interrogation techniques improved. The death sentence, from 2008, had to be cleared by provinces through the central Supreme Court, reducing the official number significantly. Evidence of the use of torture in court cases became inadmissible. But a number of factors clearly spooked the central leadership from 2007 onwards. One was the increasingly unmanageable impact of the internet (see section

'The Benefits and Threats of the Internet' below). The other was the conclusion drawn from careful study of the colour revolutions in the mid 2000s that lawyers and civil society activists, if left uncontrolled, could be agents for highly politicised objectives, and were a significant threat. The final issue was the unrest in first Tibet and Xinjiang in 2008 and 2009 respectively. Atop all this was the evidence that social unrest in society was increasing, with as many as 90 thousand events classified as 'mass unrest' each year.

The Party under Hu made it clear it prized unity above all else, and its talk of harmony was an exhortation to do this. But the final card when all else failed was the one that the CCP had used throughout its career since Mao had become the most influential leader in the late 1920s — good old fashioned violence. The role of violence in shutting up dissent, in controlling those who were causing trouble, and imposing harmony was clear in the case of Gao, who was taken in and severely tortured just as China was preparing itself to host the Olympics in 2008. Gao's testimony about this to Congress made for searingly painful reading. But in many ways, worse was to come.

Because while Hu and Wen were sticklers for following due process, the large increase in what were seen as threats in society from 2007 onwards meant that a whole 'underworld' of violence against subversive elements was set up. There was, of course, no direct link between instructions from the highest level and those on the ground who were implementing these brutal reactions. But onlookers as the situation deteriorated could not but wonder why such widespread, and well-known, use of violence could be tolerated unless there had been ways in which it has, implicitly or even explicitly, been endorsed.

Gao disappeared again, with no charges brought against him or any specific process of trial, sentencing and detention, in 2009. For many months, he was simply not heard from. His wife and children, who had been badly harassed while still in China, managed to seek refuge in the US. Gao made a brief reappearance in April 2010, when he held a disturbing interview with Associated

Press. Appearing subdued and evasive, Gao simply stated that he did not "have the capacity to persevere. On the one hand, it's my past experiences. It's also that these experiences greatly hurt my loved ones." Saying he needed to give up his 'abnormal' past life, he added "The main basis for choosing to give up is for the sake of family feelings... My children need me by their side growing up."[18] His plea, if that is what it was (the Associated Press reporters who met with him felt like he was acting like someone under heavy surveillance) evidently fell on death ears. He disappeared once more and as of the time of writing (May 2011) has not been heard from since.

Gao's case was raised by visiting foreign leaders, and received wide coverage outside of China. But the fact remained that a man with no charge laid against him seemed to be being kept against his will, and had claimed, at least in the past, to have suffered very bad torture. Those who had met him after his first disappearance confirmed that he looked disturbed and wounded, a broken man, and that extreme physical mistreatment was an explanation for this. Even in the past, those who had displeased the regime had at least been through some kind of semi-formal judicial process. The use of these extra-judicial means was particularly disturbing.

At least Gao's case was well known. For many who had decided to take on the state through the petitioning system, a whole new network of what Human Rights Watch called 'Black Jails' were set up — underground security systems, run by private companies contracted by local governments to deal with petitioners from their area who had ended up in Beijing.[19] Being a petitioner in Hu's China meant running the risk of entering a terrifying other world

---

[18] Tania Branigan, 'Chinese human rights lawyer abandons activism to reunite with family', *The Guardian*, April 7, 2011, at http://www.guardian.co.uk/world/2010/apr/07/china-human-rights-lawyer-abandons-activism [22 December 2011].

[19] See 'An Alleyway in Hell: China's Abusive Black Jails', Human Rights Watch Report, New York, 2009.

where guards were unaccountable and many just disappeared. The history of petitioning in China is a long one. It has been the method of last resort for many centuries. Under the CCP, the right of people to petition the upper levels of government has been recognised. But when the central government started to punish officials in charge of areas where there were too many protests, then local governments thought up ways of protecting their good record.

Being a petitioner in Hu's 'harmonious China' means embarking on a long journey that frequently simply drives those making the complaint mad. In a powerful report in 'Le Nouvel Observateur' in December 2010, some of the more typical cases were described. 'The quest [of being a petitioner] can last years, consuming all the resources in a family, breaking couples up, and trapping children in the torment. It invariably finishes in stalemate.' Chinese Academy of Social Sciences expert Yu Jianrong showed that 0.2 percent of petitions end up being resolved.[20] Citing the case of Guo Youdi, a thirty eight-year-old who had protested against the factory she had worked at, the report states that she had had her house burnt down, her nine year old son had suffered a suspicious 'accident', and she herself had been arrested four times, ending up in prison twice with no legal judgement against her. She had had to leave her home village, and had been threatened with three years in re-education through labour camps.[21]

Petitioners, on the whole, did not even articulate opposition to the state. They were seeking redress for specific grievances. As scholar Elizabeth Perry said,

> the protests that roil the contemporary Chinese landscape present significant challenges to the central leadership… Yet, however visible and vocal (and sometimes violent) these protests might

---

[20] Nouvel Observateur, 'Malheur aux Plaignants', December–January 2010–2011, p 76. Authors' translation.
[21] *Ibid.*, p 77.

be, participants usually go to great lengths to demonstrate their loyalty to central policies and leaders.[22]

But their reward, despite this, was increasingly to have violence used against them. This disjuncture between the ordered, prescriptive, consensus-seeking language of the elite leadership, and the unruly viciousness of thugs used by officials to force people to act in ways conducive to them achieving their ends will be discussed in the conclusion. But from 2008 onwards, partly through the shock of what had happened in Tibet, and the ways in which this had empowered elements in the security services, and partly through the general nervousness of the central government at the rise in levels of violence across society over issues like non-payment of pensions, land disputes and corruption, there seemed to be a more systematic repressiveness, which intensified as each year went on. And even the first ever visit by a Chinese Premier to a complaints centre during the New Year period in early 2011 did little to reassure that China was not entering a new repressive period.

The imprisonment of Liu Xiaobo in particular was a defining moment. Detained for a year under 'soft detention' conditions (again, extra-judicially), Liu was finally sentenced in December 2009 to 11 years for state subversion. Liu's critique of the CCP had been an extensive one, but the six internet articles which were cited in the judgement issued against him were perhaps the most significant, even though only a few thousand people had actually looked at them. Liu had mentioned the Chinese government's 'White Paper on Democracy' issued in 2005, in an article called 'Are Chinese People Only Qualified to Have "Party Democracy"'. 'In this White Paper, under the "theory of national characteristics", it stresses that China's economy is backward and its people's quality

---

[22] Elizabeth Perry, 'Popular Protest', in Joseph Fewsmith (Ed), *China Today, China Tomorrow: Domestic Politics, Economy and Society*, Rowman and Littlefield, Lanham, 2010, p 13.

is low, and then says that it is the historic choice, and the free choice of the people, that the CCP is the heart of leadership.' Sarcastically remarking that 'all successes belong to the people', Liu then states that 'above the power of the people's democracy is the power of the Communist Party. The NPC is "the puppet" of the Party, as is the CPPCC, which merely acts as a "decorative vase"'. In this system, 'the people's rights and democracy and words like these are only the outer covers for the Party… 1.3 billion people are sleeping under the Party rule.' In another essay called 'The Party's Dictatorship Patriotism', Liu stated that democracy was the sovereign choice of a country, and came from the people. The means by which the CCP maintained control were through 'violence, terror and ideological lies', not any other more legitimate means.[23] These direct attacks on the legitimacy of the CCP, and open critiques of its use of violence, were to prove too much. The award of the Nobel Prize for Peace to Liu a year later in 2010, and the huge efforts that the Chinese government put into discrediting him, and then persuading countries not to attend the award ceremony itself, for which he was not allowed out of jail in China to attend, was symptomatic of a leadership who rated repression highly in facing down threats from social and political conflict.

Hu largely remained silent on these issues. His one public statement in the US, in early 2011, at a joint press conference with President Obama, was the strongest ever made by a Chinese leader abroad. Acknowledging that "a lot still needs to be done in China in terms of human rights", he went on that while China had made "enormous progress" in human rights it:

> is a developing country with a huge population and also a developing country in a crucial stage of reform… China recognises and also respects the universality of human rights. And at the same

---

[23] Xiaobo Liu, 'Nandao Zhongguoren Zhi Pei Jieshou Dangzhu Minzhu', October 19, 2005 at www.epochtimes.com/b5/5/10/4/n1074197.htm [23 December 2011] and 'Zhonggong De Ducai Aiguozhuyi', at www.epochtimes.come/b5/5/10/4/n1074197.htm [23 December 2011].

time, we do believe that we also need to take into account the different national circumstances when it comes to the universal value of human rights. In this context, China still faces many challenges in economic and social development, and a lot still needs to be done in China in terms of human rights... At the same time, we are also willing to continue to have exchanges and dialogue with other countries in terms of human rights, and we're also going to — we're also willing to learn from each other in terms of the good practices.[24]

But on the specific cases of the lawyers Gao and Chen, and the activist Hu Jia, Hu said nothing. The official line is that they were criminals, and that they had been through due process and treated justly.

With the closure of the Open Constitution website and the project being run under academic Xu Zhiyong in July 2009, however, the government seemed to be pursuing a much more strategic line, ratchetting up the pressure. The controlling nature that was clearly part of Hu's personal make up became translated into an oppressively orderly hand in society, with the resources now in place for state security agents to implement extensive surveillance, harassment and assertive control over targets who were selected as particularly problematic. With the unrest increasing in North Africa and the Middle East in late 2010 adding to the tensions already caused by the Nobel Prize award, the authorities became even more jittery. Teng Biao, an academic lawyer based in Beijing, recounted his experiences in December of that year:

> A police officer shouted at me to sit; I pushed the chair over with my foot. Several officers rushed forward and twisted my arms, punched my head and choked me, and pushed me to the ground. They took me to another room. In the corridor I cried out, "I am a

---

[24] United Press International, 'Obama, Hu questioned on human rights', January 19, 2011, at http://www.upi.com/Top_News/US/2011/01/19/Obama-Hu-questioned-on-human-rights/UPI-87101295489952/ [22 December 2011].

law teacher, I know whether or not you are violating the law." I said this primarily to make them understand that they were dealing with someone who knew the law, to make them refrain from acting rashly and inflicting too much pain — and it was also meant for the ears of Mr. Zhang and the officers who were interrogating him.

Several police officers pushed me into a corner and one guy came up and fiercely dragged at my tie until he finally managed to pull it off, and threw it to the floor. The police officers pointed at my nose and coarsely swore at me again, and again they cried, "Do you know where you are? If we beat you, what can you do?"

After a while, a police officer came in and said that we had been detained because we had gone to Fan Yafeng's home. One officer, who I heard addressed as Xu Ping, went from merely loudly interrogating to roaring accusations at me: "O ho, that's how it is! In that case, you belong to the enemy! F- your mother, you went to see Fan Yafeng! That c-! In that case we don't have to talk about legal constraints at all! And you motherf- won't get out of here again! You traitors, you dogs! Counter-revolutionaries! The Communist Party feeds you and pays you and you still don't acknowledge how good it is! You keep insulting the Party!… We will treat you just like an enemy!"[25]

The knowledge that the Party was above the law was one that police and other security agents were united by. As 2011 wore on, figures as prominent as Ai Wei Wei, the artist and designer of the famous Bird's Nest stadium for the 2008 Beijing Olympics, were simply detained for almost two months in the Spring with no news of their whereabouts or what specifically they were being accused of. The highly systematic nature of this onslaught provoked a lot of speculation. But there was no doubt that it was mandated right from the top, by a leadership with Hu Jintao at its centre. The advances that some saw in the development of a more rules driven society in the mid 2000s were slipping away quickly. The atmosphere in mid 2011, partially because

---

[25] Biao Teng, 'A Hole To Bury You In', at http://online.wsj.com/article/SB10001424 052970203731004576045152244293970.html [22 December 2011].

of the imminent leadership transition and the nervousness and doubts that might have been provoking, but also because of the contolling mindset of the most significant figures in the leadership itself, meant that many felt that this was the worst clampdown, and the most extended, for over a decade.

## The Benefits and Threats of the Internet

In the mid 1990s, at the dawn of the internet era, China had no more than a few hundred thousand users. The CCP regarded the internet, as with any media, with extreme wariness and suspicion. But its expanding use in the rest of the world, and the ways in which it might be linked to economic production, meant that by the time Hu became Party boss in 2002, the internet had established for itself an increasingly high profile in China for communication and information.

But there was no doubt that it greatly complicated things, bringing as many potential ill effects in the eyes of the political elite as it did benefits. Even in 2000, there were reportedly 50 thousand working on the surveillance of the cyber world. Liu Di, a young student in Beijing, whose pseudonym on the internet was 'Stainless Steel Rat' was imprisoned with other activists in 2002 for a year for placing sensitive content on blogs. There were plenty of others who were about to join her. In the Jiang era and before, 'Strike Hard Campaigns' had been directed at those accused of economic crimes, political subversion, and corruption, all of it in the physical world. Now, a whole new process of surveillance was needed for viral subversion in cyberspace.

And the many gifted hackers and software engineers that the state was able to recruit to mount invasive attacks against the systems of other countries (see Chapter 4) were also able to turn their powers against their own state. Proxy servers and other systems were set up to subvert what became called the 'Great Cyberwall of China'. As Julia Lovell commented on a study of the meaning of the Great Wall in Chinese modern history, and the ways in which it had been as much a construct from the outside world as something the Chinese themselves had created, in recent years,

> underneath China's quiescent exterior, its relations with the outside world have been transformed by a quiet but radical assault on its borders, an assault no longer made by nomadic horseman, but by information and technology, and one in which China's most significant frontiers are no longer earth based, but virtual.[26]

By 2004, 64 cyber dissidents were imprisoned in China, according to the Reporters Without Borders organisation.[27] But the internet offered challenges which the government could not fudge despite all its prevarication and fears, playing "a major role in throwing open China's closed system of government to public scrutiny".[28]

Celebrated cases where the internet had helped in pressurising officials were that of the waitress in Baoding (a city in Hubei), Deng Yujiao, who knifed and killed an official who had sexually harassed her in 2009. Through an immense cyber-campaign, she had had her sentence revoked.[29] The famed Chongqing Nail House, where two home owners had held the local government at bay for a number of weeks, preventing compulsory purchase of their property, caused immense interest online in 2007.[30] Energetic internet 'lynchings' also became a feature of Chinese life, with the *China Daily*, the official English language paper of the government, stating in 2008 that "'Renrou' literally means human flesh, and 'Renrou search engine', the 'human flesh search engine' is not the search engine familiar

---

[26] Julia Lovell, *The Great Wall: China Against the World 1000 BC to AD 2000*, Grove Press, New York, 2006, p 339.
[27] *Ibid.*, p 341.
[28] *Ibid.*, p 342.
[29] See Elizabeth Corrin, 'China's Rule of Law', in Kerry Brown (Ed), *China 2020: The Next Decade of the People's Republic of China*, Chandos, Oxford, 2011, p 190.
[30] China Daily, 'Nail house in Chongqing demolished', April 3, 2007, at http://www.chinadaily.com.cn/china/2007-04/03/content_842221.htm [22 December 2011].

from Baidu and Google, but the idea of a search engine employing thousands of individuals all mobilized with one aim, to dig out facts and expose them to the baleful glare of publicity. To do this they use the internet and conventional search engines." The report went on, "A survey by the China Youth Daily last week showed that 79.9 percent of the 2,491 netizens polled believed that Renrou search should be regulated, 65.5 percent thought it might become a new way of venting anger and revenge, 64.6 percent said it infringes privacy, and 20.1 percent feared that they would become a target." The report concluded, "Internet gave people a disguise, and power without the responsibility that should come with power."[31]

Deep down, the issue was that the internet perfectly suited a society where informal links between individuals and communities were the lifeblood, and where the world of cyberspace was able to offer a bridge between any number of disparate, fragmented groups within China, allowing them the first time to create a link and a way of speaking to each other. "Since the 1990s, Chinese state power has become more decentralised and fragmented," argued one study, "...and more disciplinary and capillary on the other. The new forms of citizen activism respond to the new forms of power."[32] In this battle, the authorities had to cede territory, passing Open Governance Legislation which became effective in May 2008. According to one legal expert, this provided "the legal basis for China's first nationwide government information disclosure system",[33] and indeed had been instrumental in provinces like Guangzhou putting all of their budget online — a file so large that it had swallowed up two gigabites of space.

---

[31] China Daily, 'Human flesh search engine: an internet lynching?' July 4, 2008, at http://www.chinadaily.com.cn/china/2008-07/04/content_6821165_3.htm [22 December 2011].

[32] Guobing Yang, *The Power of the Internet in China: Citizen Activism Online*, Columbia University Press, New York, 2009, p 28.

[33] Jamie Horsley, 'China Adopts First Nationwide Open Government Information Regulations', Yale China Law Center, p 1, at http://www.law.yale.edu/documents/pdf/Intellectual_Life/Ch_China_Adopts_1st_OGI_Regulations.pdf [22 December 2011].

Hu's views on the internet were clarified in early 2011 when he summoned provincial, military and ministerial leaders just after Chinese New Year, to a study session at the Central Party School. Fresh after the impact of the news of the Jasmine Revolutions that were already toppling long established leaders in Egypt and Tunisia, he talked of the need for more effective 'social management'. According to the official report of this from Xinhua, Hu had said the purpose of the meeting was 'to properly understand the new changes and characteristics in the domestic and international situations', and outlined an eight point programme. 'Governmental and military leaders were told to step up surveillance and set up a database on the mainland's vast population,' one report stated, 'they were also told to step up control and management of cyberspace and direct online public opinion in the right direction.'[34]

One story gleaned from Wikileaks illustrated perfectly the state of the relationship between the internet and members of the Politburo Standing Committee. It involved Li Changchun, the leader responsible for propaganda, who reportedly ordered attacks on Google after entering his own name into a search engine and discovering rumours and what he considered slanders about himself and his own family circulating freely online.[35] After the withdrawal of Google support of their designated mainland China-based site in early 2010, there were yet more fears in the elite that the internet was a means of foreign infiltration to China, and of moulding a young, impressionable generation's minds. During the unrest in Xinjiang in 2009, all but government websites were shut off in the region for almost a year. The same, albeit with

---

[34] Minni Chan, 'Hu Lectures on Harmony as Protests Roil Middle East', *South China Morning Post*, February 20, 2011, and Xinhua, 'Hu Jintao Dui Sheng Bu Ji Lindao Jianghua, Cheng Zui Da Xiandu Hexie Yinsu', February 19, 2011, at http://news.qq.com/a/20110219/000838.htm [22 December 2011].

[35] Malcolm Moore, 'Wikileaks: China propaganda head oversaw Google campaign', *Daily Telegraph*, December 5, 2010, at http://www.telegraph.co.uk/news/worldnews/wikileaks/8182848/Wikileaks-China-propaganda-head-oversaw-Google-campaign.html [22 December 2011].

less intensity and for a briefer period, happened in Inner Mongolia after unrest there in May 2011. Frustrations at the unruliness of the internet meant the leadership travelled from having Facebook pages and doing talks online, to blocking out social networking sites, closing access to YouTube and other data sharing portals (while maintaining access to home-grown but more tightly policed versions like Baidu, Weibo, etc), and putting huge resources into tracking down cyber criminals. However, this did not prevent the Politburo from establishing a 'Zhongnanhai Portal', where, in theory, members of the public could email direct particular leaders.

The internet well captured the ambiguities and contradictions of China almost a decade after Hu's elevation. On the one hand, it offered ways of engaging with citizens, getting them linked more with the sort of political participation and engagement that Hu had talked of in his main speeches. On the other hand, it offered a threat. It gave scope for China to practise 'informationalised conflict' and cyber espionage, but also opened the door increasingly to what were viewed as malignant outside influences. It promoted the sort of need to educate and innovate that the leadership wanted — but also vagrant, independent thinking which they had distaste for. The internet truly was a battleground, a perfect image of the contentiousness, dynamism and complexity of a society in profound transition like China's. In that sense it acted as a massive, hidden monument of what China was becoming.

## Conclusion

# HU JINTAO: A PROVISIONAL ASSESSMENT

President Hu Jintao, what I have seen is this: your face looks calm and smiling, shown along the headlines of major newspapers; your manner of statesmanship plays well in domestic and international news; moreover, you are often found to be associated with bright events and warm scenes. But here, at this moment, I have to tell you a story that one cannot bear to listen, as if it had happened in some other world.

Thus began the testimony of Chinese human rights lawyer Gao Zhisheng, reported missing in early 2009.

Gao's words captured something important about Hu. Almost a decade after being in power, Hu maintained a low profile and remained something of an enigma. As discussed in the first chapter, this was a highly deliberate, controlled pose. But in assessing him, one is confronted with the contradictions of someone who talks of modernity and innovation on the one hand, and yet also sponsored some hugely repressive government actions in the last few years; a man who has been in charge at a time of bold economic reform, but who has also been custodian of the CCP during a period when all attempts to expand this to the political realm have been highly circumscribed. There has been innovation in China since 2002. New forms of consulting with people, new freedoms in the media, and new laws have been passed which have continued to reshape the relationship between the citizen and the state. But the underlying challenge of how to finally modernise the government's relations with the Party, and the Party's governance of itself have remained highly cautious, and often precarious. In this final chapter, I will make a provisional assessment of Hu's achievements overall.

## Not a Touchy Feely Man

In late December 2010, Hu Jintao was seen on a news item broadcast by the state owned China Central Television (CCTV) visiting the home of a woman called Guo Chunping in a poor district in Beijing. The dialogue between the two, as reported in the English language press, captured something of the public persona of the President:

> Hu: When did you move in?
> Guo: I've moved in over half a month now.
> Hu: Oh, half a month, I see. How big is this apartment?
> Guo: It's 45 square metres in all.
> Hu: 45, huh. Two rooms?
> Guo: Yes, two rooms.
> Hu: How much rent are you paying for this apartment?
> Guo: I pay RMB77 each month.
> Hu: RMB77 each month — are you able to cope with the rent?
> Guo: Yes. Secretary-General, I just wanted to say a big thank you to the Party and the government. We are so touched to have been given this fabulous apartment to live in!
> Hu: The Party and the government are very concerned with the people's daily livelihoods. We've taken up a series of measures to further improve your daily lives. Well, we're so happy to see that your lives have been improved here!
> Guo: Thank you! Thank you! Our country is really improving day by day. We never dreamed we would be living in such an apartment some day.

To more seasoned observers, the 'eye popping price of RMB77 for a 45 square metre apartment' seemed impossibly low, especially as house prices in the capital had shot through the roof in the last two years. After a vigorous 'flesh search', internet sleuths discovered that Guo was not exactly who she seemed.

> Unconfirmed reports… [wrote journalist Kenneth Tan] say that Guo is a civil servant who works with the traffic police in Beijing's Chaoyang District. According to neighbours, Guo does not live in the apartment, but has instead rented it out to others. A search on realty websites indicates that the average monthly rent for apartments at the Lijingyuan compound [where the apartment Hu visited was located] (not all of which are given to low-income families) is approximately RMB2,000.'[1]

The links to Hu's interview with the lady were removed quickly, and information about her excised.

At a time when the world was watching and scrutinising China as never before, its leadership was extremely reticent. Until early 2011, Hu had resisted doing press conferences. The event at the White House in January 2011 where he was famously unable to hear one of the reporters quizzing him on human rights was perhaps the first time he had appeared before a largely unpoliced foreign audience. Apart from meetings with Russian state TV journalists, he had given no one-to-one interviews with any other foreign journalists. His voice was mediated, controlled, and almost always highly edited.

This reluctance to speak as the President and leader of the PRC became particularly problematic during high profile moments of tension like the arguments about the Nobel Prize award to Liu Xiaobo in late 2010. Not once did Hu make any public remark, condemning the award of the prize. Nor did he speak out clearly about China's evident, and perhaps rational, disdain for a prize that had long since been highly politicised. Instead, this message was

---

[1] Kenneth Tan, 'Busted: CCTV's RMB77 low-income tenant, 2011's first internet star?', January 2, 2011 at Shanghailist, http://shanghaiist.com/2011/01/02/cctvs_rmb77_low-income_tenant_buste.php [22 December 2011].

carried by the lower level spokespeople at the Ministry of Foreign Affairs and elsewhere. That Hu was the supreme decision maker was clear on almost all the evidence that one looked at. According to one report, "after North Korea conducted a nuclear test in 2006, Hu Jintao is said to have been compelled to personally edit the wording of China's official reaction because no one else wanted to take ultimate responsibility for such a sensitive stance."[2] And yet, in presenting China to the world, Hu was absent, silent, or unreachable. Just as he had, according to some rumours, been strategically absent when the final decision had to be made about sending in the army to quell unrest in Tibet as Party Secretary there in 1989, so he managed to be invisible when China was arguing with the US over Taiwan, with Japan over disputed borders, with the EU over executions, and with anyone else over any other contentious issue. The great author and promoter of harmony within China was himself able to play this role by simply not being around when the harmonious exterior was being pierced and challenged.

Domestically, the political justification for this was clear. Hu spoke, always, as part of a collective leadership, a man who delivered consensus. He never placed himself in the position of supreme leader, avoiding the accusations of arrogance and hubris that had been levelled at the more extroverted, publicity-fond Jiang Zemin. He was perfectly aware that acting like Mao or Deng was simply not possible in the new China — there was insufficient political capital, and any case, the grim memories of late Mao megalomania were sufficiently strong for the Party to be able to jail the more fervent Mao supporters who still remained in the 2000s. His legitimacy was derived solely from the Party, and it was the Party's institutional strength that he most needed to devote his time and attention to. Party leadership was never about him and his own personal ambition and ego. That needed to be rigorously repressed.

---

[2] Linda Jakobson and Dean Knox, 'New Foreign Policy Actors in China', SIPRI Policy Paper 26, September 2010, p 5.

## The Balance Sheet: The Good

The greatest achievement of the Hu era was the maintenance of stability and economic growth. Nothing could detract from this achievement. Those who visited the PRC over the decade could see the signs of immense dynamism almost everywhere they looked. From the USD40 billion spent on the Olympics in 2008, to the equivalent spent on preparing Shanghai for the Expo in 2010, building underground lines, airports, skyscrapers, and roads, China was a massive, economic hotspot. Even the global economic crisis had limited impact. China motored ahead. Fast rail lines were built, carrying people at over 300 kilometres an hour. In the most remote parts of the country, houses were being rebuilt, bigger and better than ever before. Modernity was being etched across the landscape, removing signs of the old China by the day. Huge bridges were put up, car usage shot through the roof, and home ownership by the newly emerging wealthy pushed up the price of real estate. The fact was that increasing numbers of people could afford and aspire to the kinds of lifestyles lived in the West. China's new rich became the key target for western companies trying to crack the Mainland market. Shops in New York, Paris and London became focused on getting more visiting Chinese tourists through their doors. They proved themselves to be the biggest spenders. Ostentatious spending became as common in Beijing, Shanghai, Chengdu and Guangzhou as it was in any other wealthy global urban centres. As a sign of the dramatic changes that were now impacting China, in the 2011 census results, it showed that a little over 50 percent of people now lived in cities. It was official: China had undergone the fastest process of industrialisation and urbanisation in world history.

And whatever critics might say, this had happened, despite huge strains on the environment and society, without any major social unrest. The spectre of demonstrations in 1976 and 1989 was dispelled by a government that made its security services ever vigilant. Surveys showed that people were on the whole happy just to be allowed to get on with their lives. Some reports showed deep inward unhappiness, others showed increasing pride in what China was doing. But the kinds of unrest that had broken out in Iran, Egypt, Tunisia, Ukraine, and other countries was absent in the PRC. And as of 2011, there was simply no political alternative to the CCP.

Hu was the custodian of a hard won, and almost sacred sense of the nation's unity. His hard line on Tibet, Xinjiang, and any expressions of independence in Taiwan, from what evidence could be gleaned, were massively supported, both publicly and in the Party. The bottom line was that going soft on these would have been political suicide. But neither did he wish to be spokesperson for a nation run on a Han chauvinist agenda, cleverly arguing over Xinjiang in 2009 that the rule of law applied there as anywhere else, and that the protagonists in the events of July in Urumqi, overwhelmingly Uyghur, should be subject to the full force of the national law, as it related to all citizens of the country whatever their ethnic identity. This new sense of strength translated to international discussions on the environment, and on economic global infrastructure, where China's actions were interpreted as assertive outside of the country, but played to the increased national self-confidence within. For all the criticisms that were levelled at Hu, under his government people were broadly healthier, lived longer, were more prosperous than they had ever been before, and while society was pervaded by the sorts of contention covered in previous chapters, there was no widespread unrest.

## The Vision Thing: What was China?

For all of that, the question remained about what the country represented, and what the leadership's vision of it was. Liang Jing, the pen name used by a Beijing-based academic, accused Hu of sitting atop a government that 'ruled by rhetoric', producing nicely ordered platitudes within its own tightly policed discourse, perfect for a self-preserving elite, but having little traction in wider society. Referring to an article by Professor Ye Duchu of the

Central Party School published in an early 2010 edition of *Nanfang Zhoumo* ('Southern Weekend', a Guangzhou-based magazine), which had been proclaiming the significance of Hu's speech at the Fifth Plenary Session of the Central Discipline and Inspection Commission, Liang had said that

> …everyone sees Hu Jintao as the monarch of empty rhetoric, hence, in order to bring out the difference in this speech from previous ones, he [Professor Ye] particularly added 'not every speech of Hu Jintao's may be called a 'programmatic document'. What then was the special significance of this 'programmatic document' of Hu's? The full text wasn't found online, but the speech indeed proved to be different to his previous empty rhetoric. It turns out that Hu issued an order to punish corrupt officials, and made it clear that this time he wasn't merely sounding off, but 'really meant it'. To convince high ranking officials and people he would do as he said, Hu went out of his way to announce the crimes of two senior provincial and ministerial level leaders prior to the meeting. It is not difficult to foresee more high-ranking officials being punished this year, but that won't convince anyone that Hu can solve the problem of uniquitous corruption of high officials in the Party… The real intention of Hu Jintao's speech at the CDIC Plenary was, we learn, not in fact to 'oppose corruption and boost clean government' but rather to 'ensure government decrees are not impeded', that is, solve a problem that Hu has failed for eight years, of 'decrees not making it out of Zhongnanhai'… Hu Jintao has realised that he can't carry on ruling by empty rhetoric to the end of his term, and believes only by applying naked secret police methods can he rein in high Party officials and prevent collapse of the whole system.[3]

With rhetoric ruling over everything, and where it was not able to take effect, brutal state violence and coercion, it is not surprising that many inside and outside the PRC found it an increasingly

---

[3] Liang Jing, 'Cong konghua zhiguo dao "dongchang" zhiguo' ('From Ruling by Rhetoric to Ruling by Secret Police'), Xin Shiji, January 26, 2010, translated by Professor David Kelly (personal communication).

schizophrenic power. In Hu's words, the most he said was that the country was aiming to be 'strong and rich' but that its rise was to be peaceful, the world harmonious, and everyone would emerge from this process a winner.

It was true that the manufacture of goods in China had, on the whole, created prosperity for China and others. American and European homes were full of new goods which were affordable because they had been made in the vast factories of the PRC. Global wealth levels and living standards rose, and the Chinese government continued to lift people out of poverty with its policies. But there remained nagging questions about the sustainability of this, and what would happen when China's ever increasing energy and resource hunger brought it into direct conflict with the interests of other countries. Beneath the veneer of international camaraderie, there was plenty of evidence that other countries regarded China's rise with mixed feelings. And hovering behind this was the sense that few had worked out what China's vision of modernity and its unique contribution really was — and that may well have included the very elite in Beijing who were in charge of this.

The leadership, with their reticence, and in particular Hu's characteristic anonymity, often did not help. Their visits abroad were so tightly controlled that it was difficult to get any strong insights from them about what China really was, and as this book has tried to show, even the way they spoke internally was opaque and often confusing and contradictory. It was left, therefore, to others to try to map out what a Chinese global vision might be. For some, like British journalist Martin Jacques, it was a genuine alternative. The title of his study from 2009 says most of it: *When China Rules the World*. "We stand," he writes, "on the eve of a different kind of world," a world that changes the paradigms and parameters of "American global hegemony" which has reigned till the first decade of the 21st century for over 80 years.

> Although we are witnessing the rise of a growing number of developing countries, China is by far the most important

economically. It is the bearer and driver of the world, with which it enjoys an increasingly hegemonic relationship, its tentacles having stretched across East Asia, Central Asia, Latin America and Africa.[4]

But China is different not just in being economically and militarily powerful, but in being not a nation state but what Jacques terms a "civilisation state", a state with a cultural, developmental, historical and political nature which is radically different to elsewhere, based on a whole raft of values and beliefs which he spends a chapter of his book trying to spell out. Its views on unity, on its own cultural superiority, on race and on civilisation mean that it "has enjoyed a quite different history to that of the West".[5] It is, he goes on, "banal, therefore, to believe that China's impact on the world will be mainly and overwhelmingly economic: on the contrary, its political and cultural effect is likely to be even greater".

These were controversial statements, though the success of the Chinese translation of the book, carefully edited and adapted, showed that the central thrust of Jacques's argument was not displeasing to at least the bureaucrats in the propaganda ministry in Beijing who had to authorise its appearance locally. In the end, there were plenty of questions that scholars with deeper knowledge of China could raise about just how unified this state was, and what sense there was in dabbling with notoriously difficult concepts like 'civilisation' and 'culture' and linking them to nationalism and national identity. While it made sense as Robert Ross did to talk of China as behaving like a land-based power for much of its previous diplomatic and political history rather than a sea-based one, grand talk of it being a 'civilisational state' were much harder to defend. Political scientist Perry Anderson acidly commented on reviewing the book, that Jacques, 'once the editor of the Communist Party of Great Britain's monthly, "Marxism Today", was somehow seeking

---

[4] Martin Jacques, *When China Rules the World: The Rise of the Middle Kingdom and the End of the Western World*, Allen Lane, London, 2009, p 11.
[5] *Ibid.*, p 15.

a consolation prize in the final victorious rise of a country adhering to the old creed.

> It would not be too unfair to say that what the book at bottom represents is a belated meeting of Yesterday's Marxism with Asian Values... Certainly there is nothing to upset the authorities in Beijing, where reception should be excellent.[6]

On the other extreme was fellow British journalist Will Hutton's blockbuster of 2006, The *Writing on the Wall*. For him, there was no talk of China as being an alternative vision the West might look at. On the contrary, "if the next century is going to be Chinese, it will only be because China embraces the economic and political pluralism of the West in general, and our Enlightenment institutions in particular."[7] Hutton continues to say that "the current Chinese economic miracle is unsustainable" and that "this is why the simple extrapolation of China's continued growth at current levels for the next forty or fifty years are misleading". China is "a sophisticated civilisation beset by profound and deepening problems that is making a difficult transition from a primitive and poor peasant society to modernity".[8]

## What Makes Us Human, CCP Style

There were plenty of impassioned debates about these issues inside China, amongst the many different communities there. But if we focus on the elite, and in particular on Hu Jintao as he appears through his words as just reported in this book, the only conclusion that one can draw is that, for historic, political, and perhaps finally personal reasons, he conveyed a vision of humanity, of what motivates and inspires humans, which was rigidly materialistic. Development was

---

[6] Perry Anderson, 'Sinomania', *London Review of Books*, 32(12), January 2010, p 3–6.
[7] Will Hutton, *The Writing on the Wall: China and the West in the 21st Century*, Little, Brown, London, 2006, p x.
[8] *Ibid.*, p xi.

about 'filling stomachs', getting food, building bigger and better houses, roads, airports, shopping malls, high speed train lines… This could not be jeopardised at any cost. But when the questions shifted to what John Maynard Keynes called the 'life beyond GDP' (which is, after all, simply a primitive measure of economic output regardless of quality) the answers became either hesitant, or non-existent. Having built the 'primary stage of socialism', and heading towards achieving the second benchmark of middle income status by 2020, probably before, the haunting question of what this growth and development was all about, what sort of world it was creating for Chinese people, the kinds of freedoms and challenges and choices it was giving them, became all the sharper and more vexing. More and more, the Party-state through its economic policies had created larger spaces for people to make their own lifestyle choices in. It policed the core areas of political sensitivity with rigorous vigilance. But in terms of finding jobs, sorting out healthcare, paying for education, caring for the elderly, deciding about their sexuality, having sexual relations, choosing who they married, and then divorced (divorce levels are rocketing in Hu's China), people were mostly on their own. The state did not, and could not, prescribe much. It was too busy fighting the battles that mattered to it, with separatists, dissidents, mafia, and problem factions within its own ranks. The idea that even an organisation as vast as the CCP could regulate life the way it had done under Mao was defunct. What prevailed was an uneasy truce where people were encouraged to be intellectually free, to be innovative, but to make sure they had enough nous to avoid problem areas, and if they did want to dabble in some free thinking on these kind of issues, to make sure they did nothing practical about it, or, for that matter, express their thoughts too explicitly on the internet.

These shifting, expanding boundaries of freedom in the PRC meant that for the vast majority of people, the police state that descended on the rights lawyers and activists and dissidents, with particular intensity from 2009 onwards, was remote from their lives. No one could say with any certainty, there being no surveys that had mapped this, whether they expected anything more from their politicians than in the West. At most, they wanted some space in their lives to be left alone from state interference. In that, the new China delivered. But the mystery of why its political figures still maintained the sort of stiff, morally superior language that Hu used as the dominant register of his statements, remained. Somehow, the traditional template of the righteous, remote, high and all knowing leader remained. This lofty style was uncontentious, even if it ran the frequent danger of appearing pompous and arrogant. Beijing's streets were often shut down and its airport closed, while the great people like Hu and those around him came in and out of the capital. Their visits to the humble abodes of common people were largely regarded, internally, as inevitable set pieces of political theatre, with little, if any, relevance to daily life. Hu's vision of the bigger society, the greater society, which this wealth creation was taking China towards was, perhaps, irrelevant. Chinese people expected little more from their leaders than that, and had even more of an aversion to hearing them preach about deeper values than audiences in the West. The best that could be said is that the Party-state and its main agents left the majority of people alone. That sort of accommodation was the limits of what could be expected.

## Chinese Voices in a Changing World

After all, how easy was it to craft a common vision for the rich pageant of personalities and people that made up the China under Hu?

There was Li Yuchun, winner with over three and a half million votes, of the Chinese Super Girl competition in 2005, a talent show that had swept the country. A native of Sichuan, she had attracted viewers with her strong voice and striking individual style. But she cut against the stereotype of beauty being used to flog products in the country, with her androgynous looks, and the news that she was gay."' It [the programme] is vulgar and manipulative,' intoned an official statement from China Central TV (CCTV), the national state-run broadcaster" according to the China Daily.[9] And yet Li remained popular, appealing to independent minded young women in particular, those who, like in Japan, had increasing economic power.

It was the China of Li Wei, called Queen of Mistresses because of her ability to ensnare top level officials and business people, who had accumulated as many as 15 lovers, and managed to make a reported USD 1 billion out of them. Holding lavish parties at her mansion in the seaside resort of Qingdao, Li had continued the ancient art of concubines being closest of all to the key power holders. But her success in implicating the men who had had links with her made her case a cause célèbre when she was finally prosecuted. She turned the tables on those who had been associated with her, giving evidence against them, escaping with a short jail sentence, and ending up in Hong Kong. "You can't afford to invest everything in one person," she would say, according to one report about her,

> "You need a huge relationship net, like an umbrella." Far from prurient condemnation, many bloggers celebrated her skill: "Making money is easy in modern China... But making money without getting sent to prison for corruption takes real talent, and that's what Li Wei has done. Our market economy in China is actually a power economy. Whatever people think of her and the things she did, Li is a heroine of sorts and a morality tale for early 21st century China.[10]

It was the China of Dr Gao Yaojie, who had been instrumental in exposing the AIDS crisis in the late 1990s and early 2000s in

---

[9] 'China Rockin' to Super Girl', *China Daily*, August 30, 2008, at http://www.chinadaily.com.cn/english/doc/2005-08/30/content_473432.htm [23 December 2011].
[10] Simon Parry, 'Sleeping with the Enemy', *South China Morning Post*, Hong Kong, April 17, 2011.

the province of Henan from infected blood, and who had sought refuge in the US during a visit there in 2009. "She has been through a lot during her fight for justice," fellow activist and refugee Wan Yanhai said, "Her children have been affected too. She's been under constant monitoring and disturbance from the government for years. She feels insecure. Maybe she does not want to live her final years in fear. Her husband died in 2006 and she is all alone."[11]

But it was also the China of Chen Guangbiao, one of the country's richest new entrepreneurs from Jiangsu whose attention grabbing acts of generosity included a visit to Taiwan where he handed out red envelopes with stashes of cash in them. He performed a similar act in Wall Street, New York, arousing criticism as an arriviste from some quarters, vulgar and insensitive, and in others as a figure making highly charged points about China's newfound wealth and the uncomfortable reception of it in some parts of the world.

It was the China of the first PRC national to go into space and of the basketball player Yao Ming who was able to forge a successful career in the US. It was also the home of the rebel tennis player Li Na, whose defeat of the world women's number one in January 2011 and winning of the French Open in June the same year showed that the country's sport stars were not just dominating the Olympics. Li Na's refusal to work within the official system, her use of her own husband as her coach, and the red rose tattoo on her chest were all taken as statements of the strong individuality that existed in a country that remained authoritarian. Her success was to cause at least four cities to claim her as their own, including her real birthplace, Wuhan. It was the country of Bao Xishun, who claimed to be the world's tallest man, and of He Pingping, its shortest. It was, physically and culturally, truly a country of extremes.

---

[11] Malcolm Moore, 'Chinese Aids Activist Dr Gao in Exile in the United States', *Daily Telegraph*, UK, December 2, 2009, at http://www.telegraph.co.uk/news/worldnews/asia/china/6710901/Chinese-Aids-activist-Dr-Gao-in-exile-in-United-States.html [22 December 2011].

## Unresolved Issues

China was a country in transformation in the Hu era, but the Party itself has also been a political force going through changes. Perhaps the greatest single failure of Hu was to spell out a vision of the country's political future — a way of answering some of the increasingly urgent questions about rule of law, civil society and its status, the participation of people in political decision making, and the final great challenge of what to do about political opposition beyond simply locking people up or having them disappear. These loomed over life in the late 2000s and into the next decade, casting long shadows over large parts of the political life. China's environment after ten years of breakneck economic growth was, in the eyes of some, at a critical point. Its courts were clogged up with civil cases by disaffected citizens with a stronger awareness of their legal rights and a willingness to use them about things they were most concerned about — usually property and pensions. Petitions had increased throughout the latter part of the decade, with only a modest drop in 2010. Public protests were common. Anger over the milk scandal of 2008, where tainted milk produced by Sanya had resulted in the deaths of several babies was only one of a number of tragic cases where shoddy goods had harmed people. At the heart of this were the issues of how power was distributed, how people in positions of responsibility were selected and then legitimised, and how the public engaged with this protest. On this critical issue, the Party showed surprising paralysis, unable or unwilling to move forward. It did not clarify the legal basis of civil societies, which after all now had vast importance in many areas of life in the PRC, was reluctant to strengthen the courts at either local or national level, and steadfastly maintained that the CCP and the CCP alone could be trusted to fill all the political space necessary in society and satisfy the needs of everyone. Hu contributed little to this debate. His statements were cautious, restrictive and sometimes meaninglessly opaque. He gave no real clue to his views on either how urgent reform was in the specific areas mentioned above, or which policy direction he was in favour of. The ideas produced by the Party school and others were either ignored or hushed up.

Tactically, perhaps Hu was waiting for the time when the solution to these problems became blindingly obvious, and a strong consensus was more easily attainable in the CCP. This had happened with economic reforms, when only the most diehard then-Maoist ideologues had resisted change as the 1980s got underway. But whatever the complexities of that process, it had been relatively straightforward compared to the demands that political change might make. Hu and his generation were biased at all costs towards stability. But there was a sense in which sticking to the 'wait and watch and see' in political and legal reforms would itself, one day, become destabilising. The Jasmine revolutions in the Arab World, after all, had been inflicted on elites that had failed to read the signs of social unhappiness and had simply not moved quickly enough. For Hu's China, the greatest question was not how to get rich — many people had managed that. What was more pressing was what to do once you had made it. What was life after producing vast increased GDP?

That reforms in this area would be painful and challenging, and might carry the risk of instability, was widely recognised. But the leadership needed to start creating a path towards some longer term vision that was more convincing than simply concentrating on governance in the Party. Congresses, and their membership, and their input into decision making, seemed a relatively low risk area. More credibility for them, at local and national level, seemed a strong first move. But even here, the leadership were wary, and did nothing. Ideological worries infected the elite, with constant threats that a move in one area of reform would unravel everything else, and the whole project would collapse around their ears. Stasis and status quo became the best solution. But there was a question about whether the Party with its success in economics had now brought itself far quicker than it expected or wanted towards having to deal with the social, legal, political and structural changes that were far trickier to create consensus on and then deliver. In this context, talk about finding 'a way suitable for Chinese national characteristics' became largely irrelevant. The country was looking at the same kinds of transitional challenges as many others. Its great difference was the sheer size, and the accelerated time scale it probably needed to undergo and withstand these challenges. There the CCP truly had a monumental challenge in store for it, and the Hu era, as far as mid 2011, had done relatively little to address these.

## The Leadership Transition

That will be the problem probably left for the imminent leadership, the so-called 'fifth generation'. It is unlikely, however, that Hu will disappear after 2012. He will remain in formal positions of power, possibly up to 2015, just as Jiang Zemin had. And his influence is very unlikely to disappear even then. A politician as subtle, and patient at Hu, would be able to exercise influence deep into the second decade of the 21$^{st}$ century. Perhaps through his interest in the security services, or through significant input into Tibet, or policy on Taiwan, or leadership changes, Hu is unlikely to simply retire to a quiet backwater. As a stickler for Party process, however, it is unlikely that he will try to subvert any of the correct processes, or, for that matter, build a power base that would be potentially destabilising. That is evidently not his style. The interesting question is when, or if, critical moments of decision making occur in the decade ahead about the issues of reform outlined above. Will Hu then reveal himself finally as the supporter of much larger reform that had, once upon a time, been suspected? If the new leadership opts for quicker, deeper changes to the rule of law, or civil society, will he be a moral and intellectual supporter of these, acting like retired leaders elsewhere in simply giving his weight to new proposals and helping them through? Or will he instead be a representative of the kind of cautiousness and conservatism that has marked his era in power, setting out barriers and restrictions on younger leaders, being a formidable hurdle in their way? Will he, released from direct executive power responsibility, be a former leader who suddenly berates his successors for not now moving ahead more aggressively in key areas, or will he operate under the surface, through subtle, complicating influence, a figure whose assent or disapproval could make or break key policy initiatives?

Hu's greatest success, and the sign of his immense self-control, is that eight years after being in power, he keeps the world guessing about his personal beliefs, specifically in his own role. He may well have been nominated by Forbes as the most powerful man in the world in 2010. But the fact is that he is also one of the least known major leaders of our time. And the likelihood of him joining the international speech and punditry circuit amongst other former leaders of major countries like Bill Clinton or Tony Blair remains low. He is as likely to be as silent in retirement as he was during his years in power. He truly was, in the years of China's amazing economic growth and its rise to potential global dominance and authority, the still point in a fast changing, confusing and bewildering moving world.

# BIBLIOGRAPHY

Perry Anderson, 'Sinomania', *London Review of Books*, 32(12), January, 2010.

C Fred Bergsten *et al.*, *China, the Balance Sheet: What the World Needs to Know about the Emerging Superpower*, Peterson Institute of International Economics, New York, 2006.

Kerry Brown, *Ballot Box China: Grassroots Democracy and the Final Major One-Party State*, Zed Books, London, 2011.

Kerry Brown, 'No Reverse Gear: Chinese Sovereign Wealth Funds and Overseas Direct Investment', CLSA September 2008, at http://www.kerry-brown.co.uk/fi les/clsa_paper_final.pdf [22 December 2011].

Kerry Brown, *The Rise of the Dragon: Inward and Outward Investment in China in the Reform Period 1978–2007*, Chandos Publishing, Oxford, 2008.

John Byron and Robert Pack, *The Claws of the Dragon: The Evil Genius Behind Mao and His Legacy of Terror in the People's Republic*, Touchstone Books, New York, 1993.

William Callahan, *China: The Pessoptimist Nation*, Oxford University Press, Oxford, 2010.

Jinqing Cao, *China Along the Yellow River: Reflections on Rural Society*, Routledge Curzon, New York, 2005.

Guidi Chen and Chuntao Wu, *Will the Boat Sink the Water: The Life of China's Peasants*, Public Affairs Ltd, New York, 2006.

Jian Chen, 'The Chinese Communist "Liberation" of Tibet, 1949–1951', in Jeremy Brown and Paul G Pickowicz (Eds), *Dilemmas of Victory: The Early Years of the People's Republic of China*, Harvard University Press, Cambridge, MA, 2007.

Jie Chen and Bruce J Dickson, *Allies of the State: China's Private Entrepreneurs and Democratic Change*, Harvard University Press, Cambridge, MA, 2010.

Elizabeth Corrin, 'China's Rule of Law', in Kerry Brown (Ed), *China 2020: The Next Decade of the People's Republic of China*, Chandos, Oxford, 2011.

Bruce Cummings, *Dominion from Sea to Sea: Pacific Ascendancy and American Power*, Yale University Press, New Haven, CT, 2009.

Gloria Davies, *Worrying About China: The Language of Chinese Critical Inquiry*, Harvard University Press, Cambridge, MA, London, 2007.

Lisheng Dong, 'Direct Township Elections in China: Latest Developments and Prospects', in Kevin O'Brien and Suisheng Zhao (Eds), *Grassroots Elections in China*, Routledge, London, 2011.

Richard D Ewing, 'Hu Jintao, the Making of a Chinese General Secretary', *China Quarterly*, 2003, 173, p 17–34.

Joseph Fewsmith, '*China since Tiananmen,*' Second Edition, Cambridge University Press, Cambridge, 2008.

M Taylor Fravel, *Strong Borders, Secure Nation: Co-operation and Conflict in China's Territorial Disputes*, Princeton University Press, New Jersey, 2008.

Mark W Frazier, *Socialist Insecurity: Pensions and the Politics of Uneven Development in China*, Cornell University Press, New York, 2010.

Michael Freeden, *Ideology: A Very Short Introduction*, Oxford University Press, New York, 2003.

Alain Guilloux, *Taiwan, Humanitarianism and Global Governance*, Routledge, London, 2009.

Stefan Halper, *The Beijing Consensus*, Basic Books, New York and London, 2010.

William Hinton, 'Hundred Days War at Tsinghua University', *Monthly Review Press*, New York, 1973.

William Hinton, *Fanshen: A Documentary of Revolution in a Chinese Village*, University of California Press, California, 1967.

Jamie Horsley, 'China Adopts First Nationwide Open Government Information Regulations', Yale China Law Center, at http://www.law.yale.edu/documents/pdf/Intellectual_Life/Ch_China_Adopts_1st_OGI_Regulations.pdf [22 December 2011].

Jintao Hu, 'Zai Jinian Dang de Shiyi Jie San Zhong Quanhui Zhaokai 30 Zhounian Dahuishang De Jianghua', (Speech Remembering the Thirtieth Anniversary of the Third Plenum of the 11th Party Congress), reprinted in *Liu Ge Weisheme* ('The Six Why's'), People's Daily Publishing House, Beijing, 2009.

Jintao Hu, 'Hold High the Great Banner of Socialism with Chinese Characteristics and Strive for New Victories in Building a Moderately Prosperous Society in All Respects', Speech at the 17th Party Congress, October 15, 2007.

Jintao Hu, 'Zai Qingzhu Zhongguo Gongchandang Chengli 85 Zhounian Ji Zongjie Baochi Dangyuan Xianjinxing Jiaoyu Huodong Da Huishang De Jianghua', (Speech made at an Advanced Educational Meeting of Cadres Celebrating and Summarising the 85 Anniversary of the Founding of the CCP', Xinhua, July 1, 2006.

Yasheng Huang, *Capitalism with Chinese Characteristics: Entrepreneurship and the State*, Cambridge University Press, Cambridge, 2008.

Yasheng Huang, *Selling China: Foreign Direct Investment During the Reform Era*, Cambridge University Press, Cambridge, 2003.

Human Rights Watch, 'China: An Alleyway in Hell: China's Abusive Black Jails', New York, 2009.

Will Hutton, *The Writing on the Wall: China and the West in the 21st Century*, Little, Brown, London, 2006.

Martin Jacques, *When China Rules the World: The Rise of the Middle Kingdom and the End of the Western World*, Allen Lane, London, 2009.

Linda Jakobsen and David Knox, 'New Foreign Policy Actors in China', SIPRI Policy Paper 26, September, 2010.

Hepeng Jia, 'The Three Represents Campaign: Reform the Party or Indoctrinate the Capitalist', *Cato Journal*, 2004, 24(3), p 261–275.

Liang Jing, 'Cong Konghua Zhiguo Dao "Dongchang" Zhiguo' ('From Ruling by Rhetoric to Ruling by Secret Police'), Xin Shiji, January 26, 2010.

James Kynge, *China Shakes The World: The Rise of a Hungry Nation*, Weidenfeld and Nicholson, London, 2006.

Willy W Lam, *Chinese Politics in the Hu Jintao Era: New Leaders, New Challenges*, M E Sharpe, London, 2006.

Willy W Lam, *The Era of Jiang Zemin*, Prentice Hall, New York, 1999.

Mark Leonard, *What Does China Think*, Fourth Estate, London, 2008.

Cheng Li, 'Intra-Party Democracy: Should We Take It Seriously', *China Leadership Monitor*, Issue 30, Fall, 2009.

Cheng Li, *China's Leaders: The New Generation*, Rowman and Littlefield, Lanham Boulder, 2001.

Xiaobo Liu *et al.*, 'China's Charter 08', translated by Perry Link, New York Review of Books, December 18, 2008, at http://www.nybooks.com/articles/archives/2009/jan/15/chinas-charter-08/ [22 December 2011].

Xiaobo Liu, 'Nandao Zhongguoren Zhi Pei Jieshou Dangzhu Minzhu', October 19, 2005, at www.epochtimes.com/b5/5/10/4/n1074197.htm [accessed 23 December 2011].

Xiaobo Liu, 'Zhongguo De Ducai Aiguozhuyi', October 3, 2005, at www.epochtimes.come/b5/5/10/4/n1074197.htm [accessed 23 December 2011].

Julia Lovell, *The Great Wall: China Against the World 1000 BC to AD 2000*, Grove Press, New York, 2006.

Zedong Mao, *On the Correct Handling of Contradictions Among the People*, Foreign Language Press, Peking, 1957.

Richard McGregor, *The Party: The Secret World of China's Communist Rulers*, Harper Collins, New York, 2010.

Paul Midler, *Poorly Made in China: An Insider's Account of the Tactics Behind China's Production Game*, John Wiley and Sons, New Jersey, 2009.

Alice Miller, 'China's New Party Leadership', *China Leadership Monitor*, Issue 23, Winter, 2008.

Alice Miller, 'Hu's In Charge', *China Leadership Monitor*, Issue 16, Fall, 2005.

Alice Miller, 'The Road to the Sixteenth Party Congress', *China Leadership Monitor*, Issue 1, Winter, 2002.

James A Millward, *Eurasian Crossroads: A History of Xinjiang*, Columbia University Press, New York, 2007.

Pankaj Mishra, 'At War With the Utopia of Modernity', in Kate Merkel-Hess, Kenneth L Pomeranz, and Jeffrey N Wasserstrom (Eds), *China in 2008: A Year of Great Significance*, Rowman and Littlefield, Lanham Boulder, 2009.

Kalpana Misra, 'Neo Left and Neo Right in Post Tiananmen China', *Asian Survey*, 2003, 43(5), p 717–744.

Neil Munro, 'Democracy Postponed: Chinese Learning from the Soviet Collapse', *China Aktuell*, 2008, 37(4), p 31–63.

Jan Myrdal, *Report from a Chinese Village*, Heinemann, London, 1966.

Barry Naughton, *The Chinese Economy: Transitions and Growth*, MIT Press, Cambridge, MA, 2007.

Nouvel Observateur, 'Malheur aux Plaignants', December–January 2010–2011.

Office of the Secretary of Defense, 'Annual Report to Congress: Military and Security Developments Involving the People's Republic of China

2010', p 4, at http://www.defense.gov/pubs/pdfs/2010_CMPR_Final.pdf [22 December 2011].

Jean C Oi, Scott Rozelle, and Xueguang Zhou (Eds), *Growing Pains: Tensions and Opportunity in China's Transformation*, Walter A Shorenstein Asia Pacific Research Center, Stanford, 2010.

Elizabeth Perry, 'Popular Protest', in Joseph Fewsmith (Ed), *China Today, China Tomorrow: Domestic Politics, Economy and Society*, Rowman and Littlefield, Lanham, 2010.

Frank Pieke, *The Good Communist: Elite Training and State Building in Today's China*, Cambridge University Press, Cambridge, New York, 2009.

Joshua Cooper Ramo, *The Beijing Consensus*, The Foreign Policy Centre, London, 2004.

Sophie Richardson, *China, Cambodia, and the Five Principles of Peaceful Co-existence*, Columbia University Press, New York, 2010.

Alan D Romberg, 'Ma at Midterm: Challenges for Cross Straits Relations', *China Leadership Monitor*, Issue 33, Summer, 2010.

Daniel H Rosen and Zhi Wang, 'Deepening China-Taiwan Relations Through the ECFA', Peterson Institute Policy Brief PB10-16, June 2010.

Robert R Ross, *Chinese Security Policy: Structure, Power and Politics*, Routledge, London, 2009.

David Shambaugh, *China's Communist Party: Atrophy and Adaptation*, Woodrow Wilson Centre Press, New York, 2008.

Fang-Cheng Tang et al., 'Knowledge Acquisition and Learning Strategies in Globalization of China's Enterprises', in Alon and McIntyre (Eds), *Globalization of Chinese Enterprises*, Palgrave Macmillan, Basingstoke, Hampshire, 2008, p 31–43.

Ian Taylor, *China's New Role in Africa*, Lynne Rienner, Boulder, 2009.

Biao Teng, 'A Hole To Bury You In', at http://online.wsj.com/article/SB10001424052970203731004576045152244293970.html [22 December 2011].

John C Tkacik, 'Who's Hu? Assessing China's Heir Apparent, Hu Jintao', Lecture at the Heritage Foundation, US, April 19, 2002, at http://www.heritage.org/ Research/Lecture/Whos-Hu [22 December 2011].

Victoria Tuke, 'China's Soft Power Development by 2020', in Kerry Brown (Ed), *China 2020: The Next Decade of the People's Republic of China*, Chandos, Oxford, 2011.

Andrew G Walder, *Fractured Rebellion: The Beijing Red Guard Movement*, Harvard University Press, Cambridge, MA and London, 2009.

Hui Wang, *The End of the Revolution: China and the Limits of Modernity*, Verso, New York, 2009.

Shaoguang Wang, 'Openness, Distributive Conflict, and Social Insurance: The Social and Political Implications of China's WTO Membership', at http://www.gateway2china.com/report/CUHK_paper.htm [22 December 2011].

Xiaodong Wang et al., *Zhongguo Bu Gaoxing* ('China is Unhappy'), Phoenix Media Publishing and Jiangsu Publishing House, 2009.

Jonathan Watts, *When a Billion Chinese Jump*, Faber and Faber, London, 2010.

Teresa Wright, *Accepting Authoritarianism: State-Society Relations in China's Reform Era*, Stanford University Press, California, 2010.

Guobing Yang, *The Power of the Internet in China: Citizen Activism Online*, Columbia University Press, New York, 2009.

Xiaohua Yang and Clyde Stoltenberg, 'Growth of Made-in-China Multinationals: An Institutional and Historical Perspective', in Ilan Alon and John R McIntyre (Eds), *Globalization of Chinese Enterprises*, Palgrave Macmillan, Basingstoke, Hampshire, 2008, p 63–66.

Jingtao Yi, 'China's Rapid Accumulation of Foreign Exchange Reserves and its Policy Implications', China Policy Institution, Nottingham, Briefing Series No 10.

Peter Yu, 'Hu's the One to Succeed Jiang Zemin?' *The Straits Times*, Singapore, August 28, 1998.

Bijian Zheng, 'China's "Peaceful Rise" to Great-Power Status', *Foreign Affairs*, 2005, 84(5), p 18–24.

Tianyong Zhou, Changjiang Wang, and Anling Wang, *Gong Jian: Shiqida hou Zhongguo Zhengzhi Tizhi Gaige Yanjiu Baogao*, ('Storming the Fortress: A research report on political reform after the 17th Party Congress'), Xinjiang Production Corps Publishing House, Xinjiang, 2007.

Slavoj Zizek, 'Can you Give My Son a Job', *London Review of Books*, 32(20), October, 2010.

# INDEX

9th Party Congress   13
12th Five   86
12th Party Congress   48
17 Point Agreement   17
17th Party Congress   xix, 46, 51, 53, 64, 79, 151, 163
1992 Consensus'   126

accountability   36, 43, 175
Africa   59, 60, 92–94, 102, 138, 173, 190 135, 205
African   59, 60, 93, 94
agricultural   21, 41, 78, 169
aircraft carriers   124, 135
Ai Wei Wei   191
Akmal Shaikh   116
Anhui   2, 38–39
Anti Rightist Campaign   4
ASEAN   131
Asian   206
Asian Financial Crisis   87
Asian values   161
Association of South East Asian Nations (ASEAN)   130
Attlee, Clement   146
autonomous regions   4, 69

Ba Jin   6
baby milk powder scandal   85
Bandung Conference   103
Bao Xishun   210

Beijing   109, 114
Beijing Consensus   109, 114, 132
Beijing Olympics   xx, 24, 82, 191
Beijing University   7, 9, 63, 141, 161
Belgrade   106
big character poster   7
Bird   57
Black Jails   186
Blair, Tony   xx, 104, 214
blood inheritance   7
blood line   9
Bo Xicheng   48
Bo Xilai   7, 48
Bo Yibo   10, 15, 20, 48
British Virgin Islands   89
Bush, George W   xx, 106, 111, 112
business   xxii, 31, 40, 42, 44, 48, 60, 62, 81–85, 88, 91, 92, 95, 97, 122, 128, 130, 133, 134, 141, 161, 169, 176, 209

Callahan, William   122
Cambodia   103, 104
Cao Jinqing   38
carbon emission   115
Cayman Islands   89
CCP 17th Party Congress   175
CCP power   38
Central Asia   12, 95, 205

Central Committee  16, 48–50, 52, 53, 55, 157, 162, 173, 175
Central Committee of the CCP  19
Central Cultural Revolutionary Group  7, 9, 10
Central Discipline and Inspection Commission (CDIC)  203, 229
Central Leading Small Group  58
Central Military Commission (CMC)  xvii, 22, 75, 126
Central Party School  21, 64, 195, 203
Central Party school, Zheng  107
characteristics  160
Chiang, P. K.  131
Cheng Li  3, 13, 55, 176
Chen Guangcheng  184
Chen Guidi  38
Chen Liangyu  33, 43, 45, 51
Chen Shui-Bian  124
Chen Shunyao  14
Chen Xitong  xvii, 43
Chen Yun  15, 48
Chen Yunlin  130, 131
China Democracy Party  183
China Federation of Youth  16
China National Overseas Oil Corporation (CNOOC)  xi, 91, 94
China of Chen Guangbiao  210
China People's Political Consultative Conference (CPPCC)  54, 189
China's economy  xxiii, 20, 21, 86, 96
Chinese Communist Party (CCP)  xvii, xviii, xxii, xxiv, 3, 5, 13–16, 19, 21, 23, 24, 27–29, 30, 31, 36, 43, 47, 48–50, 55, 56, 64, 69, 79, 82, 83, 103, 121, 143, 147–153, 155, 156, 159, 164, 167–177, 179, 181, 182, 185, 187–189, 192, 197, 202, 207, 211–213
Chinese Investment Corporation (CIC)  89, 90, 94, 95
Chongqing  131, 142, 193
citizen activism  194
civil society  63, 151, 178, 182, 185, 211, 213
class  xxii, 3, 5, 6, 9, 97, 106, 122, 163–166
class struggle  79, 143, 148, 162
climate change  115, 116
Climate Change Summit  114
CMC  22, 29, 32, 33, 49, 75
collective leadership  51, 75, 157, 182, 200
colour revolutions  172, 177, 185
Committee of the Politburo  19
Communist Party  xiii, xiv, xvii, xxiv, 2, 5, 16, 20, 21, 33, 37, 63, 101, 134, 189, 205
Communist Party elite  23
Communist Youth League  15, 23
Confucius  109, 161
consensus  24, 26, 29, 31, 32, 46, 109, 114, 123, 140, 143, 147, 153, 154, 182, 188, 200, 212
conservatives  9, 20
constitution  xix, 65, 81, 69, 141, 149, 150, 153, 181
Consultative Conference  54
contradictions  4, 156, 161, 165–167, 170, 196, 197

Copenhagen 114
core interests 138, 139
corruption xvii, 18, 28, 39, 42, 47, 57, 71, 171, 174–176, 188, 192, 203, 209
counter-terrorism 107
Cultural Revolution 2, 4–7, 11, 15, 27, 17, 47, 54, 66, 70, 79, 105, 133, 143, 147, 148, 157, 162, 174
Cummings, Bruce 136
cyber attacks 93, 137

Dai Bingguo 68, 118, 138
Dalai Lama 18, 58, 117
democracy 64, 65, 74, 124, 128, 132, 145, 156, 157, 164, 177, 175, 181, 188, 189
Democracy Wall 183
Democratic People's Republic of Korea (DPRK) 118–120, 121, 124
Democratic Progressive Party (DPP) 124–126, 130
Deng Liqun 29, 52, 81
Deng Xiaoping xxiii, 4, 14, 18, 19, 23, 27, 47, 48, 49, 60, 75, 79, 149, 177
Deng Yujiao 193
Derrida, Jacques 151
dialectic materialism 164
Dickson, Bruce J 148
discourse xiv, 144, 145, 146, 164, 202
dissent 149, 185
D'Long 88
Domestic consumption 86
DPRK's energy 120
DPRK-style 121

East China Sea 123
Economic 111
Economic Cooperation Framework Agreement (ECFA) 111, 130, 131, 133, 140
economic crisis xxiii, 67, 80, 83, 86, 94, 95, 96, 98, 112, 123, 201
Economic Dialogue 138
economy 148
Eight-Point Proposal 127
elite xvii, xxiii, xxiv, 1, 2, 3, 7, 9, 10, 13–15, 19, 28, 29, 48, 49, 52, 62, 64, 67, 82, 108, 122, 132, 133, 142, 143, 146, 151, 153, 154, 157, 165, 169, 178, 181, 182, 188, 192, 195, 202, 204, 206, 212
elite discourse 153
elite dissent 172
elites 85, 147, 149, 167, 168, 169, 212
energy 38, 54, 71, 90, 91, 93, 95, 102, 159, 180, 120, 204
entrepreneurial class 31
entrepreneurial energy 45
entrepreneurs 31, 40, 82, 148, 148–150, 167, 168, 183, 210
European Union (EU) xxiii, 89, 96, 106, 112, 115, 116, 200
Exchange 95
export market 91, 96, 106

faction 8, 11, 23, 28, 32, 51, 56, 75, 164, 175, 181, 207
Falungong 183, 184
famines 13, 37
Fang Binxing 92

farmer   xxii, 6, 30, 37–39, 40, 46, 77, 164, 168, 169
Five Antis Movement   4
Five Principles of Peaceful Co-Existence   103
Five Year Plan   86
Flowers Movement   4
Forbes   84, 214
forces   150, 157
foreign investment   21, 80
Foxconn   84, 98
Frazier, Mark   43
Free Trade Agreements   130
Fudan University   151

G20   98
Gang of Four   20, 47
Gansu   xx, xxii, 7, 12–15, 25, 33, 101, 182
Gao Yaojie   209
Gao Zhisheng   184
GDP growth   86, 110
Geely   95
Giddens, Anthony   151
Gini   41
'Going Out' policy   88
Goldman Sachs   42, 86, 96
Gome   82
governments   44
Great Hall of the People   52
Great Leap Forward   13, 37
growth   xxii
Guangmei   10
Guangxi   xxii, 69
Guangxi, Hunan   16
guanxi   15
Guiquan   40
Guizhou   16, 17
Guo Chunping   198

Guo, Terry   98
Guo Youdi   187

Habermas, Jurgen   151
Hainan spy plane incident   106
hardliner   21, 83, 170, 175, 179
harmonious society   26, 41, 109, 143, 153, 154, 158, 161
harmony   114, 133, 158, 159, 162, 167, 185, 200
healthcare   97, 207
hegemony   88, 93, 108, 204
He Guoqiang   54, 169
Henryk Szadziewski   73
He Pingping   210
He Yafei   117
Hilary Clinton   124
Hinton, William   6
HIV-contaminated blood disaster   55
Hong Kong   xx, 34, 77, 89, 89, 91, 92, 126, 128, 130, 179, 180, 182, 209
Hu Haiqing   14
Hu Jia   184, 190
Hu Jintao   ix, xiii, xiv, xvii, xviii, 1, 3, 8, 11, 14, 16, 17, 18, 21, 22, 24, 25, 27, 29, 33, 41, 43, 50, 55, 58, 61, 64, 75, 90, 93, 94, 97, 102, 112, 124, 128, 134, 141, 143, 153, 179, 191, 197, 198, 200, 203, 206
Hu Yaobang   13, 15, 23, 27, 33, 178, 179
Hua Guofeng   27
Huang Guangyu   82
Huang Ju   33, 45, 51, 54
Huawei   92, 93
hukou   38

human rights   63, 65, 114, 117, 139, 186, 189, 190, 197, 199
Hunan   27, 37
Hundred Flowers Campaign   148
Hutton, Will   206

ideology   xix, xxiv, 29, 30, 64, 53, 82, 108, 132, 141–143, 145, 149, 151, 153, 159, 161, 165, 169, 171
Ilham Tohti   74
indicators   110
inequality   xvii, xix, xxiv, 25, 37, 40, 41, 101, 147, 152
Inequality   86
informationalised   93, 137, 196
Inner Mongolia   12, 69, 196
inner Party democracy   xix, xxiv, 174, 175
innovation   8, 31, 158, 159, 171, 172, 182, 197
institutionalisation   48
international affairs   53, 101, 138, 136, 172
International Monetary Fund (IMF) 98
International Olympic Committee   62
internet   58, 62, 72, 93, 116, 131, 137, 176, 184, 185, 188, 192, 193, 194, 195, 196 207
Iraq   xxiii, 70, 104, 136, 107

Jacques, Martin   204
Jiang Nanxiang   3, 8, 9
Jiang Qing   4, 7, 10 105, 161
Jiang Yanyong   35
Jiang Zemin   xvii, xviii, xix, xx, 1, 2, 18, 14, 20, 22, 28, 29, 32, 43, 47, 49, 56, 70, 82, 106, 108, 124, 126, 149, 183, 200, 213
Jia Qinglin   33, 54, 169
Jie Chen   148
Jixi, Anhui   1
John Maynard Keynes   207
Jon Huntsman   139

Kang Sheng   8, 105
Kant, Immanuel   25, 26
Kashgar   71, 73, 74
Kim Dae Jung   121
Kim Jong Il   118–121
Kim Yong-un   119
KMT   5, 125, 126, 148
Koizumi Junichiro   122
Korean Peninsula   104, 119
Korean Workers Party   119, 120
Kuai Dafu   9, 10
Kuomintang   3
Kynge, James   90

labourers   38
land border   102, 103
Lanzhou   12 13
League   15
legitimacy   9, 21, 43, 69, 120, 148, 153, 157, 162, 169, 170, 174, 189, 200
Lhasa   18, 58, 59 67, 69
Li Changchun   51, 54, 169, 195
Li Junru   53
Li Keqiang   53 54, 55
Li Na   210
Li Peng   1, 21
Li Wei   209
Li Yuanchao   55, 56
Li Yuchun   208

Liandong Red Guard faction  6
Liang Jing  202
liberalisation  16, 20, 49, 79, 181
Libya  94, 138
Lin Biao  27
Liu Di  192
Liu Guijin  60
Liujiaxia  12
Liu Shaoqi  4, 5, 10, 27
Liu Shaoqi, Wang  10
Liu Xiaobo  63, 64, 85, 116, 124, 172, 182, 188, 199
Liu Yandong  56
Liu Yongqing  14
Liu Zhaoxing  138
Liu Zhihua  57
local governments  40, 43, 61, 96, 186, 187, 193
London Stock  95
Luo Jiwen  95
Luo Gan  33, 54
Luo Jiwei  95
Lushun Meeting  4

manufacturing  80, 84
Mao Zedong  3–5, 7, 8, 14, 27, 47, 136, 146, 151
Mark Leonard  141
marketise  21
Marx, Karl  37, 160
Marxism  144, 146, 147, 155, 156, 159, 160, 163, 164, 173, 176, 205, 206
Marxism, socialism with Chinese  160
Marxist  141, 154, 156, 161, 162
Marxist discourse  169
Marxist ideology  143

Ma Ying-Jeou  125, 130, 131
McGregor, Richard  132
media  xxiv, 1, 4, 36, 61, 62, 109, 171, 182, 192, 197
Mencius  161
Midler  84
Migrant  38
migrant labourers  37, 38, 60, 168, 169
military budget  133
Miller, Alice (Lyman)  31
Millward, James  68
Ministry for Propaganda  36
Mishu  13, 23, 33
models  175
modernisation  xiv, 117, 128, 147, 159, 154, 164
Mongolian People's Republic  12
multipolarity  108

National Congress  52, 83
National People's Congress  83, 87 135
NATO-led attack on Yugoslavia  22
Naughton, Barry  40, 79
Nest stadium  57
Nie Yuanzi  7
Ningxia  69
Nixon, Richard  105, 124
Nobel Peace Prize  66, 124
non-interference  102, 103, 104, 107
non-state  xxiii, 31
non-state sector  30, 80, 81, 83, 148
North Korea  111, 117, 118, 120, 200

OECD   xxii, 82
Olympics   56, 57, 59, 60, 62, 63, 92, 93, 109, 111, 113, 132, 185, 201, 210
'one country, two systems'   128
O'Neil, Jim   86
Open Constitution   190
Opium Wars   116
Organic Village Election Law   174
Organisation Department   13, 15, 19, 55
Organisation for Economic Co-operation and Development (OECD)   80

Pan Wei   141
Party Branch Secretaries   171
Party Secretariat   49
patronage   15, 23, 29, 32, 33
peaceful rise   109, 114, 123, 133, 135
Pearl River Delta   84
Peng Dehuai   4
Peng Zhen   15
pension   43, 44, 188, 211
People's Armed Police   72
People's Daily,   1 ,7, 51, 78
Perry, Elizabeth   187
Peterson Institute for International Economics,   131
petition   187, 211
petitioner   186, 187
petitioning   186, 187
Pew Foundation   98
Pieke, Frank   142
power   xvii, xix, xx, xxi, xxiii, xxiv, xxv, 1, 2, 5, 10, 14, 17, 19, 20–24, 27–29, 31–33, 37, 39–

42, 48–51, 53, 55–57, 65, 66, 68, 69, 71, 76, 81, 92, 93, 98, 102, 104–106, 108–110, 112, 114, 115, 122, 123, 133–135, 137, 138, 140, 154, 164, 165, 167–171, 175, 177, 178, 180, 184, 189, 192, 194, 197, 204, 205, 209, 211, 213, 214
pragmatism   104, 144
President   130, 131
princelings   23
private sector   44, 81–83, 150, 167, 168
productive forces   30, 150
Public Security Bureau   72
Pudong   45, 46
Pyongyang   118, 119, 120

Qian Liqun   146
Qian Zhongshu   154
Qinghai   12, 59

Ramo, Joshua Cooper   109
Red Army   133
reform era   15, 38, 66, 158, 167
reform process   27, 28, 37, 79, 162, 163, 183
Ren Zhengfei   92
Ren Zhichu   11
repression   72, 75, 105, 166, 183, 189
Resolution on Party History   47
Responsibility System   168
Revolution   166
rhetoric   69, 135, 162, 167, 182, 202, 203
rhetorical   117, 144
Richard   132
Richard McGregor   55, 171

rights 65, 73
Ross, Robert 105, 205

Severe Acute Respiratory Syndrome (SARS) xxiii, 33–35, 37, 107
Security Council 104
security services 8, 58, 63, 71, 188, 201, 213
self control 23, 214
Senegal 93
sent down youth 6
September 11th 70, 107
sessions 6
Severe Acute Respiratory Syndrome (SARS) 33
Shaanxi 15, 37
Shanghai xxiii, 2, 4, 14, 16, 28, 33, 38, 43–47, 49, 51, 98, 113, 120, 130, 139, 201
Shanghai Expo xiii, 130
Shanghai Group 23, 31–33, 36, 47, 51
Shanghai Miracle 45
Shanghai Pension 44
Shanghai SIA 44
Shanghai Social Insurance Agency 43, 44
Shanghai Xi 53
Shenzhen 84, 92, 98, 120, 175, 180
Sichuan xx, 12, 16, 60, 175, 208
Silk Route 12
Sino-Japanese 121
Sino-Japanese war 3, 5, 15, 123
Six Party Talks 118, 119, 121
socialism xiv, 30, 41, 46, 144, 163, 164, 176, 207
socialism with Chinese characteristics 83, 120, 144, 153, 154, 156, 163, 173, 176
socialist countryside 41, 155, 159
social management 195
soft power 60, 109
Song Ping 13, 14, 19, 23, 33
Sophie Richardson 103
South Africa 94
South China Sea 102, 124, 135
Southern Tour xviii, 18, 20, 28, 49, 144
sovereignty 102, 103, 126, 127, 128, 129, 164
Soviet Union 16, 18, 21, 144, 148, 172, 173
Spielberg, Stephen 60
stability xiii, xiv, 21, 66, 67–69, 71–73, 110, 120, 124, 151, 156, 159, 161, 164, 165, 201, 212
Stainless Steel Rat 192
Standing Committee 19, 22, 33, 48, 53, 55, 170, 195
Standing Committee of the Politburo 45
State Administration for Foreign Exchange 95
state capitalism 110
state constitution 30
State Economic Commission 9
state owned enterprise xviii, 40, 46
State Planning Commission 15
Stockholm International Peace Research Institute (SIPRI) 134
Strategic and Economic Dialogue 112
Strike Hard Campaigns 183, 192
struggle 6
struggle sessions 9, 11

successors   27, 124, 214
sustainability   158, 161, 204

Taipei   124, 125, 130
Taiwan   xxv, 3, 84, 103, 111, 105, 117, 124–128, 130–132, 135, 140, 163, 200, 202, 210, 213
Taiwanese   126, 128, 130, 131
Taiwan's soft power   132
Taiwan's sovereignty   130
Taiwan Straits   127
Taizhou   2
Tang Jiaxuan   138
Taylor, Ian   59
taxation   39, 40
technocrat   23, 28, 33
Teng Biao   190
Third Way   151
Three Antis Movement   4
Three Representatives' theory   30
Three Represents   149, 150, 152, 157
three stresses   149
Tiananmen Square   xvii, xviii, 11, 49, 56, 105, 148, 179
Tibet Autonomous Region   17
transition   xix, 22, 29, 32, 48, 75, 79, 87, 105, 107, 162, 192, 196, 206
Tsinghua   xxii, 2, 3, 6–11, 13, 14, 23, 33
two systems   128

United Nations (UN)   104
Union   172
United Front   54
Unocal   91
Urumqi   67, 68, 69, 71, 202

Urumqi, Xinjiang   116
United States (US)   xviii, xx, 1, 17, 42, 63, 77, 79, 89, 91–96, 101, 102, 105, 106–109, 111, 116, 118, 112–115, 117–119, 123, 124, 134–137, 139, 168, 183, 185, 189, 200, 210
US energy   91
US hegemony   137
USSR   4, 28, 38, 172, 173
US Strategic and Economic Dialogue   138

Values   206
Vietnam   34, 104, 136
Vietnamese   104
village elections   43, 174
violence   4, 6, 7, 10, 18, 22, 67, 147, 183, 185, 189, 203

Wan Yanhai   210
Wang Guangmei   12
Wang Hongwen   47
Wang Hui   26, 136, 147
Wang Huning   53, 142, 151
Wang Lequan   71
Wang Qishan   56
Wang Shaoguang   77
Wang Xiaodong   62, 85
Wang Yang   56
war on terror   107
Waseda University   122
Washington Consensus   109
Wedeman, Andrew   42
Wei Jingsheng   183
Wenchuan   xx, 60
Wen Jiabao   xiv, 13, 14, 32, 33, 49, 87, 96, 112, 115, 123, 152, 178, 180

Western   175
western models   164
Wikileaks   xix, 19, 117, 118, 195
Willy Lam   1, 181
Workers Party of Korea   120
work report   52, 53, 79, 81, 171
World Health Organisation (WHO)   xvii, xviii, xxi, 29, 32, 34–36, 77–81, 84, 86, 88, 89, 96, 106, 125
Wright, Teresa   167
Wu Bangguo   33, 51, 83, 118, 120, 169
Wu Chuntao   38
Wu Guangzheng   54
Wu Han   4

Xi Jinping   53, 54, 55, 64, 71
Xi Zhongxun   55
Xi'an   123
Xiaokang   42
Xiaoping   xxii, xxiii, 149
Xibaipo   151
Xidan   183
Xinhua   50, 120, 141 195
Xinjiang   xxiii, 67, 68, 70–74, 93, 103, 107, 111, 116, 126, 132, 172, 185, 195, 202
Xu Kuangdi   43
Xu Wenli   183

Xu Xiaonian   42
Xu Zhiyong   190

Yan Xuetong   131
Yan'an   8
Yang Jisheng   157
Yao Ming   210
Yasheng Huang   45, 82, 83, 92
Ye Duchu   202
Yu Jianrong   187
Yu Jie   182

Zeng Qinghong   31, 33, 49, 50, 51, 54, 64, 107
Zhang Chunxian   71
Zhang Guiquan   39, 40
Zhang Mingqing   130
Zhang Wenkang   34
Zhao Ziyang   13, 17, 28, 33, 178, 179
Zheng Bijian   107
Zhou Enlai   9, 103
Zhou Tianyong   66
Zhou Yongkang   54, 120, 169
Zhou Zhengyi   44
Zhu Junyi   44
Zhu Rongji   xviii, xxi, 29, 33, 50, 80, 87, 154
Zizek, Slavoj   167